The
Food Lover's
TRAIL GUIDE TO ALBERTA

Mary Bailey & Judy Schultz

BlueCOUCH**Books**

National Library of Canada Cataloguing in Publication
Bailey, Mary, (date)
The food lover's trail guide to Alberta / Mary Bailey, Judy Schultz

ISBN 1-894739-02-7

1. Food industry and trade–Alberta–Guidebooks.
2. Restaurants–Alberta–Guidebooks. 3. Alberta–Guidebooks. I. Schultz,
Judy. II. Title.
TX360.C32A52 2003   381'.45641'0257123   C2003-910249-1

Cover and author photos: J.Alleyne Photography
Map: Wendy Johnson, Johnson Cartographics Inc.
All interior photos are by Mary Bailey except where indicated.

Acknowledgments: Thank you, thank you!
Our most sincere gratitude goes to several people who had a hand in this book.
Without their help, we'd still be eating and worrying. A big thanks to Kieran Black and Jennifer Cockrall-King in Edmonton and Julie Van Rosendaal in Calgary. We're also grateful to the *Edmonton Journal, City Palate*, and the individuals and agencies that kindly gave us permission to use their file photographs. For their assistance with restaurants in Calgary and district, we thank Dee Hobsbawn-Smith, Linda Green and Ellen Kelly. In Lethbridge, our gratitude goes to Ward and Samantha Schultz. We thank the growers, ranchers, producers, chefs and other food people who were so generous with their time and information, answering our questions at all hours, from the middle of their busy days to after midnight. And a special thank you to those we tracked down at home on their days off.

Blue Couch Books
an imprint of Brindle & Glass Publishing
132 Hallbrook Drive Southwest
Calgary, Alberta
T2V 3H6
www.brindleandglass.com

Brindle & Glass is committed to protecting the environment and to the responsible use of natural resources. This book is printed on 100% post-consumer recycled and ancient forest-friendly paper. For more information please visit www.oldgrowthfree.com.

2   3   4   5 06   05   04   03

PRINTED AND BOUND IN CANADA

To the farmers and ranchers of Alberta,
without whom a book like this could not have been written.

CONTENTS

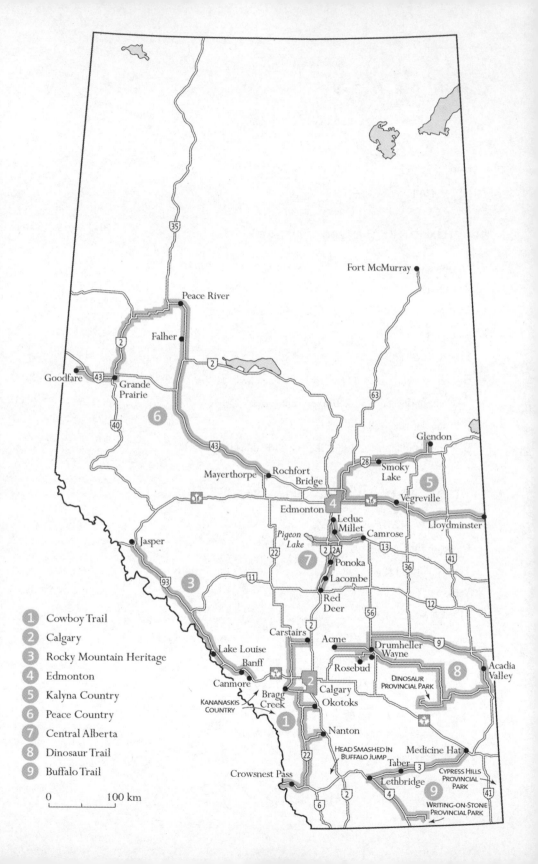

1 Cowboy Trail
2 Calgary
3 Rocky Mountain Heritage
4 Edmonton
5 Kalyna Country
6 Peace Country
7 Central Alberta
8 Dinosaur Trail
9 Buffalo Trail

Fort McMurray

Peace River
Falher
Goodfare
Grande
Prairie

Glendon
Smoky
Lake
Vegreville
Lloydminster

Mayerthorpe
Rochfort
Bridge
Edmonton
Leduc
Millet
Camrose
Pigeon
Lake
Ponoka
Lacombe
Red
Deer

Jasper

Carstairs
Acme
Drumheller
Wayne
Rosebud
Acadia
Valley
Lake Louise
Banff
Canmore
Bragg
Creek
KANANASKIS
COUNTRY
Calgary
Okotoks
DINOSAUR
PROVINCIAL PARK

Nanton

HEAD SMASHED IN
BUFFALO JUMP
Medicine Hat
Taber
CYPRESS HILLS
PROVINCIAL
PARK
Crowsnest Pass
Lethbridge

WRITING-ON-STONE
PROVINCIAL PARK

0   100 km

INTRODUCTION

Welcome to our Alberta table.

As we travelled from meal to meal around the province, we found a food community in the making and a landscape populated by a host of dedicated culinary artisans, from growers in their fields to chefs in their kitchens. At a time when food is increasingly an industrial by-product, when we forget that milk and cheese begins with cows and bread begins in a grain field, meeting these people was a revelation. We also found a developing connection between chefs and producers that will effect the entire food scene in Alberta.

We talked to bakers who source and grind their own grains. We stood in the middle of a goat herd while nannies nibbled our pockets, sampled their milk while it was still warm and tasted amazing cheeses while the cheese maker's eyes glowed with pride.

These dedicated food artists don't do it for prestige; few people know the names and faces behind the food they buy. They certainly don't do it for the money; on a per-hour basis, they could make more in almost any other field. They do it for love. For most of these remarkable people, food is not a job—it's a passion.

But hard work and good intentions won't result in great cheese if the milk is second-rate, and behind the artisans we discovered a motherlode of first-class ingredients—the local and regional specialties that are available here in this fortunate province, from heirloom tomatoes to oat groats and tender, succulent meats and fowl.

Because we think food people are a special breed, and we enjoy them so much, we've profiled a few of them here. We've also included some of their favourite recipes and shared a few secrets about where they find their best ingredients and why their food tastes the way it does.

This book is a taste of the way things are, here and now. *The Food Lover's Trail Guide to Alberta* is not intended to be an encyclopedia, and we encourage you to keep track of your own finds. It is, however, a generous selection of our favourites, with producers and restaurants ranging from tiny and quirky to grand gourmet—a highly personal guide to the places, people and products we enjoy so much.

We hope you'll enjoy them, too. Bon appetit!

We have divided Alberta into nine culinary trails, starting in the Crowsnest Pass. We go west to the Mountains, north to the Peace River Valley, west to Lloydminister and all points in between. Consult our trail map on page vi for reference but please use a good road map for navigating.

Restaurant Listings

Every effort has been made to ensure that the information featured is accurate. However, prices, credit cards accepted and days and hours of operation could change. We have assumed all businesses take cash, and those that don't take any other form of payment we've listed as "cash only." Please call ahead to verify when making plans to visit a restaurant, store or event.

Pricing Symbols

$ under $10 for one person, without alcohol, tip or taxes
$$ under $20 for one person, without alcohol, tip or taxes
$$$ over $20 for one person, without alcohol, tip or taxes

An "R" after the telephone number indicates that reservations are recommended.

Stores

Standard retail hours for most stores are 10:00 AM–6:00 PM, Monday through Saturday. Hours of operation are listed where available and applicable but are always subject to change. Please call ahead for verification.

Other Businesses

The producers, farmers and ranchers featured in this book operate enterprises that are affected by such things as the weather and the natural whims of livestock. Check out their web sites and call before visiting.

We've included phone numbers and web sites for producers who are set up for retail. To purchase products from the producers not set up for visitors, please inquire at your local grocery or health food stores, which often stock such items.

If you have any comments or would like to tell us about a favourite producer, farmer, rancher, chef, restaurant or supplier not included here, fill out the form on our website. Further contact information is available there as well.

ALONG THE COWBOY TRAIL

1 FROM THE CROWSNEST
TO CARSTAIRS

Southern Alberta is celebrated for its cowboys, both mythical and real, and this we know—cowboys love to eat. From the Calgary Stampede to the working ranches in the foothills of the Rockies, the traditional food of the cowboy trails—the flapjacks and biscuits, baked beans and barbecued beef—has become the stuff of legend. We're happy to report that authentic cowboy cuisine is alive and well, with a style all its own.

In the southwestern corner of the province near the Frank Slide is the historic coal mining town of Coleman. Here in the gorgeous high country, where prairie meets mountain, our cowboy trail begins.

DINING OUT ALONG THE COWBOY TRAIL

$$ **Pick's Roadhouse**

Highway 3 Coleman, Crowsnest Pass   Tel: (403) 564-5100

Open Sunday–Thursday 11:00 AM–10.00 PM

Friday, Saturday 11:00 AM–11:00 PM

V, MC, DEBIT

Just on the edge of town, next door to the Heartland County Store, sits Pick's Roadhouse, the latest creation from Witold Twardowski, Calgary's favourite restaurant impresario. Pick's, named after local character Emilio Picariello, offers typical roadhouse fare: burgers, chicken, steaks and pizzas cooked in the handmade applewood-burning oven. All baking is done in-house in the lower-level bakery. On weekends, go for the briskets, pork shoulder and butt, ribs, loin or chicken smoked in a pit over applewood coals.

The building, once the church hall, has been restored, its interior filled with found objects reflecting local pursuits (fishing, mining) and the history of the area. Huge wooden beams and an open kitchen contribute atmosphere. A touch of the theatrical is supplied by the enormous ornate bar—from the set of the movie Showboat. It's fantastic!

3

$
Black Diamond Bakery and Coffee Shop

119 Centre Avenue, Black Diamond   Tel: (403) 933-4503

Open Monday–Saturday 7:00 AM–6:00 PM

V, MC, AE, DEBIT

A visit to George Nielsen's bakery, housed in a former school (they moved it from Longview), is a taste of southern Alberta history. He has seven tables, and the rush starts early, when the local cowboys come in for the rancher's breakfast: four pancakes, three sausages, two eggs, hashbrown patties and toast. For those who can't handle a "real man's" meal, there's the lonesome (and skinny) dove: one egg, one piece of toast. Hardly anyone orders it.

"We have two soups every day, but people really love the chili," says George. "It's my own recipe, the same one I've been using every day since 1993." We hint shamelessly, but he doesn't bite. "No, you can't have the recipe," says the sly dog.

George has been baking everything from scratch for the past 15 years. His favourite bread is the big round sourdough he calls the Trail of the Cowboy Sourdough. George also makes a very fine eccles cake. It goes like this: layer of puff pastry, layer of currants, second layer of puff pastry, sugar and cinnamon. He rolls the whole thing flat, so the currants sneak up into the top layer. Yum.

$$
Boundary Ranch

www.boundaryranch.com

Highway 40, Kananaskis   Tel: (403) 591-7171 R

Open summer daily 11:00 AM–8:00 PM; Open winter for groups only

V, MC, AE, DEBIT (DINNER IS RESERVATION ONLY)

The Guinn family has been in the Kananaskis area since the 1930s when Alvin and Eva Guinn operated one of the earliest guest ranches in the mountains. In those days, Alvin roped and broke wild mustangs to take his guests on trail rides.

Working up an appetite.

TRAILRIDERS ASSOCIATION OF ALBERTA

In 1987 the family, with three tents and a string of ten horses, started Boundary Ranch on the same land that had supplied Alvin with his wild mustangs. Year by year the ranch has expanded, adding more facilities: a beer garden, a veranda and a giant fire circle.

Boundary Ranch offers a taste of ranch life and aboriginal culture for groups, including authentic Stoney tipis and a sweat lodge. After a trail ride, guests gather around the fire while the rib-eyes sizzle. Then, the cook whips up a batch of bannock to eat with maple syrup, and they finish off the evening with a marshmallow roast. Trips and events include guided horseback and outfitting trips, rodeos, barbecues, hayrides, whitewater rafting and trail rides for groups of 25 to 500. The restaurant, open for non-group visitors during the summer, also produces rustic and tasty fare: burgers, baked beans, steaks and chili.

$ **High Country Café**

Highway 22 & Secondary Highway 549, Millarville   Tel: (403) 931-3866

Open Monday–Saturday 8:00 AM–3:00 PM

    Sunday 9:00 AM–3:00 PM

DEBIT

Karen Orum bakes butter tarts and pie every day, and they're a big hit with everyone who tastes them. The other big hit here is the grilled bison burger, served all dressed (mushrooms, onions, cheese) on a kaiser roll. The rolls are baked just down the road at George Nielsen's Black Diamond Bakery.

On Sunday morning, the High Country gets a bit fancy and serves eggs Benedict, but Saturday there's a full rancher's breakfast: pancakes, bacon and sausage, eggs and home fries. "We can't do this in the summer when there's a farmers' market on Saturdays," says Karen. "The crowd gets too big, and we can't fit it all on the grill."

$$ **The Home Quarter Prime Rib Steak & Seafood**

216 1st Street W, Cochrane   Tel: (403) 932-2111

Open Monday–Friday 10:00 AM–10:00 PM

    Saturday, Sunday and holidays 9:00 AM–10:00 PM

V, MC, AE, ENR, DEBIT

The "home quarter" is an old farming term, referring to the quarter section that was first homesteaded. "Joan and I are both from a farming background," says owner Clarence Longeway. "It was just the right name."

The Home Quarter began as a bakery, but 12 years ago the Longeways took it over and turned it into a pie shop. Now, two local women make everything from scratch, including the toothsome, flaky crust. They'll bake 50 varieties of fresh pies—flapper, banana cream, coconut cream and their famous lemon meringue. "Saskatoon pie is a big seller," says Clarence. "We go through 1000 pounds of saskatoons a year." There are even a number of sugar-free pies made with Splenda.

The dining room with two big wood-burning fireplaces seats 105 guests. The signature dish is certified Angus prime rib. Every Sunday there's a hefty roast turkey dinner with gravy, stuffing and cranberries. For dessert? Pie, of course!

$$ Memories Inn

Morrison Road, Longview   Tel: (403) 558-3665 R
Open Friday–Saturday 5:00 PM–10:00 PM
  Sunday buffet 12:00 PM–7:00 PM
V, MC, AE, DEBIT

"No ribs on Sunday," says Rudy Vallee, the chef with the secret recipe stored in his head. "Yes, I'm really Rudy Vallee. I've been stuck with that name all my life!"

Everybody wants his recipe, and Rudy has turned down big money from big people, but there'll be no parting with the secret of the fabulous ribs. We know this much: they're beef. They're big. They're meaty. They're trimmed by Vallee himself before they hit the heat, and they're finger-lickin' good when they hit the plate.

"No eggs either," says Vallee, dismissing the lowly egg now and forever. "This is beef country, and we do our own thing. And one more thing: if you don't like the food, you don't pay. We're open 10 years, and so far everybody pays."

$$$ La P'tite Table

                                        www.la-ptite-table.com
52 North Railway Street, Okotoks   Tel: (403) 938-2224 R
Open Tuesday–Friday 11:00 AM–1:30 PM, 5:30 PM–10:00 PM
  Saturday 5:30 PM–10:00 PM
V, MC, DEBIT

La P'tite Table has considerable charm, and serves well-made country French dishes. House-smoked salmon makes an excellent starter. The rilettes of duck is lovely with a glass of red wine. For main course try the braised sweetbread tart with caramelized shallot sauce, or the lovely woodsy flavours in the grilled chicken breast with wild mushroom sauce. Rabbit gets a gently perfumed tarragon sauce, and ostrich medallions are sauced with a sweet-piquant blend of black currant and juniper berry.

For dessert, indulge in the tarte tatin, the lemon curd tart or a freshly made sorbet. Or try the memorable version of île flottant—floating island to the Anglophones—airy meringue in a vanilla cream, finished with toasted almonds. With the addition of their takeout, Au P'tit Gourmet, locals can now take dinner home to heat-and-eat. Think of the picnics!

Mountain Bistro and Pizzeria

$$

Bragg Creek Shopping Centre, Bragg Creek   Tel: (403) 949-3800

Open Monday–Sunday 11:00 AM–8:00 PM; open later in summer

V, MC, AE, DEBIT

> Stop in for the substantial blue plate specials: rosemary-mustard chicken breast, pyrohys served with Spolumbo sausage, vegetarian mushroom burgers or a creative version of ratatouille. Good pizzas, burgers, several pastas and the all-day breakfast round out this casual menu. It's not fancy, but nobody goes away hungry.

MacKay's Cochrane Ice Cream

www.mackaysicecream.com

220 1st Street W, Cochrane   Tel: (403) 932-2455

Open May–September daily 10:00 AM–10:00 PM

Open October–April daily 10:00 AM–6:00 PM

DEBIT

> To a lot of Albertans, the MacKay name means ice cream. This second-generation family business operated by sisters Rhona and Robin MacKay began as a grocery store owned by their dad. Long after the ice cream had become their best seller, he insisted on keeping the groceries. "When he died we didn't want to dust those soup cans anymore, so we took them home and became an ice cream shop," says Robin.
>
> Some of the flavours—saskatoon, chokecherry, rhubarb ripple—reflect their prairie roots. "The rhubarb used to come from the patch in our backyard," says Robin. And about the chokecherries: "Dad used to pick me up from swimming and we'd go pick chokecherries. I still have a scar from where I fell down the hill."
>
> MacKay's ice cream is luxurious—high butterfat and low overrun (very little air). Whenever possible they use fresh fruit. But they also do all the fun flavours: bubblegum, cookie dough, Smarties. "The kids go wild when we do tours. They've never seen so many Smarties in one place." ✍

PaSu Farm

$$$

www.pasu.com

Carstairs   Tel: (403) 337-2800 R

Open Tuesday–Saturday 12:00 PM–4:00 PM

> Sunday buffet 12:00 PM; tea, 2:30 PM–4:00 PM

Call for evening fine dining and special events.

V, MC, AE, DEBIT

> Noah would have loved this place. Llamas, sheep, donkeys, elk and geese roam the farm where Sue and Patrick de Rosemond operate their lovely country restaurant. They could scarcely have designed a more beautiful backdrop than this—somewhat softer than the southern landscape along our cowboy trail, but

equally moving. Before you go, know that dinner will be a leisurely affair amounting to several hours.

Starters might include a plate of pristine mixed baby greens with Natricia chèvre, possibly with saskatoon vinaigrette. PaSu specializes in lamb, and Patrick refuses to cook it beyond medium rare, so don't even ask. Roast stuffed leg of lamb for six or eight is available by prearrangement. Delicious stuffed profiteroles, fresh fruit pies, cheesecake, several chocolate choices and a good cheese tray served with port round out the selections.

HOW TO GET THERE: From Highway 2A, turn on Highway 580, go west 12 km, then south on Range Road 203, 2.5 km. Watch for signage.

◎ FOR a longer journey, here are two guest ranches offering typical cowboy cooking and western hospitality.

$$ **Bloomin' Inn Guest Ranch**　　　　　　　www.bloomin-inn.com
3 miles east of Pincher Creek on Highway 785　　　　Tel: (403) 627-5829
V, MC (RESTAURANT SERVES TO GUESTS ONLY)

Colleen and Francis Cyr run a ranch vacation on their third-generation land, homesteaded by Francis's family in the early 1900s.

After a big farmhouse breakfast, guests are encouraged to help feed the animals, and after that they're on their own to wander the property or tour nearby sites such as Head-Smashed-In Buffalo Jump. A trip to this UNESCO heritage site is an absolute must.

Colleen does all of her own baking, from bread and buns to pies and cookies. For guests, the meals are a taste of true ranch life, with everything on the table coming from the land, including their excellent bacon and ham. One year the pigs were named Bacon, Ham, Pork and Sausage. Oh, well.

COLLEEN'S BLOOMIN' INN GUEST RANCH CRAB APPLE JELLY

This is more method than recipe, but it makes delicious jelly. Simmer 3 lbs crab apples in 3 cups of water until tender, about 20 minutes. Drip through a jelly bag. Cook 4 cups juice and 3 cups sugar to jelly stage, about 15 minutes. Skim foam and test for gel point. Pour into 4 1–cup sterilized jars. Seal. Use within a few weeks.

Bloomin' Inn Guest Ranch Meatball Stew

Colleen says, "This down-home stew is a favourite with guests and family at our ranch. We use our own beef and local garden vegetables, and we think it's the best in the West."

1 medium turnip
6–8 large carrots
6–8 large potatoes
6 stalks celery
1 large onion, chopped
1 tbsp (15 mL) canola oil
4 cups (1 L) chicken or beef stock
2 cups (500 mL) water (optional)
1 cup (250 mL) green beans
1 bay leaf
meatballs (recipe follows)
salt and pepper to taste

Cut turnip, carrot, potatoes and celery into bite-sized pieces. Sauté onion in oil. Put vegetables in Dutch oven and cover with chicken or beef stock. Add up to 2 cups water if needed. While vegetables are cooking, brown meatballs in large frying pan, a few at a time. Drain on paper towels and reserve. Add meatballs and green beans to pot. Simmer for about 30 minutes. Serve with dumplings or biscuits.

MEATBALLS
1 lb (500 g) lean ground beef
½ lb (250 g) ground pork
1 envelope dry onion soup mix
1 egg
2 handfuls oatmeal
salt and pepper

Combine all ingredients in mixing bowl. Do not overmix. Shape into 1 ½ inch diameter meatballs to make approximately 5 to 6 meatballs per serving. Serves 6 to 8.

$$ **Willow Lane Ranch**   www.willowlaneranch.com

Granum   Tel: (403) 687-2394 or (403) 687-2284

Open May–October

V, MC

Willow Lane Ranch, a working cattle and horse ranch, is located near Granum, about an hour and a half from Calgary. Guests of Keith and LeAnne Lane are invited to climb on a horse and get involved in the working duties of the ranch.

LeAnne's cooking is substantial and homey. Her baking—bread, cookies, cakes, pies—is all from scratch. She's too busy to look after a vegetable garden, but buys produce from local farmers. One of her favourite salads is a delicious combination of romaine and radishes with a honey-poppy seed dressing, and everybody loves her baked beans. Menu items run from fluffy saskatoon berry pancakes to a hefty boxed lunch for the riders, and a rib-sticking dinner of roast chicken or roast beef. For the steak lover, dinner is often prime Alberta beef raised right there on the ranch.

WILLOW LANE RANCH BAKED BEANS

4 lb (2 kg) navy (pea) beans
2 large onions, chopped
1 meaty ham bone
salt and pepper
2 cups (500 mL) catsup
1 cup (250 mL) brown sugar
1 cup (250 mL) vinegar (see note)
½ cup (125 mL) molasses
1 tbsp (15 mL) dry mustard
½ cup (125 mL) barbecue sauce
2 tbsps (30 mL) Worcestershire sauce
4–5 drops Tabasco sauce

Soak beans overnight in cold water. Drain. Add onion, ham bone, salt and pepper to the beans, cover with fresh water and bring to boil. Reduce heat and simmer for two hours. Remove ham bone and cut off meat. Place meat in roaster and add remaining ingredients. Give it a stir.

Bake 4 to 5 hours at 250 F (125 C) with the lid off, stirring occasionally. Serves 15 to 20, generously.

NOTE: If you have a jar of sweet pickles and it's down to its last pickle, use 1 cup (250 mL) pickle juice instead of vinegar.

CALGARY

2

It's brash, exciting, a big city and proud of it. Proud of its history, as historic buildings along Stephen Avenue downtown have been rehabilitated and turned into glamourous settings for sophisticated, big-ticket dining. A surprise for visitors perhaps, but not for the worldly citizens of this burgeoning city.

Calgary is blessed in its location, rapidly emptying on weekends as everyone heads to the Rockies or Kananaskis to play. You'll find great food, great food places—markets, purveyors and shops of all description—and a wide-open friendly attitude here.

◉ CALGARY PANTRY
WHERE GOOD COOKS SHOP

Some cooks would rather eat soap than divulge their sources, but we're here to spill the beans. We'll tell you where to find ancho chili powder, red Thai rice, white truffles, the best smoked trout, game meats, local cheeses—whatever your heart or your recipe desires. For convenience, our not-so-secret sources are divided alphabetically, by category.

ℐ CANDY

Bernard Callebaut Chocolaterie

Meet our favourite Belgian—Bernard Callebaut. Each of his stores is a superb presentation of the chocolatier's art with soft light bathing trays and trays of the most delicious bonbons. Fabulous packaging—exquisite coffrets in the signature bronze colour, ribbons, bows, faux-fruit, all for the luxurious, handcrafted Belgian chocolates made in Calgary. (See also page 239.)

Main location and chocolate factory   Tel: (403) 266-4300
1313 1st Street SE
Open Monday–Wednesday, Saturday 8:30 AM–6:00 PM
    Thursday, Friday 8:30 AM–9:00 PM; Sunday 12:00 AM–5:00 PM
V, MC, AE, DEBIT
    Other locations: 5771 Signal Hill Centre SW, 217-1700; 1123 Kensington Road
    NW, 283-5550; 847 17th Avenue SW, 244-1665; 124–5403 Crowchild Trail NW
    (Crowchild Square), 286-2008; A123–1600 90th Avenue SW (Glenmore
    Landing), 259-3933; 318–100 Anderson Road SE (Southcentre Mall), 271-4100.

Olivier's Candies
919 9th Avenue SE   Tel: (403) 266-6028
Open Monday–Saturday 9:00 AM–5:00 PM
V, MC, DEBIT
    Olivier's has been a Calgary landmark since 1909. With much of the original
    equipment, including magnificent old copper pots, Glade Roberts and Bonnie
    McKinnon carry on the craft of handmade candies: ribbon candy, old-fashioned
    spice mix, coconut candy, peanut brittle, peppermints, butterscotch and big
    twirly lollypops. "We still have candy molds dated 1904. We use century-old
    recipes for our barley sugar candy and our peppermint patties," says McKinnon.
        Before Christmas they're elf-busy, hand-pulling thousands of candy canes
    and flavouring them with real peppermint oil.

CHEESE

The Cookbook Co Cooks   www.cookbookcooks.com
722 11th Avenue SW   Tel: (403) 265-6066
Open Monday–Friday 10:00 AM–8:00 PM
    Saturday 10:00 AM–5:30 PM; Sunday 12:00 PM–5:00 PM
V, MC, AE, ENR, DEBIT

This small selection of fine
cheeses is carefully chosen
and sold only at the point
of ripeness. Of special note
is the amazing number of

*Savoury selection of chèvre at
the Cookbook Co Cooks*

artisinal goat cheeses from France, Ontario and Quebec (Chevre Noir) and of course, Natricia Dairy from Ponoka.

Italian Centre

824 1st Avenue NE   Tel: (403) 263-5535
Open Monday–Saturday 9:00 AM–6:00 PM
V, MC, AE, DEBIT

> The selection here offers all the classic Italian cheeses: gorgonzola, mozzarella di bufala and, of course, good grating cheeses.
>
> They take it to another level with their lesser-known choices, such as the hard to find Taleggio, an outstanding cow's milk cheese from northern Italy, handmade in small batches from gently pasteurized Valtellina milk of the highest quality. This is a washed-rind cheese, available young (six months) or aged to a nutty, almost meaty flavour. Look for it when it's not quite runny inside, but developing that rich, buttery texture similar to Pont-l'Evêque. This truly is one of the world's great cheeses.

Janice Beaton Fine Cheese

                                                     www.jbfinecheese.com
1708 8th Street SW   Tel: (403) 229-0900
Open daily 9:00 AM–7:00 PM
V, MC, DEBIT

> This amazing shop is home sweet home for the cheese lover, whether you want a cheese sandwich with pristine tomatoes and herbs from Hotchkiss to eat in, or a nibble of Stilton to go with your port at home. The focus is French, Swiss and Canadian cheeses, including Alberta's own Natricia and Sylvan Star.
>
> The shop specializes in cheeses that Janice and her crew are passionate about: fine handmade cheese from goat, cow and sheep's milk. Don't get Janice started on the arcane and byzantine quota rules and regulations that prevent the shop from selling several unique artisan cheeses from other provinces—you'll be there for a very long time. (Which would be fun.)
>
> We found lots of things that go with cheese: Valbella Meats ham, garlic sausage and bunderfleisch (air-dried beef), baguettes from Manuel Latruwe and Tour Eiffel bakeries, lovely cornichons, and fabulous terrines from Quebec. We also found gadgets for cheese cookery such as a T-Fal raclette maker and fondue pots.

Boyd's Lobster Shop

1515 14th Street SW   Tel: (403) 245-6300
Open Monday–Saturday 9:00 AM–7:00 PM
      Sunday 11:00 AM–6:00 PM
V, MC, DEBIT

In spite of its name, Boyd's is more than a lobster shop. They carry a wide variety of fresh fish and seafood, including exotic species.

Manager Paul Cormier says the big demand is for lobsters, especially during the spring season. Once the barbecues come out, their customers start looking for deep-sea fish like marlin, mahi mahi, tuna and shark. "These big fish make wonderful steaks, and we cut them to order," he says. "Shark steak can be a little dry, but if you marinate it and don't overcook it, it's delicious."

Billingsgate Seafood Market

630 7th Avenue SE   www.billingsgate.com
                                 Tel: (403) 269-3474 (ANY FISH)
Open Monday–Saturday 9:00 AM–6:00 PM
V, MC, DEBIT

Mark Pulfer, manager of Billingsgate's retail division for Alberta, is proud of the variety of fish he sees coming into his shop every week. "Our customers want the fish they've eaten in Cuba or Mexico or wherever they spend their winter holidays, and we can get it for them. Right now we're seeing a lot of wild exotics like sea bass, mahi mahi and Nile perch, a mild, white-fleshed fish from Lake Victoria in South Africa."

Lobster is big in May, then fresh salmon. At Christmas they go crazy with all the party favourites: lobster, king crab legs, and about 50 different options of shrimp, including spotted prawns, tiger prawns, Mexican shrimp, Louisiana and green shrimp, cooked or frozen.

∥ MEATS AND FOWL

4th Street Meats

2100 4th Street SW   Tel: (403) 229-3661
Open Tuesday–Friday 10:00 AM–6:00 PM; Saturday 10:30 AM–5:30 PM
V, MC, DEBIT

We like this store because of its emphasis on chemical-free and free-range meats, and on quality. Meats are properly aged for better flavour. They also offer game and custom cutting services.

Bon Ton Meat Market

1941 Uxbridge Drive NW
(Stadium Shopping Centre)
Tel: (403) 282-3132
Open daily 9:00 AM–6:00 PM
V, MC, DEBIT

Along with an excellent selection of well-aged beef, pork, free-range eggs and fowl, there are cooked ribs (both beef and pork) roast chickens, wings and assorted deli fare ready for take-away. And they cook for their customers. "During the holiday season, scads of turkeys and roasts will be cooked here" says owner Fred Keller. Bon Ton's philosophy is of the "if it ain't broke don't fix it" variety. Their unique meat pie recipe remains unchanged in 60 years. "We sell hundreds daily," says Fred.

Calgary Bison Company

www.bisoncentre.com
Delacour
Tel: (780) 280-1747
Open daily but call ahead
CASH ONLY

Owners Linda and Jerry Ruhl were among some of the first bison ranchers in the province and their experience shows. On hand to provide cooking tips, recipes and just general bison lore, they make the trip more than worthwhile. Lean steaks, roasts and a variety of jerky, smokies and ground meat are available.

Life After Football: Spolumbo's

Spolumbo's Fine Foods and Deli
1308 9th Avenue SE
Tel: (403) 264-6452
www.spolumbos.com
Open Monday–Saturday 8:00 AM–5:30 PM
V, MC, AE, DEBIT

The name Spolumbo, so beloved of diners in Calgary, was born when cousins Tom and Tony Spoletini got together with former teammate Mike Palumbo. The quartet of ex-football players was complete when Craig Watson signed on in mid-1992. (Note the four football jerseys, framed and mounted on the walls.)

Today their sausage-making business builds on fine Italian tradition in a low-fat, thoroughly modern manner. These links are what you came for—chicken, sun-dried tomato and basil, chorizo made with turkey, chicken or pork, whisky-fennel spiked with Jack Daniels, merguez made with lamb and harissa, turkey-sage with pine nuts, chicken with roasted peppers. No additives, preservatives, fillers or binders—just sausage. The leader of the pack is the link that started it all, a spicy Italian sausage, aromatic with fennel. New flavours include a Louisiana-style pork andouille and the spicy Diablo spiked with salsa. You can buy your links and take them home, or choose from the lunch menu, sausages, sandwiches or Mamma's meatloaf on panini (Thursday to Saturday only).

Only in Calgary, you say? Nope. It's a federally inspected plant, and they ship all over the continent. ⸞

Canadian Rocky Mountain Ranch

West on Highway 22, South 4 km on 69th Street

V, MC

www.crmranch.com

Tel: (403) 256-1350

> The raison d'être of the ranch is to raise game meats (elk, bison and caribou) for the Canadian Rocky Mountain Resorts, Buffalo Mountain Lodge, Deer Lodge and Emerald Lake Lodge. Now, they seem to have enough for us regular joes as well. Check out their excellent web site for pricing, availability, recipes and tour times.

Specialty Fine Foods and Meats

3630 Brentwood Road NW (Brentwood Village Mall)

Open Monday–Saturday 10:00 AM–6:00 PM

Sunday 11:00 AM–5:00 PM

DEBIT

Tel: (403) 282-7412

> Need a little Kobe beef for your next dinner party? Or, how about the wild meats? Take your pick of venison, buffalo, elk, ostrich or caribou. Barbara Jackson and her husband Steven operate this fine butcher shop specializing in fresh and wild products. Ask Barbara to put you on the phone list to let you know the next time they have some fresh game meats coming in. Fresh sockeye salmon is carried in season and all meats and fowl are sourced from local farms. The sausage is delicious, from a family recipe with no fillers or preservatives, "Just meat and spice," says Barbara.

Tong Ky BBQ House

114 3rd Avenue SW

Open daily 10:00 AM–6:00 PM

CASH ONLY

Tel: (403) 269-4990

4301 17th Avenue SE

Open daily 10:00 AM–6:00 PM

CASH ONLY

Tel: (403) 248-3122

> Tong Ky BBQ House is not the only one in town, but it is one of the more memorable. For less than $15, take home a whole barbecued duck, or ask the butcher to wave his cleaver over the carcass and turn it into chopstick-friendly bites.

ASIAN & SOUTH ASIAN

Calgary Spiceland

3–5320 8th Avenue SE   Tel: (403) 273-1546

Open Monday–Friday 10:00 AM–7:00 PM

    Saturday 10:00 AM–6:00 PM; Sunday and holidays 11:00 AM–4:00 PM

V, DEBIT

    They aren't kidding about the spices. Looking for garam masala or tamarind? Want to make your own vindaloo paste? Stop here for fenugreek seeds, cumin seeds, ginger and chilis. On the sweeter side, they carry cinnamon sticks, cardamom pods, star anise, and many more exotic ingredients that distinguish East Indian cuisine. You'll also find a variety of rices, pulses, lentils, spicy snacks and condiments.

Continental Food & Spices & Produce Market

3253 34th Avenue NE   Tel: (403) 250-2448

Open Monday–Saturday 10:00 AM–7:30 PM

    Sunday and holidays 11:00 AM–5:00 PM

V, MC, DEBIT

    This produce section stocks items you won't find at your regular supermarket— okra, curry leaves, cassava and karela (bitter gourd)—plus the usual cilantro, pea shoots and tiny eggplant. Fresh and frozen ghee and paneer are available, as are almond and rose oils, all the favourite brands of pickle and chutneys, plus all the aromatics and spices. Look for beans, pulses and grains in abundance.

Dalbrent Spice Rack

3604 52nd Avenue NW

Tel: (403) 289-1409

Open Monday–Saturday 10:00 AM–7:00 PM

    Sunday and holidays 11:00 AM–5:00 PM

MC, AE, DEBIT

    There is a good selection of frozen Indian breads—naan, paratha, roti and chapati— and an inspiring array of pickle and chutneys here. They also carry mustard oil, rose and orange flower waters, and of course all the spices for your own masala.

Joy's Caribbean Foods

5–630 1st Avenue NE   Tel: (403) 234-9940
Open Monday–Friday 10:00 AM–7:00 PM
     Saturday 10:00 AM–6:00 PM
V, DEBIT

Come for roti—goat, veggie, chicken, shrimp or beef—or for the substantial, spicy Jamaican patties. Check out the selection of Caribbean essentials: callaloo, ackee (canned or fresh in season), jerk sauces and spices to make your own secret jerk rub.

Lambda Oriental Foods Market

1423 Centre Street North   Tel: (403) 230-1916
Open Sunday–Thursday 10:00 AM–7:30 PM
     Friday 10:00 AM–8:00 PM
     Saturday 9:00 AM–8:00 PM
V, DEBIT

This is a great little store, an excellent source for fresh meat and Asian ingredients like miso, wonton wrappers, rice vinegars, unusual condiments and teas of all sorts—for health, longevity, a slender figure, a sharper brain, a restful sleep, and simple drinking pleasure. The lemongrass is always fragrant, the greens fresh and the Japanese eggplant firm. Lambda has a terrific selection.

Nha Trang Market

101–575 28th Street SE   Tel: (403) 248-3301
Open daily 8:00 AM–9:00 PM
DEBIT

Nha Trang specializes in Vietnamese groceries, both fresh and frozen. It's a small selection, but it's authentic and worth checking out.

Shun Fat International Supermarket

3215 17th Avenue SE   Tel: (403) 272-8888
Open Monday–Saturday 9:00 AM–9:00 PM
     Sunday and Holidays 9:00 AM–8:00 PM
V, DEBIT

This is the place for East Asian ingredients—Thai, Vietnamese, Filipino, Korean and some Japanese. At the meat counter, the fresh pork, beef and poultry always looks great. The barbecued duck is platter-perfect and never skimpy—one duck, crisp of skin and juicy of breast, will make warm duck crepes for four. Frozen fish covers three aisles. There are at least 15 kinds of rice (basmati, scented, red, black

and so forth) in large economy-sized bags. Expect produce in season and all the
fresh herbs and greens—bok choy, suey choy and so forth—at good prices.

T & T Supermarket

800–999 36th Street NE (Pacific Place Mall)   Tel: (403) 569-9333
Open Monday–Saturday 9:30 AM–9:00 PM
    Sunday 12:00 PM–5:00 PM
V, MC, DEBIT

T & T is well known for its extensive selection of Chinese, Japanese and Southeast
Asian specialties. Count on a large selection of both imported and made-in-
Canada Asian foodstuffs, especially the delectable little Chinese sausages made by
Wing's. We like to poke about this mall as there are some fascinating Japanese
stores that carry lovely tableware and other hard goods.

EAST COAST

The Newfoundland Store

3501 17th Avenue SE   Tel: (403) 272-9092
Open Monday–Thursday 10:00 AM 6:00 PM; Friday 10:00 AM–7:00 PM
    Saturday 10:00 AM–6:00 PM; Sunday 10:00 AM–5:00 PM
V, MC, DEBIT

Homesick easterners from the Rock shop at this store for a taste of home. Prime
time for lobsters is Mother's Day. During lobster season they also have a standing
order from High River Rotary for 575 lobsters, plus one 10-pounder that they
raffle for charity.

The fish is frozen, including the requisite cod cheeks, cod tongues, digby scallops, Atlantic clams (fresh in season) and Nova Scotia lobster. Salt beef is available
for making a Jig's dinner: pea pudding, carrots, turnip, cabbage and potatoes. They
also carry some hard-to-find soft drinks like the top seller, Pineapple Crush, and
birch beer, which tastes like a mixture of cream soda and root beer. You'll find
Purity brand specialties: biscuits, hard bread, candies and flavoured syrups, and
Maple Leaf bologna, AKA Newfie steak, and salt cod for fish and brewis—a traditional dish of cod with soaked hard tack (a dried biscuit) and potatoes.

Evans' family also owns Da' Rock Restaurant across the street at 3460 17th
Avenue, where they do all that can be done with Newfie steak—bologna fried,
bologna sandwiches, bologna and eggs. Friday night is fish and brewis, Saturday
is pea soup, Sunday they make Jig's dinner. There's live entertainment Friday and
Saturday with traditional music: lots of reels and jigs, old son.

EUROPEAN

Dutch Cash and Carry

3815 16th Street SE (off Ogden Road)   Tel: (403) 290–1838
Open Monday–Friday 8:00 AM–4:30 PM; Saturday 9:00 AM–3:00 PM
V, MC, DEBIT

> Two very good reasons to be relentless in your search for this hard-to-find store
> are the great variety of Gouda cheeses, all of exceptional quality, and classic Dutch
> liquorice. You'll also find close to 400 imported Dutch and Indonesian foodstuffs.
> Do check out the wide variety of sambal sauces and other condiments used in
> Indonesian cooking such as fried onions for nasi goreng and peanut sauce.

Troyka Foods International

300–9737 Macleod Trail SW (Southland Crossing Plaza)   Tel: (403) 258-3344
Open Monday–Friday 10:00 AM–8:00 PM
        Saturday, Sunday 10:00 AM–7:00 PM
        Holidays 12:00 PM–4:00 PM
V

> Troyka is all about Russian specialties: fish, pickles, cakes and candies, for starters.
> For that special occasion, Sevruga caviar may be ordered with a deposit.
> Homemade favourites such as blintzes, pyrohy, cabbage rolls and borscht are avail-
> able for takeaway.

LATIN AMERICA

Atlantic Pacific

4907 17th Avenue SE (Saigon Mall)   Tel: (403) 235-5313 .
Open Monday–Friday 9:00 AM–6:00 PM; Saturday 9:00 AM–5:00 PM
DEBIT

> This store carries Portuguese specialties with a Brazilian flavour. Fresh saffron,
> sardines, olive oils and lots of fish including the ubiquitous salt cod. Brazilian soda
> pop and canned goods are also available.

El Bombazo Latino Market

2881 17th Avenue SE   Tel: (403) 204-3757
Open Wednesday–Saturday 9:00 AM–9:00PM; Sunday–Tuesday 9:00 AM–8:00PM
V, MC, AMEX, DEBIT

> The smallish grocery store on the busy 17th Avenue SE strip carries salsas, chipo-

tles in adobe, corn and wheat flours for tortillas, all for authentic Latin cooking. If you're hungry, huevos rancheros, yummy pupusas (stuffed tortillas) and enchiladas are on the menu at the in-store café.

La Tiendona

1836 36th Street SE   Tel: (403) 272-4054
Open Monday–Friday 10:00 AM–8:00 PM
    Saturday 10:00 AM–5:00 PM
DEBIT

This is a lively store that carries Mexican and Central American ingredients. Expect to find frozen tortillas, hot sauces, corn flours, and canned and dried peppers. There are also cactus leaves and a wide selection of condiments.

Boca Loca Fine Mexican Foods

1512 11th Street SW   Tel: (403) 802-4600
Open summer Monday–Friday 10:30 AM–7:00 PM
    Saturday 10:00 AM–5:00 PM
    Sunday 12:00 PM –4:00 PM
Open winter Monday–Friday 10:30 AM–6:00 PM
    Saturday 10:00 AM–5:00 PM
    Sunday 12:00 PM–4:00 PM
V, MC, DEBIT

Renette Kurz lived in Guadalajara and it shows. You'll find fresh cactus leaves, tamarind, tomatillos, Spanish onion, Mexican avocados, epazote (an herb used in soups and quesadillas), hominy corn for pozole, white hominy soup and cuitlacoche, a corn fungus similar in flavour to mushrooms, considered a delicacy.

Two Mexican cheeses, queso fresco (goat's milk) and queso crema (cow's milk) are stocked. Also, piloncillo (sugar cane cones) and organic Mexican Blue Mountain coffee for making cinnamon-scented Mexican coffee; and just the thing for our cold winters: Ilbarra and Abuelita brand hot chocolate.

They also carry really, really ripe plantains. "Latins like plantain when it's almost black," Kurz explains.

We also discovered a wide variety of dried peppers, mole sauces, hot sauces, Mexican vanilla and condiments, not just from Mexico but from Costa Rica and Belize as well. Talvera pottery (lead-free, dishwasher safe) from Puebla is gorgeous on the wall or for serving. We found tools for tortilla making, the warmers and flat pans (comals) that are also perfect for roasting tomatoes. Corn tortillas, salsa and tamales for takeaway are made fresh daily. ✎

The Cookbook Co Cooks

722 11th Avenue SW

Open Monday–Friday 10:00 AM–8:00 PM

    Saturday 10:00 AM–5:30 PM; Sunday 12:00 PM–5:00 PM

V, MC, AE, ENR, DEBIT

www.cookbookcooks.com

Tel: (403) 265-6066

Desiring to purchase white truffles? Black truffles? Truffles in oil? Gail Norton's busy shop would have been called an emporium of gustatory delights in some

other century. Pantry basics: demi-glace, several varieties of salt, fresh produce, luscious figs and tomatoes in season, all the newest condiments, sauces, spreads and dips—often laid out to sample. There is an extensive selection of locally sourced items as well as the cookbooks, of course. (See also pages 12, 199, 200.)

Salt and more salt, artfully displayed at The Cookbook Co Cooks.

MEDITERRANEAN

A&A Foods and Deli

1401 20th Avenue NW

Open Monday–Saturday 8:00 AM–10:00 PM

    Sunday 10:00 AM–8:00 PM

DEBIT

Tel: (403) 289-1400

It looks like a standard corner grocery store, until you notice the deli section filled with Lebanese specialties: flaky filo desserts, toothsome spreads and salads. The chicken schwarma—hot peppers, garlicky tahini sauce and smoky spit-roasted chicken rolled with tomatoes and lettuce in a pita—is a must. There is a good selection of pantry items from the Mediterranean basin if you want to DIY.

Atlas Supermarket

116 16th Avenue NE   Tel: (403) 230-0990

Open Tuesday–Saturday 10:00 AM–9:00 PM

      Sunday 11:00 AM–7:00 PM

DEBIT

It's part grocery store, part restaurant, with a few tables set up beside the racks filled with Middle Eastern grocery items—pomegranate molasses, quince jam,

preserved lemons and a really superb house-made yogourt. Order the outstanding fesenjan stew, chicken with walnuts and pomegranate. Nice touch: the jar of za'atar on each table for dusting, like the ubiquitous hot pepper flakes in a pizza joint.

Green Cedrus

4710 17th Avenue SE   Tel: (403) 235-9983

Open daily 9:00 AM–10:00 PM

V, MC, AE, DEBIT

It's a well-stocked grocery carrying Mediterranean specialties such as bulgur wheat, couscous and lentils. One of the best things about this shop is the tremendous olive selection from Egypt, Lebanon and Greece. You'll also find Turkish delight and halal meats. The aromatic coffee is ground to order the Arabic way, with cardamom.

Italian Centre

824 1st Avenue NE   Tel: (403) 263-5535

Open Monday–Friday 9:30 AM–6:00 PM

      Saturday 9:30 AM–5:30 PM

V, MC, AE, ENR, DEBIT

There are groceries, homemade fresh and frozen foods and a wide variety of dried pastas, along with an excellent cheese and meat selection including hard-to-find Italian cheeses and the real Parma ham. Don't miss Uncle Luigi's oil from Sardinia (yes, there really is an Uncle Luigi) and don't let the obviously homemade label throw you. This mild nutty oil is a good choice when you want a softer flavour. We love this place.

The Heart of Bridgeland
8 Street & 1 Avenue NE

Scuola de Cucina • Italian Gourmet Foods • Italian Centre • Merlo Vinoteca

Consider: We have an exclusive wine store with a cooking school on top, next door to a fresh pasta place, across the street from a traditional Italian grocery. Yeehaw!

Peter and Franca Beluschi have created a gourmet corner in Bridgeland, Calgary's Little Italy, and it looks, sounds, smells and tastes just like a corner in an Italian village.

Franca searches out rare and delicious wine for Merlo Vinoteca. At the cooking school upstairs, Peter explains the mysteries of Italian cuisine to enthusiasts, 16 at a time, throughout the year. Students learn to cook with Italian style. It could be pasta, it could be veal, but it's always fresh and authentic, and students eat what they've cooked. The classes are a bargain—three courses with wines for only $65 (at our deadline).

Meanwhile, across the street, Franca's family holds forth in the grocery store making sandwiches, advising on cheeses, choosing the right pasta for your sauce. This is where you'll find a ceramic platter for your marinated mushrooms and grilled peppers, a pasta maker if you must do it yourself, and a great selection of estate olive oils. It's everything you would expect from an Italian grocer, including the banter, with hams hanging from the ceiling, Italian cheeses, the real Parma ham (identified by the ducal crest on the label), all the wonderful Italian vegetables—radicchio, fennel—and Uncle Luigi's extra-virgin olive oil from Sardinia. Big sandwiches, too, with hot peppers, to go. ⬸

The Italian Store
5140 Skyline Way NE
Open Monday–Saturday 9:00 AM–5:00 PM
V, MC, DEBIT

Tel: (403) 275-8222

This is essentially the retail arm of Scarpone's, an excellent producer of canned goods available throughout the province. Check out this location for the full selection. There's a well-stocked grocery and deli, fresh and frozen foods, fresh seasonal produce and an outstanding meatball sandwich. Yum.

Kalamata Grocery
1421 11th Street SW
Open daily 8:00 AM–11:00 PM
DEBIT

Tel: (403) 244-0220

Here's a great little grocery store with a real neighbourhood feeling and Mediterranean flavour. The focus is on Greek deli items and specialties, particularly feta cheeses of high quality.

Lina's Italian Market

2202 Centre Street N Tel: (403) 277-9166

Open Monday–Friday 9:00 AM–8:00 PM

　　Saturday and Sunday 9:00 AM–5:00 PM

V, MC, DEBIT

The best reason to go to Lina's (besides groceries, that is) is to have a pizza and pick up the fennel in oil at the deli along with a lovely loaf of ciabatta. Lina's also carries good-looking produce, all sorts of cooking equipment and gadgets, dishes, coffee-makers and Mediterranean canned specialties like hearts of palm. The combination deli, lunch counter, cappuccino bar and grocery has an extensive selection of Italian oils, vinegars, pastas and some Latin American products such as chipotles in adobe.

Nicastro Foods

2418 Edmonton Trail NE Tel: (403) 230-5424

Open Monday–Thursday 9:00 AM–7:00 PM

　　Friday 9:00 AM–9:00 PM

　　Saturday 9:00 AM–6:00 PM

V, MC, DEBIT

The Nicastro family has been in this location for over 20 years, selling fresh produce in season: cactus pears, persimmons and chestnuts in early winter, fresh favas in the spring and of course those fabulous peppers and eggplant in the fall. At the deli, hundreds of panini will be made at lunchtime, not counting the orders that get spirited away to downtown office towers. It's the usual fillings— capicolla, mortadella, salami, provolone (only the best quality)—with vegetable spread on only the freshest bread. The Nicastros see their customers becoming more knowledgable about Italian food. For example, they now carry 12 kinds of Aceto Balsamico de Modena, two of which are 12 years old. Also on the shelf is a variety of pastas, oils, condiments, pasta makers and stovetop espresso makers. Son John grew up in the store and likes the neighbourhood aspect of it.

"We've become a part of a lot of families," he says.

Amaranth Whole Foods

7 Arbour Lake Drive NW   Tel: (403) 547-6333

Open Monday–Friday 9:00 AM–8:00 PM

    Saturday and Sunday 9:30 AM–6:00 PM

V, MC, DEBIT

    In this old-timey grocery store ambiance you can buy organic fruits and vegetables and over 300 bulk items, including grains and baking supplies. Free-range eggs, beef, turkey and bison are popular items, as is organic milk.

Community Natural Foods

                    www.communitynaturalfoods.com

202 61st Avenue SW (Chinook Station)   Tel: (403) 541-0606

Open Monday–Saturday 9:00 AM–8:00 PM

    Sunday 10:00 AM–6:00 PM

V, MC, DEBIT

1304 10th Avenue SW   Tel: (403) 229-2383

Open Monday–Saturday 9:00 AM–8:00 PM

    Sunday 10:00 AM–6:00 PM

V, MC, DEBIT

    Started in the '70s as a co-op, Community has grown to two stores selling a wide variety of healthful, wholesome, natural and organic foods. There is an ample

bulk section. Look for TK Ranch Natural Meats and vegetables in season from local organic farms like Poplar Ridge, Lund's Organic Farm and Hotchkiss.

Cornucopia

16–1941 Uxbridge Drive NW   Tel: (403) 284-9700

(Stadium Shopping Centre)

Open Monday–Friday 9:00 AM–8:00 PM

      Saturday 9:00 AM–7:00 PM

      Sunday 10:00 AM–6:00 PM

V, MC, DEBIT

Fresh produce, baked goods, cereal and condiments plus foods to go are available here. You'll also find a small organic bulk selection of nuts, dried fruits and grains. There's a terrific selection of fresh sandwiches, salads and the like for takeaway.

Planet Organic Fresh Market

10233 Elbow Drive SW (Southwood Corner)   Tel: (403) 252-2404

Open Monday–Friday 9:30 AM–8 PM

    Saturday 9:30 AM–7:00 PM; Sunday 11:00 AM–7:00 PM

V, MC, DEBIT

    Just-opened in the old Debaji's location, Planet Organic Market brings its unique blend of good-for-you hedonism to Calgary. Soft lighting and funky music belies the fact that there is a lot of old-style health foods and potions for the skin and supplements for the body. Look for an extensive selection of local products, both organic and conventional, and an excellent bulk section, plus meats and a large array of packaged goods.

Sunnyside Market

10–338 10th Street NW   Tel: (403) 270-7477

Open Monday–Wednesday, Saturday 10:00 AM–7:00 PM

    Thursday, Friday 9:00 AM–7:00 PM

    Sunday 11:00 AM–6:00 PM

V, MC, DEBIT

    A friendly neighbourhood grocery that concentrates on fresh organic fruit, vegetables and grains. There are organic meats in the freezer and a small dairy section.

Sunterra Market   www.sunterramarket.com

803 49th Avenue SW (Britannia)   Tel: (403) 287-0553

Open Monday–Saturday 9:00 AM–9:00 PM

    Sunday 9:00 AM–8:00 PM

V, MC, DEBIT

    Other locations: 200–1851 Sirocco Drive SW (West Market Square) 266-3049; 855 2nd Street (Bankers Hall), 268-3610; Village Marche (Trans-Canada Tower), 450 1st Street SW, 262-8240

    Sunterra, popularized the "eat-in or takeout, and pick up a few groceries at the same time," in Calgary. It's a shopping style for busy people. (See also pages 46, 234.)

Wrayton's Fresh Market   www.wraytons.com

590–5111 Northland Drive (Northland Village Shops)   Tel: (403) 269-3663

Open Monday–Friday 9:00 AM–9:00 PM

    Saturday 8:00 AM–8:00 PM; Sunday 10:00 AM–6:00 PM

V, MC, DEBIT

    This store opened to great fanfare just this fall in the old Debaji's north-end location and promises to be a superb destination for those who love food. Heaps of organic and conventional produce beguile with colour, texture and shape, and there is a fully stocked fishmonger, meat counter and bakery. We especially like the stock market which has a variety of daily-made stocks for soups and sauces in a bevy of flavours.

Former Teatro chef Michael Allemier has signed on to direct the food operations of the in-house bakery, café, and the creation of a full range of ready-to-go meals. We expect a few changes as they work out the wrinkles inherent in any new operation, but so far it looks and tastes great.

Michael Allemeier

Wrayton's Fresh Market executive chef, Michael Allemeier, came to Alberta from the west coast, after six years cooking with his mentor, John Bishop, with whom he co-authored *Bishop's, The Cookbook*. He joined Calgary's Teatro Restaurant as executive chef.

"Cooking in BC is easier," he says. "It's easy to keep it fresh, seasonal, regional." But it's a little harder to accomplish in a climate like Calgary's and he immediately began searching out local sources for high-quality produce, meat and dairy. "I believe in seasonal menus. The secret

Michael Allemeier with Janet Lewis, production sous chef.

is using what we have in creative ways. Taber corn is an example. In season, I use it fresh in a crème brûlée, which suits the natural super-sweet properties of that corn."

He's excited about the local regional products he is able to cook with like wild boar, range beef, artichokes and stinging nettles, oat groats, heirloom tomatoes, cold-smoked trout, native black cherries and a dozen different potatoes. Allemeier doesn't see all this largesse as exotic ingredients. "It's just Alberta," he says.

His recent move, to Wrayton's Fresh Market, is a challenge and a change in direction. He's in overall charge of the in-house bakery, all meal replacement services, the restaurant and 65 staff.

Between taping the third season of the *Cook like a Chef* TV show, his duties at Teatro and then the run up to getting Wrayton's open, Michael somehow found the time to write his Certified Chef de Cuisine papers. "I have a fabulous wife," he says. "Maybe at Wrayton's, I'll have fewer late nights." ✎

Calgary has a community of bakers who make fine French pastries. In shop after shop, we find exquisite examples of the art of patisserie—small, tender gems that melt in the mouth. The city also has its share of bakers-of-conscience, people who go out of their way to use organic or ancient grains, grind the grains themselves, and give the loaves time to rise slowly.

Brûlée Patisserie

722 11th Avenue SW   Tel: (403) 261-3064
Open Tuesday–Friday 10:00 AM–6:00 PM; Saturday 10:00 AM–5:00 PM
V, MC, AE, DEBIT

Rosemary Harbrecht's Brûlée sells indulgence. Breakfast fans looking for the perfect accompaniment to their morning latte or cappuccino will love the pecan sticky buns, glazed with brown sugar and richly caramelized pecans. For those with no time to fill the cookie jar, homestyle cookies come in a wide variety of flavours and fillings. We love the lavender- and orange-scented shortbread. Her heavenly and complicated tortes and specialty cakes follow the seasons, expect a hazelnut lime roulade in spring or the blackberry dacquoise filled with whipped cream and beautiful berries in summer. Chocolate, of course, is seasonless, welcome at any time of the year. Brûlée does not disappoint, whether it's the spicy Diablo, a dark chocolate masterpiece enlivened with some chili heat, or the decadent Chocolatissimo.

In the exquisite Brûlée Patisserie, indulgence is at hand.

Byblos Bakery   www.byblosbakery.com

2479 23rd Street NE   Tel: (403) 250-3711

Open Monday–Saturday 9:00 AM–5:00 PM; Sunday 9:00 AM–4:00 PM

CASH ONLY

> You can buy this bakery's pita bread, tortilla wraps, bagels and baklava at most major stores around the province. It's a family business success story. But it's most fun to go to the source if you're looking for Middle Eastern breads, pies, sweets or specialties—think of fatayer and za'atar, for openers. The baklava is syrup-drenched and tooth-achingly sweet, but so delicious with good coffee.

Decadent Desserts

103 1019 17th Avenue SW   Tel: (403) 282-3392

Open Monday–Friday 8:30 AM–4:00 PM; Saturday 8:30 AM–1:00 PM

V, MC, DEBIT

> Dessert maven Pam Fortier purchased Decadent Desserts (and the recipe for the city's best chocolate chunk cookies) from its co-founder, Bev Polsky. She continues to produce delectable sweet things for restaurants, retailers and the shop—a tantalizing seasonal array of tarts, cakes, cookies and tortes.

Eiffel Tower French Bakery

121–1013 17th Avenue SW   Tel: (403) 244-0103

Open Monday–Saturday 7:00 AM–6:00 PM; Sunday 9:00 AM–5:00 PM

V, DEBIT

102–502 25th Avenue NW   Tel: (403) 282-0788

Open daily 7:30 AM–7:30 PM

MC, DEBIT

> This classic French boulangerie is known city-wide for its baguettes and croissants, brioche, pain de compagne and petit pain. It is also the place to practice chocolate stress relief therapy. Sweet things recommended (apart from everything chocolate) are the raspberry mousse, which features fresh raspberries and whipped cream sandwiched between layers of almond cake, and the Royale, a confection of chocolate pastry cream on a crunchy hazelnut layer with almond cake base. In season, don't miss the fresh strawberry tarts.

Gunther's Fine Baking

4306 17th Avenue SE   Tel: (403) 272-0383

Open Tuesday–Friday 10:00 AM–5:30 PM; Saturday 9:00 AM–3:00 PM

CASH ONLY

> When Elizabeth and Gunther Stranziger celebrated their 30th year in the bakery

business a few years ago, Elizabeth said it was just another day. Another day of rustic, wholesome European baking.

Choose from a dozen different ryes, the medium Tyrolian rye or the heavy Vienna black among them. Or try the loaf made with oat bran and sunflower seeds. Rounding out the selection are various cheesecakes, mousse-filled cakes, rum and mocha tortes, and the German specialties: Zuckerkirsch torte and French and Danish pastries.

Heritage Recipes Organic Breadworks
7A–7640 Fairmount Drive SE (Astral Centre)
Open Tuesday–Friday 10:00 AM–6:00 PM
    Saturday 9:00 AM–5:00 PM
CASH ONLY

www.invisabl.com/organicbakery
Tel: (403) 640-0005

Martha Fincati took over this successful bakery, and her hands are the flour-dusted hands of a bread-loving baker. Try the fig and anise sourdough, the peasant seed loaf and the Austrian hiker's loaf, for starters.

Lakeview Bakery
6449 Crowchild Trail SW
Open Monday–Friday 8:00 AM–6:00 PM
    Saturday 8:00 AM–5:00 PM
    Sunday 12:00 PM–5:00 PM
V, MC, DEBIT

Tel: (403) 246-6127

Their excellent signature loaf is the ancient grains, made with quinoa, amaranth and spelt. They also do egg-free, dairy-free, sugar-free special orders, plus gluten-free pies, cakes, brownies and Christmas cakes for those with celiac disease. Lots of specialty breads here, some wheat free, some organic.

Patisserie Manuel Latruwe
1333 1st Street SE
Open Tuesday–Friday 7:30 AM–6:00 PM
    Saturday 7:30 AM–5:00 PM
V, MC, DEBIT

Tel: (403) 261-1092

This is where the sugarplums live, next door to Bernard Callebaut. The desserts are jewel-like, presented in a jewel box of a bakery. It's pastry as art, and everything—the fruit tarts, the mousse-filled cakes, the mille feuille, and at Christmas, the bûche de noël—is truly elegant. Even better, the desserts taste every bit as delicious as they look. Latruwe also makes wonderful bread, including baguettes, croissants and pain au chocolat.

Prairie Mill Bread Company

129–4820 Northland Drive NW   Tel:(403) 282-6455
Open Monday–Saturday 6:00 AM–6:00 PM
V, MC, DEBIT

26–7337 Sierra Morena Blvd SW   Tel: (403) 686-2500
Open Monday–Saturday 6:30 AM–10:30 PM
V, MC, DEBIT

919 Centre Street North   Tel: (403) 277-1137
Open Monday–Saturday 10:00 AM–6:00 PM
V, MC, DEBIT

The true bread specialists at this organic bakery buy organic grains and flours
and stone-mill their own wheat. There's a great selection, including the standards—whole wheat, honey white, cinnamon raisin—as well as the more
inventive sweet and savoury options: muesli, cranberry-orange, apple crunch,
nine grain, sunflower seed, Mediterranean (with black and green olives and
onion), jalapeno cheddar and Italian herb. The sourdough bread is especially
toothsome.

Rustic Sourdough

1305–17th Avenue SW   Tel: (403) 245-2113
Open Monday–Saturday 8:00 AM–5:00 PM
V, MC, DEBIT

Rustic Sourdough is known for hand-formed sourdough-based breads, from
heavy multi-grain to baguettes. Ryes are best sellers, but don't miss the cranberry-

pecan round or the European
muesli made with nuts and dried
fruits. Sweets include Danish pastries, tarts, cookies, cakes and
pies. We love the cream puffs,
poppy seed slices and the dobos
slice made with caramel and but-
tercream. The deli counter serves
sandwiches of cheeses and cold
cuts on house-made breads, and an
assortment of salads.

Caffe Beano
1613 9th Street SW
Tel: (403) 229-1232
Open Monday–Friday 6:00 AM–12:00 AM
Saturday, Sunday 7:00 AM–12:00 AM
CASH ONLY

Here's a coffee shop with history. Janice Beaton opened Beano many years ago, and it's now in the hands of good cook Rhondda Siebens, one of the authors of *Women Who Dish*. Enlarging the space has not altered its cozy nature or the personalized service. This coffee is roasted locally, and there's a lengthy list of choices. Yes, they have tea: black, green and herbal. Really good sandwiches: try the tomato, basil and white cheddar, or artichoke, tomato and goat cheese. The baking is done in-house and the muffins and the apple blackberry pie are especially noteworthy.

Conversations Tea Room
10816 MacLeod Trail South, 222 Willow Park Village   Tel: (403) 271-8886
Open Monday–Wednesday 10:00 AM–6:00 PM
Thursday 10:00 AM–8:00 PM; Friday, Saturday 10:00 AM–6:00 PM
Sunday 10:30 AM–3:30 PM
V, MC, DEBIT

Conversations serves some of the most delicious cakes and pastries you'll find in these parts. The cakes are all home-baked by owner Krystyna Stefan, whose finest creation may be the Hansel cake, a fudgy flourless chocolate. The ginger cake with warm lemon sauce is delicious. Tea for two, served from 2:00 PM, includes a savoury tray (mini-quiche, egg salad triangles, pinwheel sandwiches, cheese, vegetable crudités and dip) and a sweet tray with dainty pastries, scones and tarts.

Higher Ground

2nd floor, 1126 Kensington Road NW   Tel: (403) 270-3780
Open Monday–Thursday 7:00 AM–11:00 PM
    Friday 7:00 AM–12:00 AM; Saturday 8:00 AM–12:00 AM
    Sunday 8:00 AM–11:00 PM
V, MC, DEBIT

> There's a bit of la dolce vita about this second-floor coffee house. Terrific grilled sandwiches: the Sicilian, the Venetian, and a good old turkey with Swiss. Baked goods include toothsome muffins, cinnamon twists and cheesecake.

Joshua Tree

805 Edmonton Trail NE   Tel: (403) 230-9228
Open Monday–Thursday 7:00 AM–11:00 PM
    Friday, Saturday 8:00 AM–11:00 AM; Sunday 8:00 AM–10:00 PM
V, MC, DEBIT

> This is a funky little spot with its own quirky personality. The coffee is from Calgary's Planet Coffee Roasters, and the tea is Tazo. If you're hungry, try the tree-burger with chicken, mushroom and fried onions. The usual quick fare applies as well: panini, quesadillas, yummy house-made muffins and banana bread.

Planet Coffee Roasters

2212 4th Street SW   www.planetroasters.com
Open daily 7:00 AM–12:00 AM   Tel: (403) 244-3737
V, MC, DEBIT

> Other locations: 101–83 Beauridge Drive NW, 288-2233; 3605 Manchester Road SE, 243-9992.

> The 4th Street location roasts for all of the Planet Coffee Roasters. When the roaster is going, the neighbourhood fills with the pungent toasted-bean aroma. Keep in mind that this is not the heavenly brewing-coffee aroma that makes getting up in the morning worthwhile, but a much less attractive smell. Actually, it's quite stinky. But it's worth it for fresh-roasted beans.
>
> You can buy the roasted beans here or take the green beans home and go through the whole process yourself, including the roasting thing. They also sell home roasters, espresso machines and the other accessories so dear to the heart of the coffee lover.

JUDY SCHULTZ

Primal Grounds   www.primalgrounds.com
3003 37th Street SW   Tel: (403) 240-4185
Open Monday–Friday 7:00 AM–11:00 PM
        Saturday 8:00 AM–11:00 PM; Sunday 8:00 AM–10:00 PM
CASH ONLY

Westside Recreation Centre (inside)
Corner of 17th Avenue and 69th Street SW
Open Monday–Friday 10:00 AM–9:00 PM; Saturday, Sunday 10:00 AM–6:00 PM
CASH ONLY

Primal Grounds on 37th Street has a handy drive-through window, but this is more than your usual coffee shop. Both locations have great home cooking. Check out the turkey and cranberry sandwich, the macaroni and cheese and the chicken suiza. All the baked goods are made from scratch, with a ginger-laced pumpkin cake you won't soon forget.

Steeps the Urban Tea House   www.steepstea.com
880 16th Avenue SW   Tel: (403) 209-0076
Open Monday–Thursday 9:00 AM–11:00 PM; Friday 9:00 AM–12:00 AM
        Saturday 10:00 AM–12:00 AM; Sunday 10:00 AM–11:00 PM
V, MC, AE. DEBIT

"We have a sorta kitchen," says the friendly guy behind the counter of the busy Urban Tea House. "We have a teeny grill, and make sandwiches to order." Food runs to soups, sandwiches, panini, Jamaican patties and some good pastries. Owner Brendan Waye's trademark chai is the big tea story here—vanilla, green, herbal and traditional chais, less sweet than some, and very full-flavoured. We love the mysterious aromas wafting off the steaming cups—what spices be these, what herbs?

CAFÉS, BISTROS, DINERS
& NEIGHBOURHOOD JOINTS

Everybody in this dynamic young city wants to be a restaurateur, or know a restaurateur. Calgary's food scene is one of rapidly revolving doors, with the occasional shriek of glee or dismay as new players join the game.

New restaurants, diners, grills, cafés, trattoria, bistros . . . they pop up overnight, reinventing themselves, opening and closing at an amazing rate. The joints, hangouts and eateries in this list have one thing in common: a certain character that makes them memorable.

$ **The Arden**

1112 17th Avenue SW   Tel: (403) 228-2821

Open Monday–Friday 11:00 AM–12:00 AM
    Saturday 9:00 AM–12:00 AM
    Sunday 9:00 AM–10:00 PM

V, MC, AE, DEBIT

    The Arden looks like a classic diner from the outside. Inside, it's a trendy upscale space—diner-as-hangout-and-bar with lots of stools for perching and some cozy booths for two, co-owned by singer-songwriter Jann Arden and her brother Patrick Richards. Try the hot turkey sandwich, a guilty pleasure complete with white bread and salty gravy. The Blue Arden, a hefty burger with melting blue cheese and sautéed mushrooms served with crisp fresh-cut fries, is a model of its kind, as are liver and onions, macaroni and cheese like Mom used to make, sloppy Joes and classic meatloaf (the siblings' mother's own recipe).

$$$ **Bonterra**

1016 18th Street SW   Tel: (403) 262-8480 R

Open Monday–Friday 11:30 AM–3:00 PM; 5:00 PM–11:00 PM
    Saturday 5:00 PM–11:00 PM
    Sunday 5:00 PM–10:00 PM

V, MC, AE, DC

    Bonterra, operated by the Creative Restaurant Group, is a beautiful space with indulgent staff to care for you. Don't expect traditional Tuscan fare, but do look for the high quality for which chef Josef Wiewer is recognized.

    This menu changes seasonally, reflecting what's new and fresh at the market. Try the pasta amatriciana with wild boar bacon, go on to the lumache (giant snail-shaped pasta) with artichokes, spinach and a thyme-cream velouté. The cornish hens, inspired by chef Wiewer's favourite dish from Siena, are roasted with black olives, Marsala, herbs and garlic. To end, we had the excellent panna cotta, scented with lemon, orange and vanilla, served with a strawberry and rhubarb coulis.

$$ **Boyd's**   www.calgarymenus.com/boydsseafood

5211 Macleod Trail South   Tel: (403) 253-7575 R

Open Monday–Wednesday 11:00 AM–9:00 PM
    Thursday–Saturday 11:00 AM–10:00 PM
    Sunday 12:00 PM–9:00 PM

V, MC, DEBIT

    The founder, Blaise Boyd, made his reputation as a cook with superlative fish and chips, and his son Jason offers halibut, haddock, cod and pollock in batter, from a one-piece dinner of pollock to a family pack of halibut (eight pieces of fish, coleslaw and fries) available for takeout only. The fish and chips page of the menu explains clearly what to expect from each species. We love the detailed paragraph at the end of the page that explains concisely and without apology just how and why fresh French fries vary throughout the year.

$$ Brava Bistro

723 17th Avenue SW   Tel: (403) 228-1854 R

Open Monday Saturday 11:00 AM 3:00 PM, 5:00 PM 11:00 PM

    Sunday 5:00 PM—10:00 PM

V, MC, AE, DC

They call it Canadian Provençal, we call it bistro cooking. Whatever you call it, it's consistently good. We've found ourselves back at Brava more times than we can count. We love the grilled rack of lamb, perfectly cooked, pink throughout, tender, juicy, with braised leek and fennel. Then there's the luxurious truffled wild mushrooms with soft polenta. The menu changes often, but this is fine cooking at any time. You could go to Brava just for the selections of wines by the glass. It's enormous—50 at last count and well-priced too, most under $8.

$$ Buon Giorno

823 17th Avenue SW

Tel: (403) 244-5522 R

Open Monday Friday 11:30 AM—2:00 PM

    Saturday 5:00 PM—11:00 PM

V, MC, ENR, AE, DEBIT

Here is a bit of Italy the way we like to pretend it would be: busy, aromatic with garlic, tomatoes and olive oil. The menu has all the favourites, alfredo, carbonara, bolognese and, our personal favourite, spaghetti aglio olio. This is simple food, expertly prepared. These people could cook in their sleep. It's not trendy, but there's nothing quite so satisfying as a plate of well-made pasta with just the right sauce.

$$ **Calzoni's**

825 12th Avenue SW   Tel: (403) 216-0066

Open Monday–Wednesday 11:00 AM–8:00 PM

     Thursday–Saturday 11:00 AM–9:00 PM

V, MC, AE, DEBIT

You have to admire chef-owner Colin Kryski's sense of humour. How about that business card with the black and white photograph of a nude male sculpture shot from the ankle and looking waaay up, which proclaims: "Size DOES matter!" Ya gotta love it. Flip over the card and read through a list of Kryski's best pizzas, including Three Wise Guys, The Tenth Commandment or The Garden of Good and Evil. The pizza is not cheap, but it's great. The business is mostly takeout and delivery, but there are six seats for dining in.

$ **Cedars Deli Café**

225 8th Avenue SW   Tel: (403) 263-0285

Stephen Avenue Mall

Open Monday to Friday 10:00 AM–7:00 PM

     Saturday 11:00 AM–4:00 PM

V, MC, AE, DEBIT

Other locations: Cedars Deli, 200 Barclay Parade SW (Eau Claire Market), 264-2532; Cedars Falafel Hut, MacEwan Hall, University of Calgary, 282-0713

Founded by Mary Salloum and her family nearly 20 years ago, The Cedars now has three locations, including a prime spot on Stephen Avenue Mall.

Try the dolmades, the spinach filo, the tabbouleh with its great bash of parsley and lemon and the saffi salad with chickpeas. Undecided diners like the combo plates, either the vegetarian or the Mediterranean, which is a feast including felafel, hummus, tabbouleh, dolmades and kibi (ground sirloin and bulgur wrapped around a mixture of pine nuts and ground beef). The hot eggplant casserole is also a winner, with sliced eggplant layered with filo, spinach, zucchini, mozzarella and eggs.

Table service or takeout is available at the café; takeout only at the other two locations. There are lineups at lunch.

$$ **Chili Club Thai House**   www.calgarymenus.com/chiliclub

125–555 11th Avenue SW   Tel: (403) 237-8828

Open Monday–Friday 11:30 AM–2:00 PM; 5:00 PM–9:00 PM

     Saturday 5:00 PM–10:00 PM; Sunday 5:00 PM–9:00 PM

V, MC, ENR, AE, DEBIT

Beware: red chili icons on the takeout menu warn the diner of heat levels, but ask

Mary Salloum

Back in 1983, Mary Salloum had no intention of becoming a restaurateur. But when her first cookbook, *The Taste of Lebanon*, turned into a best-seller, she suddenly had a following. "And that's how it started," she says. Her small deli opened in 1985, a tiny space with only 13 chairs, and the catering business took off like a rocket. "The menu was about half the size it is now. Felafel and shawarma (grilled steak on a stick) were our best sellers, but the tabboulch, the hummus and the baklava were big items too."

Salloum still loves to cook. "For years I was the only cook here. We have four now, but I'm still in the restaurant every day." Her son Daniel and daughter Dana are both involved in the business. Every October Salloum packs her bags and hits the trail looking for new and interesting food in Europe, the Middle East, the Mediterranean and North Africa. "I get into the kitchens and prowl through the food markets," she says. "And I eat!" ⬸

your server for guidance when in the restaurant as there are no icons on the eat-in menu.

The hot and sour soup with prawns is enlivened with slivers of lemongrass and kaffir lime leaves. The hottest curry is the green shrimp, but there's another layer of flavour here: the subtle sweetness of coconut milk. Cooling slices of cucumber are served alongside. Try the Panang duck curry, which pairs succulent boneless duck with eggplant.

The best title on the menu belongs to a vegetable dish: evil jungle prince mixed vegetables.

$ **Diner Deluxe**
804 Edmonton Trail   Tel: (403) 276-5499
Open Monday–Friday 7:30 AM–9:30 PM
    Saturday, Sunday 8:00–3:00 AM, 5:00 PM–9:30 PM
V,MC, ENR, AE, DEBIT
> Calgary chef Dwayne Ennest and wife Alberta have opened a retro diner serving tasty '50s-style comfort food including toothsome breakfasts. The cooking is seasonal and all the jams pickles, desserts and pies are made in-house. Dwayne is well known in Calgary for pioneering organic ingredients and developing long-standing relationships with local farmers. Opening soon next door is their Art Deco-themed supper club, to be open three nights a week with more sophisticated food.

$$ **Grand Isle Seafood Restaurant**
200–128 2nd Avenue SE   Tel: (403) 269-7783 R
Open Monday–Friday 10:00 AM–10:00 PM; Saturday, Sunday 9:00 AM–11:00 PM
V, MC, AE, DEBIT
> We like this Cantonese restaurant for its daily dim sum. Cheerful servers push their carts around the room and you hail them as best you can in order to snag delicate pork-filled steamed buns, shrimp or pork dumplings, salted turnip (or parsnip) cake with its slightly oily texture, cold rice rolls, ribs, chicken feet and sticky rice on lotus leaf. In the evening this seafood house offers a giant menu with hundreds of choices. Fresh lobster and crab repose in the big tank. Freshwater and saltwater fish are available fresh according to season. Fresh oysters are lovely, steamed in black bean sauce or simply with ginger.

$$ **Indochine**
244–315 8th Avenue SW, Bankers Hall   Tel: (403) 263-6929 R
Open Monday 11:00 AM–7:00 PM
    Tuesday, Wednesday 11:00 AM–8:00 PM; Thursday–Saturday 11:00 AM–9:00 PM
V, MC, ENR, AE, DEBIT
> This small, charming restaurant on the second level of Bankers Hall presents contemporary fusion food based on classic Vietnamese-French cuisine. Dishes are given a playful tweak in the translation: nicoise salad is made with grilled lemongrass salmon, mahogany quail (in a sugar-soy sauce glaze) is served on mixed greens with fresh fruit and coconut rice with a bizarre sounding yet tasty dressing of balsamic vinegar and blue cheese. There are lots of vegetarian dishes, including vegan. Dairy is replaced with coconut milk and the pasta is all rice, which is good news for celiacs. The fresh-cut French fries, seasoned with rosemary, sea salt and garlic, are noteworthy.

$$$ **The Kashmir**

507 17th Avenue SW   Tel: (403) 244-2294 R

Open winter Tuesday–Thursday 11:30 AM–1:30 PM; 5:30 PM–9:30 PM

 Friday 11:30 AM–1:30 PM; 5:30 PM–10:00 PM

 Saturday 5:30 PM–10:00 PM

 Sunday 5:30 PM–9:00 PM

Open summer evening hours only

V, MC, ENR, AE, DEBIT

Here we have classic Moghali cooking—subtle, rich and elegant. Begin with the samosas and pakoras, the samosas filled with your choice of lamb, chicken, prawn or vegetable, and the crisp, golden vegetable pakoras made of lentil or chickpea flour.

A wide array of vegetable-based dishes ranges from kabuli chana (puréed chickpeas cooked in a spicy sauce) to bhindi (okra with onions) and mutter paneer (a mild white homemade cheese with green peas in a mild curry). Breads are wonderful, especially the naan topped with sesame seeds, garlic or butter, and worth every bite for mopping up sauces and crumbs.

Meat eaters can choose their heat, from the spicy lamb vindaloo to the gentle flavours of butter chicken. In between are chicken Jalfrazie, a dry curry with capsicum and tomato; rogan josh, the most famous of lamb curries; Goa-style beef with coconut sauce; and a half-dozen or so prawn dishes.

$$ **La Tasca**

2138 Crowchild Trail NW   Tel: (403) 210-5566

Open Tuesday–Friday 11:30 AM–2:30 PM, 4:30 PM–10:00 PM

 Saturday, Sunday 4:30 PM–10:00 PM

V, MC, AE

Tony Luque and Jose Galeano are the gregarious owners of this bistro specializing in the cooking of their native Spain. Come especially for the tapas and the paella. Start off with Alubias Y Pimento, a salad of white beans with garlic-roasted red pepper, the Pisto Manchego, vegetables sautéed in the style of the La Mancha region, and the Salchicha Asturiana, veal sausage cooked in cider and olive oil. There are three different paellas to choose from, including vegetarian, saffron rice with a varying assortment of fresh vegetables.

Of course we can't go to a Spanish restaurant and not have flan, the Iberian version of crème caramel. La Tasca's is delicious, subtly flavoured with fresh orange.

The Latin Corner

$$

109 8th Avenue SW   Tel: (403) 262-7248 R
Open Monday–Friday 11:30 AM–9:00 PM; Saturday 6:00 PM–10:00 PM
V, MC, ENR, AE, DEBIT

Fans will remember the original location in an old Dairy Queen on 4th Street, and the earthy, flavour-packed black bean soup. The new location on Stephen Avenue Way is bigger and better looking and still serves the black bean soup accompanied,

at lunch, by a grilled tortilla filled with cheese, salsa and cilantro. Seafood and meat dishes are your best bets. The paella della casa of clams, mussels and lobster is built on a golden rice base fragrant with saffron. There are several platters for sharing, the signature being the toothsome el gaucho Sâu Paulo style, with grilled skewered chicken, beef ribs tamarindo, chorizo sausage served with rice and beans.

Owners Gustavo Yelamo (a former bullfighter) and his wife Nadia are ebullient hosts. It's a fun place that gets livelier as the evening moves on. If your idea of livin' la vida loca includes (perhaps) a little hip-swinging to the beat as you move through the restaurant, you'll love the Latin corner.

Livin' la vida loca at the Latin Corner.

The Living Room

$$$

514 17th Avenue SW   Tel: (403) 228-9830 R
Open Monday–Friday 11:30 AM–12:00 PM
     Saturday–Sunday 5:30 PM–12:00 PM
V, MC, ENR, AE, DEBIT

They call their style of cooking contemporary interactive in this chic and comfortable room with the friendly waiters. There are several plates for two: an almost 40-ouncer of Alberta beef, succulent roast chicken on a platter piled high with roasted potatoes and vegetables, steaming bowls of pho and bouillabaisse and fondue. The seasonal menu includes first courses and well-priced entrees for smaller appetites. The tasting menu, called a five-course culinary experience, reflects who's cooking in the kitchen. For now, executive chef duties are split between Kenny Kaechele and Janice Hepburn. Excellent wine list.

We made dessert interactive, sharing a darkly delicious molten chocolate cake, served in a big white bowl with two large spoons. It's a great spot.

JULIE VAN ROSENDAAL

Luxor Emporium and Café

3919 Brentwood Road NW Tel: (403) 282-0030

Open Monday–Thursday 9:00 AM–10:00 PM

    Friday, Saturday 9:00 AM–11:00 PM; Sunday 11:00 AM–10:00 PM

V, MC, DEBIT

    Luxor is a definite find. It lays claim to being Calgary's first Egyptian restaurant. The house specialty and best-seller is beef shawarma, the beef thinly sliced and marinated, then grilled to order before being wrapped in a pita with tahini and vegetables. The Egyptian version of baba ghanoush is made with roasted eggplant, tahini, salt, pepper, garlic and lemon juice, and served with a little diced tomato. For dessert try the baklava, delicious filo filled with a variety of nuts and honey, and kataifi, a shredded wheat pastry made with pistachios and honey.

    Luxor is rather like an Egyptian bazaar, with 45 seats scattered amid shelves stocked with the raw materials of Eastern Mediterranean cooking: dried hibiscus flowers for tea, orange blossom water, rose syrup, Israeli couscous, Turkish delight, halvah, and coffee scented with cardamom for brewing in a rakwee, the definitively shaped Turkish coffee pot.

Mescalero

$$

1315 1st Street SW

Tel: (403) 266-3339 R

Open Monday–Thursday 11:30 AM–11:00 PM

    Friday 11:30 PM–1:00 AM

    Saturday 5:00 PM–1:00 AM

V, MC, ENR, AE, DEBIT

    The food is spicy, cross-cultural fare from the Americas. The menu is extensive and changes often, as all good menus should. Recent favourites have included mussels steamed in a light sauce laced with chipotle; a tapa of coconut curry prawns with rice, onion and red and green pep per; and a burrito filled with a memorable combination of salmon, asparagus and goat cheese. From the page of inventively named desserts we

The rustic charm of Mescalero.

chose an encounter with a Fallen Angel, chocolate angel food cake drizzled with Jack Daniels, layered with chocolate mousse and topped with banana cream.

    Mescalero has a well-lived-in, south-of-the-border look, especially on the evocative patios. It's bigger than life, with an upbeat, occasionally raucous atmosphere. If you don't have fun here, it's your own fault.

Witold Twardowski: Renaissance Cowboy in Calgary

He's a food lover, a wine lover, a dog lover. He's also been described as a scrapper, a charmer, a Polish prince, a bit of a rogue. Whatever else this unusual man may be, Witold Twardowski is an original, and he's been the mover and shaker behind Calgary's most exciting restaurants, reinventing himself on a regular basis.

In the past, there was beautiful Ambrosia and the Soup Kitchen, the ambitious Phoenicia and Divino. There was a creative stint with the interior design of Buffalo Mountain Lodge, Deer Lodge, Emerald Lake. He was the co-creator of Cilantro and part of what was once dubbed the Mescalero Group, which developed the River Café, Mescalero and Teatro. There was also a brief fling with Turqueza. "The building had great bones and I was trying the Nuevo Latino trend before its time. But the vision didn't come together," he explains. Still, it's vision that keeps him going. "Our restaurants were all designed to satisfy our own definition of great food in a great space. We always had beautiful outdoor patios. The food was always based on wholesome, natural materials. Still is."

The Mescalero Group split a few years ago and he went on to expand Mescalero, revitalize The Ranche, become a partner in The Latin Corner with Gustavo and Nadia Yelamo and develop Pick's Roadhouse in the Crowsnest Pass. His next project is the Hotel California on the Baja Peninsula. Influential Calgary chef Dany Lamotte, most recently of Wild Sage, will be in charge of the restaurant.

He sees Calgarians developing more sophisticated palates and a greater understanding of food. "But they aren't easily fooled by the next trendy thing. The restaurants that have endured look after the basics: good food, good service, attention to detail." ✑

$$$ **Passion Vietnamese Fusion Cuisine**   www.passionrestaurant.com
611 6th Street SW   Tel: (403) 261-9888 R
Open Monday–Thursday 11:30 AM–2:00 PM, 5:00 PM–9:00 PM
    Friday 11:30 AM–2:00 PM, 5:00 PM–10:00 PM
    Saturday 5:00 PM–10:00 PM
V, MC, ENR, AE

> Passion presents a thoroughly upscale approach to the delicacy and beauty of Vietnamese cooking in a lovely, restrained space. Chili oil and chili paste are used more than fresh chilies, resulting in a concentrated heat with layers of flavours: sweet, salty, sour, hot. The vermicelli combination involves marinated barbecued beef, chicken and shrimp with a garnish of peanuts and lettuce. We like the starter of tamarind-glazed ribs, and the lemongrass chicken is a flavour-packed dish marinated in a fish sauce laced with sugar, pepper, fresh herbs and lemongrass. The orange crème caramel is rich and delicate. With a scoop of coconut ice cream, it makes a satisfying tropical conclusion to an outstanding meal.

The Savoury Caterer: Calgary's Judy Wood

$$

Savoury Café & Catering
101–322 11th Avenue SW
Open Monday–Friday 7:30 am–3:30 pm

www.savourycatering.com
Tel: (403) 205-4002

V, MC, ENR, AE, DEBIT

Judy Wood hates catsup; at least the commercial variety. It's one of the reasons she is now co-owner of Savoury, a café and catering operation in downtown Calgary. "I'm not a rice krispie squares, sweet and sour meatballs kind of caterer," says Wood. "We make everything from scratch and use lots of fresh herbs."

Wood started her career at a young age. At 15 she knew she wanted to be a chef and started cooking for her parents' friends. She was starry-eyed about France, went there, and graduated from La Varenne in 1981. After kicking about France, she landed a job with the Calgary Four Seasons Hotel as its first female chef. A stint in Toronto followed, but Calgary beckoned. Wood came back to the West to head up the kitchen for Buchanan's opening. "It was during the Olympics, a really exciting time to be back in Calgary. Very heady," she says. Wood then worked with the Price family developing the concept, recipes and catering department for the Sunterra stores.

Eager to be out on her own, Wood opened Savoury with partner Linda Cockburn in 1999. Behind the café/deli that acts as the visual showpiece for

Judy Wood behind the counter at Savoury.

Savoury, Wood works with six full-time staff, including a pastry chef, cooking the way she likes to. "I won't use that awful pre-peeled garlic," she says. ✎

Pau Hana Grille

$$

420–1851 Sirocco Drive SW (West Market Square)   Tel: (403) 217-3000 R
Open Tuesday–Friday 11:00 AM–2:00 PM; Tuesday–Thursday 5:00 PM–9:00 PM
Friday, Saturday 5:00 PM–11:00 PM; Sunday 5:00 PM–9:00 PM

V, MC, ENR, AE, DEBIT

We love the pretty room, but the food's the thing. Owner John Aihoshi has a different vision—a felicitous marriage of Pacific flavours and classic French techniques. Roast half duckling finished with a maple balsamic vinegar is served with a fontina and wild rice risotto—more European than Asian.

Be clear about this: no pupus. But there's a touch of Polynesia here after all.

Try the fantastic crab stack, a salad of mango, tomatillo, pea shoots, cucumber and avocado with a ginger-kaffir lime vinaigrette and two large crab claws riding side-saddle.

$$ Smuggler's Inn

6920 Macleod Trail South   Tel: (403) 253-5355
Open Monday–Thursday 11:30 AM–11:00 PM
    Friday, Saturday 11:30 AM–12:00 AM
    Sunday 10:00 AM–2:00 PM, 4:30 PM–10:00 PM;
V, MC, ENR, AE, DEBIT

Smuggler's is a '70s-style beef house, so dark you can barely see the person across the table. But when a restaurant is as consistently full of happy eaters as this one, it has to be doing something right. This is one of the few restaurants that still has a huge salad bar with dressing choices in small crocks. You could start with steak soup, go on to the salad, and eventually try the house specialty prime rib, which is cut from the best Alberta beef. Or just stick with steak. Yes, there's chicken and fish, but the beef's the thing.

$$ Sunterra Market, Bankers Hall

www.sunterramarket.com
Plus-15 Level, 855 2nd Street SW
Tel: (403) 269-3610
Open Monday–Wednesday 6:30 AM–6:30 PM
    Thursday and Friday 6:30 AM–8:00 PM
    Saturday 9:30 AM–5:30 PM
V, MC, DEBIT

Other locations: 3rd Floor, 401 9th Avenue SW, 263-9755; 200–1851 Sirocco Drive SW, 266-3049

Breakfast and a coffee bar, lunch and dinner to eat-in, takeout, or reheat at home, these folks have covered all the bases. Leave yourself extra time to browse the store itself, from soup packages to olives, cheeses and nuts, before or after you dine. The departments are extensive. The bakery produces breads and sweets, baguettes and demi-baguettes as well as Bohemian pumpernickel and Vienna breads. Desserts include fresh fruit tarts, mousse cups, squares, cakes, cookies and a 10-inch chocolate mousse torte. A stroll through the takeout section reveals sushi, samosas, spring rolls, focaccia and baguette sandwiches, layered like Dagwood's best, salads, vegetables and dips, pizza ready to bake in two sizes, and a case full of entrees ready to eat. Salmon steaks, BBQ chicken parts and wings, oversized pork meatballs encrusted with herbs, ribs, roast potatoes . . . a busy person need never cook! The other side of the stand has soups, ready and waiting, and short order cooks on call to feed your whims.

$

Thai Sa-On Restaurant

351 10th Avenue SW   Tel: (403) 264-3526

Open Monday–Friday 11:30 AM–2:00 PM, 5:00 PM–10:00 PM

Saturday 5:00 PM–10:00 PM

V, MC

The Chanhao family arrived in Grande Prairie from Thailand in February 1982. Remarkably, they held on, eventually moving to Calgary, where they've operated Thai Sa-On for a decade.

This comfortable, unprepossessing spot is a family affair: Sanit (everybody calls him Sam) is host, sisters Vida and Sonthaya are in the kitchen along with mother Wan and mother-in-law Kalayarat. The cooking reflects that the family is from the northeastern part of Thailand, featuring lean, subtly spiced dishes such as the larb moo, a pork dish with toasted rice. The 99-item menu goes far beyond the ubiquitous pad Thai. Pork comes in a red, yellow or green curry, each with a different degree of heat and flavour.

Beef is curried Masaman style, a southern Thai specialty, tangy and just slightly sweet. The manager's special is toothsome: spicy steamed shrimp with Thai pepper, basil, fresh chilies, garlic and ginger. There is an extensive vegetarian selection.

$

Thi-Thi Submarine

209 1st Street SE

(behind Harry Hays building)

Tel: (403) 265-5452

Open Monday–Friday 10:00 AM–7:00 PM

Saturday 10:00 AM–5:00 PM

CASH ONLY

We think Thi-Thi is the best Vietnamese subhouse in Calgary. The wonder of the place is that they serve anything at all, considering the cramped quarters and minimal equipment. Yet the two people behind the counter manage to put out a steady stream of well-filled, hot and tasty subs. Order the beef saté with hot chilies. This isn't complicated stuff. It's street food, Vietnamese style.

$ **Vietnam Restaurant** www.calgarymenus.com/vietnam
2nd floor, 227 12th Avenue SE Tel: (403) 263-0995 R
Open Sunday–Thursday 11:00 AM–10:00 PM
　Friday, Saturday 11:00 AM–12:00 AM
V, MC, AE, DEBIT

For nearly 20 years the Nguyen family has been cooking simple, hearty Vietnamese food for an appreciative audience. Spring rolls, fresh and tender salad rolls, noodle dishes and a tasty lemongrass chicken are among the most popular items. The number one dish on the menu is #65: spring rolls with barbecued pork, rice and vermicelli.

OTHERS WE LIKE
Anpurna,175B 52nd Street SE, 235-6028; **Barclay's (at the Eau Claire Sheraton)** 255 Barclay Parade SW, 517-6666, **Booker's BBQ Grill & Crab Shack**,316 3rd Street SE, 264-6419; **Centini**,160 8th Avenue SE, 269-1600; **Cross House,** 1240 8th Avenue SE, 531-2767; **Heartland Café**, 940 2nd Avenue NW, 270-4541; **King and I**, 822 11th Avenue SW, 264-7241, **Nellie's** 738 17th Avenue SW, 244-4616 (other locations as well); **Open Sesame**, 6920 Macleod Trail South, 259-0123; **Rimrock Dining Room (Palliser Hotel)**, 133 9th Avenue SW, 262-1234; **Rocky's Burger Bus**, 1120 46th Avenue SE, 272–1623; **Sugo** 1214 9th Avenue SE, 263-1115; **Sushi Hiro**, 727 5th Avenue SW, 233-0605; **Sushi Yoko**, Centre Street N, 230-1516; **Tandoori Hut,** 5201 10th Street NW, 270-4012; **Wrayton's Café**, Northland Drive NW; 590–5111. We also like **Divino** a lot but they are under renovation.

BIG NIGHTS, SPLURGES, CELEBRATIONS

$$$ **The Belvedere**
107 8th Avenue SW (Stephen Avenue Mall) Tel: (403) 265-9595 R
Open Monday–Friday 11:30 AM–2:00 PM, 5:30 PM–10:00 PM
　Saturday 5:00 PM–10:00 PM
V, MC, ENR, AE

The Belvedere has become one of Calgary's premier dining experiences, a prime spot for power lunches and leisurely dinners. The cooking is complex and serious. For starters, try the foie gras, seared for only three seconds per side, then served on corn spoon bread with onion marmalade and poached apple with a sherry reduction.

The menu has a section called tastings which changes seasonally: duck, seafood, savories (pâté and terrines), served as variations on a theme. The caviar served with iced vodka is of sevruga, whitefish roe, salmon roe and tobiko (Japanese caviar, smaller than salmon roe, pink to white in colour, with a nice, poppy texture). For dessert, the dark chocolate sticky toffee pudding makes a superb ending. Fabulous cocktail bar.

$$$ **Buchanan's**   www.calgarymenus.com/buchanans
7th Street & 3rd Avenue SW, on the corner   Tel: (403) 261-4646 R
Open Monday–Friday 11:00 AM–10:00 PM
    Saturday 5:00 PM–10:00 PM
V, MC, ENR, AE

For a decade, this fine example of the North American chop house on the western edge of downtown has served high quality chops and steaks, precisely grilled to taste, and the best burger in the city.

Owners Mike and Carol Buchanan have created a classic, with a strong wine list and a wide selection of single malts. It's a fine place to while away the evening or consummate a business deal.

$$$ **Catch**
100 8th Avenue SE
Tel: (403) 206-0000 R
Open Monday–Friday 11:30 AM–10:00 PM
    Saturday, Sunday 5:00 PM–10:00 PM
V, MC, ENR, AE

Think of six perfect oysters, impeccably fresh, and six thimble-sized sauces, from wasabi to mildly-scented tarragon to peach vinaigrette. Only in the oyster bar at Catch.

How does an oyster bar play in Calgary, so far from the tide lines? Very well, when it's part of a restaurant captained by Michael Noble, late of Vancouver's Diva at the Met, the Bocuse d'Or, and (yes) television, with a gutsy

CREATIVE RESTAURANT GROUP

The upstairs dining room at Catch is sleek and sophisticated.

appearance on *The Iron Chef*. Noble is uncompromising about quality, and he favours Canadian regional ingredients.

Catch is delightful. Every aspect of food, wine, service and decor has had meticulous attention. Step into the oyster bar where everything is informal and fun, or ascend to the burnished perfection of the upstairs dining room. Both rooms have that damn-the-expense-just-make-it-glow look that is only possible in certain heritage buildings, with enlightened, deep-pocket management, where the chef is one of the owners. It's a felicitous combination that doesn't happen often enough.

$$$ **Cilantro**

338 17th Avenue SW   Tel: (403) 229-1177 R

Open Monday–Thursday 11:00 AM–11:00 PM; Friday 11:00 AM–12:00 AM

Saturday 5:00 PM–12:00 AM; Sunday 5:00 PM–11:00 PM

V, MC, ENR, AE

This has been a long-time favourite in Calgary, prized for both its inventive cooking and its pretty, sheltered patio, possibly the most sought-after spot in town on summer evenings. Downstairs bustles while the upper level is a lovely, intimate setting for a long dinner.

We like the pear and gorgonzola pizza to start, followed by the rack of lamb with roasted shallots and Hunan barbecue sauce, served with mashed potatoes, spaghetti squash and roasted yam. The lean, juicy elk burgers are from the owners' ranch in the Bow Valley. For dessert, the goat cheese cheesecake with port-poached apples and a sauce of fresh and dried cranberries won rave reviews at New York's James Beard House.

$$$ **Fleur de Sel**

2–2015 4th Street SW   Tel: (403) 228-9764 R

Open Tuesday–Friday 11:30 AM–2:00 PM, 5:00 PM–12:00 AM

Saturday 5:00 PM–12:00 AM; Sunday 5:00 PM–10:30 PM

V, MC, ENR, AE, DEBIT

Fleur de Sel, the fluffy white top layer of the hand-raked sel de gris, is the current darling of the Mediterranean kitchen. The aptly named Fleur de Sel restaurant has its own fans, who love this bistro for the excellence of its unpretentious cooking. Patrice Durandeau is a creative chef, whether he's making a classic Marseille-style fish soup—tomato-based and laced with saffron—or a simple salad of duckling on fresh mixed greens with a mustardy vinaigrette. An authentic cassoulet (a rare dish in these parts) is made with the traditional flageolet beans and a delicious confit of pheasant. Durandeau has a relaxed approach to closing time. "If you see someone in the restaurant, we're open," he says.

$$ **The Highwood at SAIT**

1301 16th Avenue NW (John Ware Building)   Tel: (403) 284-8615 R

Open Monday–Friday 11:30 AM–2:00 PM

    Monday–Thursday 5:00 PM–9:00 PM (hours vary depending on curriculum)

V, MC, DEBIT

    This dining room provides students with real-world experience in all sorts of challenging situations, from handling the lunch rush to customer complaints. The Highwood is so popular that reservations are essential and must be made well in advance. Cindy Findlay, academic program coordinator, feels that the students are their big draw. "They're so enthusiastic, they have those big smiles and they're so glad to see everyone."

    One of the great pluses of the Highwood is the low cost of dining in a truly professional room. For the equivalent food and service, you'd expect to pay considerably more elsewhere.

$$$ **Hy's Steak House**

316 4th Avenue SW   Tel: (403) 263-2222 R

Open Monday–Friday 11:30 AM–11:00 PM

    Saturday 5:00 PM–11:00 PM; Sunday 5:00 PM–10:00 PM

V, MC, AE, DC

    Great beef is the hallmark of Hy's, where tux-attired waiters glide among the red banquettes as they have since the '60s. The chain, named for its founder, Hy Aisenstat, was the original great Canadian steak house.

    The dry-aged, AAA Alberta beef is flawless. Order the steak of your choice in the size of your choice and they'll cut it to order. You don't have to eat steak— you could have chicken, fish, seafood or the Chinese chicken salad with fried wonton chips and rice noodles, or the production number: a Caesar salad prepared tableside. But this place is about beef, and that's what they do best.

$$$ **Il Sogno**

24 4th Street NE   Tel: (403) 232-8901 R

Open Monday–Friday 11:30 AM–2:00 PM, 5:00 PM–10:00 PM

    Saturday 5:00 PM–10:00 PM

    Sunday brunch 10:30 AM–2:00 PM; dinner 5:00 PM–10:00 PM

V, MC, ENR, AE

    This smartly designed room in Bridgeland suits the subtle, assured cooking of chef and owner Giuseppe di Gennaro. Look for robust flavours in fish, roasted meats, and various pastas and risottos, depending on the season. Or sit at the chef's bar by the open kitchen and let Giuseppe feed you whatever looks good that day.

$$$ **La Chaumière**
139 17th Avenue SW   Tel: (403) 228-5690 R
Open Monday–Friday 11:30 AM–2:00 PM, 6:00 PM–10:00 PM
        Saturday 6:00 PM–10:00 PM
V, MC, ENR, AE

> This is still the place to spoil yourself or pamper your significant other. Fresh flowers, candles, deep, soft armchairs, immaculate table settings and impeccable service are the order of the day. Chef Robert Mathews, an alumnus of Culinary Team Canada, maintains the high standards of this dining room. Duck with rosemary is roasted so the skin is crisply bronzed and the flesh is fork-tender, then served in thin slices. Sautéed sea bass is presented on a green pea risotto with a julienne of spring vegetables. In this room you can still have chateaubriand, carved tableside. It's classic cooking without excessive flash.
>
> There's an excellent wine list, running to more than 700 selections. The cellar has some fine French choices, and depth in Italian and Californian wines.

$$$ **The Ranche**   www.theranche.com
15979 Bow Bottom Trail SE, Fish Creek Park   Tel: (403) 225-3939 R
Open Monday–Thursday 11:30 AM–9:00 PM
        Friday 11:30 AM–10:00 PM
        Saturday 5:00 PM–10:00 PM
        Sunday 10:30 AM–9:00 PM
V, MC, DC, AE, DEBIT

> At historic Bow Valley Ranche in Fish Creek Park we have a lovely setting far from the madding crowd. The menu presents contemporary versions of traditional ranch cooking. For openers, we like the salad of slow-roasted steelhead trout (from Valbella Meats in Canmore) on mixed greens with a blackberry vinaigrette. Main courses run to traditional prairie meats: roast duck, pork tenderloin, roast venison and, of course, Alberta beef.
>
> For dessert, there's a chocolate plate: homemade truffles, a chocolate cup filled with chocolate mousse, chocolate cake glazed with (you guessed it) chocolate, and chocolate ice cream! Should you want a tad less chocolate, there are some nice, homey desserts: the apple tart and bread pudding are both fine. The Ranche was purchased recently by the excellent Canadian Rocky Mountain Resorts, owners of Buffalo Mountain Lodge in Banff among others.

$$$ **River Café**

www.river-cafe.com

Prince's Island Park

Tel: (403) 261-7670 R

Open Monday–Friday 11:00 AM–11:00 PM

    Saturday, Sunday 10:00 AM–11:00 PM

    closed in January

V, MC, ENR, AE, DEBIT

If we could go to only one Calgary restaurant for the rest of our lives, it would be the River Café on Prince's Island. You must walk to it, over the little bridge, and there's always a smell of woodsmoke in the air. It's magical.

Chef Glen Manzer goes to considerable trouble to highlight locally raised game and meat. He sources true culinary gems: Leoni Grana cheese and heirloom tomatoes from Hotchkiss Farms. Breads are fabulous, made in house from organic grains and flours and cooked in the wood-burning ovens that also turn out deliciously thin-crusted pizzas. Think of buckwheat honey-glazed duck breast, or wild sage and oat groat cake with tomato confit and pumpkin seeds, or carpaccio of Alberta beef with sunchoke chips and a surprising foie gras aoili.

Away from it all at the River Café.

On weekends, brunch at the River Café offers wonderful platters to share, such as the fish and game, with smoked trout, candied salmon, tea-smoked duck, venison pâté with grilled apple and turnip relish. We love the confit of duck and white bean hash with a poached egg, and the pumpkin waffle with fruit butter and spiced apple syrup. The wine list is lovingly chosen.

$$$ **Teatro**   www.teatro-rest.com

200 8th Avenue SE   Tel: (403) 290-1012 R

Open Monday–Thursday 11:00 AM–11:00 PM; Friday 11:00 AM–12:00 AM

    Saturday 5:00 PM–12:00 AM; Sunday 5:00 PM–10:00 PM

V, MC, ENR, AE, DEBIT

Chef Andreas Wechselberger carries on the glorious menu for which Teatro is

known—a celebration of Italian market cuisine, Alberta-style, using what's fresh, local and in season.

This menu begins with a selection of appetite-sparking antipasti—warm hazelnut-crusted goat cheese on mixed greens with onions and apple; rosemary flatbread with roasted eggplant pesto, cured olives and a subtle anchoyade; carpaccio of beef with Leoni-Grana cheese and extra-virgin olive oil. The wood-burning pizza ovens feature calzone with chicken sausage, brie and spinach. The applewood-roasted salmon is served with a fondue of smoked lentils with tomato confit. Look for free-range chicken, succulent rack of lamb, rack of pork glazed with maple liqueur. Desserts are the combined efforts of Wechselberger and pastry chef Clark Adams. Try the lemon tart or the signature crème brûlée made with Taber corn.

Teatro presents dining as theatre in this dramatic turn-of-the-century bank building. Big ticket, upscale, worth the splurge.

The bar at Teatro.

$$$ **Thomsons Restaurant**

700 Centre Street South (Hyatt Hotel)   Tel: (403) 537-4449 R

Open Sunday–Thursday 6:30 AM–10:00 PM

Friday–Saturday 6:30 AM–11:00 PM

V, MC, ENR, AE, DEBIT

Thomsons opened in the Hyatt along the burgeoning Stephen Avenue Mall, keeping the old brick and sandstone character of the original Thomson brothers' structure, circa 1890s. Although it's open all day, typical of many hotel dining rooms, we'll speak of dinner—the foie gras and the ravioli from executive chef Max Labhardt are outstanding. They do a great steak, with mashed potatoes and a caramelized onion sauce. Or there's the breast of duck with maple glaze.

Classic, elegant plate presentation, globally-inspired flavours and a selection of handsome sweets. Service is simply excellent.

$$$ **Wildwood Grill and Brewing Company**

2417 4th Street SW

Tel: (403) 228-0100 R

Open Monday–Thursday 11:30 AM–2:30 PM, 5:00 PM–10:00 PM

Friday, Saturday 11:30 AM–2:30 PM, 5:00 PM–11:00 PM

Sunday 5:00 PM–10:00 PM

V, MC, AE

The Wildwood Grill is in a beautiful room, with layers of wood and stone against the gleaming copper of the beer tanks and the open kitchen. The style of cooking is European classic, but the ingredients are definitely regional, with emphasis on wild foods such as berries, wild game, locally produced vegetables and grains and Alberta cheeses. Chef Josef Wiewer is fond of braising, roasting and smoking. In winter, we like the roast rabbit risotto and the double pork chop cured in vanilla, roasted and served with sage, sautéed apples, five spice powder and calvados. Try the Swiss chard leaves stuffed with roasted eggplant, mushrooms, spinach and tomato, served with a velvety tomato cream.

JULIE VAN ROSENDAAL

On a cold and rainy night, nothing suits better than the lamb, braised slowly and served with barley (from Hamilton Farms) and finished with roasted garlic, fresh sage and a splash of red wine. Desserts continue the warm and comforting theme with ginger butterscotch cake, a moist gingerbread with a soft butterscotch center, served with ginger/green tea ice cream. The restaurant holds several winemaker's dinners and other special events throughout the year.

Feast of Fields   www.slowfood.com

Celebrate the harvest. This autumn food festival brings local producers and growers together with Calgary's talented chefs to bring you the best of the season. Festival goers watch chefs at work in the great outdoors, roasting bison, grilling sausages and harvest vegetables. Meanwhile, they mix and mingle with the people who grew all this bounty. The Calgary Slow Food chapter sponsors the earthy harvest picnic at Prince's Island Park. It's a casual, walk around event held rain or shine, an excellent opportunity to meet and greet the who's who of the Calgary food scene. ✎

ROCKY MOUNTAIN HERITAGE
3
FROM YAMNUSKA TO JASPER

We come to the mountains, the wild, awe-inspiring places, mindful of those who came before: the aboriginals who first taught the white man how to survive an unforgiving alpine environment; the surveyors, outfitters and characters: Tom Wilson, the first of those white men to see Lake Louise; Bill Peyto and Jimmy Stewart, the Swiss guides; Cornelius Van Horne, builder of railways, visionary, lover of good food and drink; women like Mary Schaffer, explorer and naturalist. We'd have enjoyed meeting them all.

Happily, today's travellers have no need to roast a Richardson's ground squirrel over a campfire—the world is discovering an emerging Rocky Mountain cuisine.

CANMORE

Canmore started life as a coal mining town. When the coal was gone, so were the jobs, and the future of the town seemed uncertain. Today, it's been transformed into the administrative centre of the Rockies, an occasional movie shoot location, and prime real estate.

From rustic miners to movie stars and million dollar homes, Canmore is hip and happening, much to the chagrin of some of its longtime residents. The good news for food lovers? Great little restaurants, quirky pubs and shops where you can buy everything for a picnic basket or a camping trip, all in a small town atmosphere.

CANMORE PANTRY
WHERE GOOD COOKS SHOP

Valbella Meats & Deli
104 Elk Run Boulevard (Elk Run Industrial Park)
Open Monday–Saturday 8:00 AM–5:30 PM
V, MC, DEBIT

www.valbellameats.com
Tel: (403) 678-4109

Founded in 1978 by Walter von Rotz, this excellent smokehouse and butcher shop supplies not just Canmore residents but most of the good restaurants in the province. Its excellent products can also be found at Janice Beaton in Calgary and Sunterra in Edmonton and Calgary.

Valbella provides custom meat cutting, and produces unique charcuterie—venison ham, chimneystick, landjaeger, and a phenomenal duck liver pâté, plus a variety of wonderful sausages. The shop is especially famous for its air-dried beef.

A big plus has been the addition of inventive sauces and condiments, fabulous foils for sausages and game. The mustard melon is a superb accompaniment for any meat or cheese, and people have been known to eat it right out of the jar.

Bella Crusta Italian Flat Bread and Pizza Therapy

902 6th Avenue (across from Marra's)
Tel: (403) 609-3366
Open Monday–Thursday 10:00 AM–6:00 PM
    Friday, Saturday 10:00 AM–8:00 PM
CASH ONLY

Bella Crusta makes excellent cook-at-home pizzas on their secret recipe focaccia, fresh or frozen, ready to pop into your oven. You could buy a single slice of hot pizza or a sandwich—barbecued beef, chicken salad, or a toothsome all vegetable with hummus and cream cheese. Edmontonians may remember Bella Crusta from its days in the Old Strathcona Farmers' Market. There is a smattering of Italian specialty items, but the pizza's the thing.

Marra's

638 8th Street
Tel: (403) 678-5075
Open Monday–Saturday 8:00 AM–8:00 PM; Sunday 10:00 AM–6:00 PM
V, MC, DEBIT

Range-fed beef from Bragg Creek, plus conventional beef in custom cuts, beautiful lamb and pork, breads from Canmore Bakery, lots of choices in dry goods and produce. All this, plus competitive pricing in a convenient main street location—what's not to like? Marra's is a great little grocery store.

Mustard Melon

Make this condiment at least one week before you require it.
3 tsps (45 mL) Keen's mustard powder
1 cup (250 mL) water
2 cups (500 mL) white vinegar
2 cups (500 mL) sugar
approximately 3.5 lbs ripe cantaloupe

Combine all ingredients except for melon in plastic or stainless steel container. Peel cantaloupe and cut in half. Remove seeds and cut flesh into 3/4-inch chunks. Combine melon and mustard mix and refrigerate for 48 hours. Transfer melon and liquid to pot and cook at light boil. Cook until liquid thickens slightly, transfer into sterilized jars, cool and refrigerate. Keeps well in refrigerator, but use within a couple of weeks.

$$ **Crazyweed Kitchen**
2–626 Main Street   Tel: (403) 609-2530
Open Monday–Saturday 11:00 AM–7:00 PM; Sunday 11:00 AM–6:00 PM
V, MC, DEBIT

> You can eat in, at one of the few tables against the wall. You can take out—choose
> from a variety of sandwiches. Think roast lamb with rosemary, roast chicken with
> smoky chipotle; pizza; a variety of wraps; or one of their wildly creative soups.
> You can look in the cooler for tea-smoked salmon, curried seafood, other treats
> to take home and warm up.
>
> Crazyweed inspires rabid fans. We cannot go to Canmore without stopping at

> this cheerful spot,
> even if it's just for a
> latte and a cookie.
> Recent renovations
> have increased seat-
> ing somewhat and
> improved flow, but
> you'll never get a
> busload of people
> into Crazyweed—
> give thanks.

Cheese selection at Crazyweed Kitchen.

$$ **Musashi Japanese Restaurant**
7A–1306 Bow Valley Trail   Tel: (403) 678-9360
Open Monday–Saturday 5:00 PM–10:30 PM; seasonal closings
V, MC

> A compact Japanese restaurant close to the Trans-Canada, Musashi is good to
> know about if you're traveling through. The chef has a sure hand with sushi, teryi-
> aki and yakitori. The tempura has a feathery crisp exterior, the udon (noodle soup)
> is blessed with a full-flavoured broth. Finish with a bowl of green tea ice cream.

$$ **Zona's**
710 9th Street   Tel: (403) 678-6111
Open daily 5:00 PM–10:00 PM for dinner, 10:00 PM 12:00 PM for tapas and drinks
V, MC, ENR, JCB, DEBIT

> Zona's funky atmosphere and unique food—the menu changes seasonally—keep
> us coming back. After 10:00 PM a full range of tapas are available. We love the
> spring roll, the feta, dill and spinach empanadas with olives, and the spicy butter-
> nut squash, roast garlic and jalapeno dip is perfect with a glass of full-bodied red
> wine. We especially like the dishes, odd-shaped pieces of clay, vaguely plate-
> shaped, fired in earth and stone colours, perfect for this quirky little spot.

BIG NIGHTS, SPLURGES, CELEBRATIONS

$$$ **Chez François**   www.bestwestern.com
1604 2nd Avenue (Green Gables Best Western, Bow Valley Trail)   Tel: (403) 678-6111 R
Open daily 7:00 AM 2:00 PM, 5:00 PM–9:00 PM
V, MC, AE, DEBIT

> Sylvie and Jean François Gouin have operated this fine French restaurant for 13
> years. Don't let its setting in a Best Western fool you, there's real talent in the
> kitchen. Jean François is a master saucier. Everything is from scratch, the quality
> of ingredients is top notch, the stocks are full-flavoured, the sauces silken and
> delicious. There are a number of table d'hôte menus available on any given
> evening and one at lunch—three courses for $12.95, great value and an exten-
> sive à la carte menu with an emphasis on fresh fish: orange roughy, red snapper,
> salmon, trout. The atmosphere is elegant and airy with big, big windows framing
> the view of the Three Sisters.

$$$ **Des Alpes Restaurant**   www.telusplanet.net/public/desalpes
702 10th Street   Tel: (403) 678-6878 R
Open Tuesday–Sunday 5:00 PM 10:00 PM
V, MC, AE

> Marianne and Xaver Schurtenberger have run this cozy Swiss-style restaurant for
> 12 years. Through the years they have concentrated on simple, classic food, made
> from scratch daily—a menu of enduring classics where the deft hand of the chef
> and the quality of the ingredients is paramount. They like to serve escargot, Caesar
> salad and three different versions of steak au poivre. Veal is prepared Zurich-style,
> with a mushroom and onion cream sauce. Cheese fondue is available in winter
> only. The trout is cooked with herbs and lemon, finished with Noilly Prat.

Features of the day depend on what's fresh and in season. "The menu changes when we feel like it," says Marianne. We hope it doesn't change too much.

OTHERS WE LIKE
Copper Door, 726 9th Street, 678-5233; **Melange**, 107–722 8th Street, 609-3221; **Summit Café**, 102–1001 Cougar Creek Drive, 609-2120; **Vic's (Radisson Hotel)** 511 Bow Valley Trail, 678-3625.

◉ THINGS TO DO BETWEEN MEALS

Take a hike: Di Grassi Lake Trails. Look for the trailhead sign about a kilometre past the Nordic Centre.

Take a dip: On the way to the Nordic Centre on Spray Lakes Road you'll find the old quarry, perfect for a refreshing dip.

Go for a ski: The Nordic Centre Provincial Park offers a quick (or longer) ski on the track and on groomed trails. Lessons and rentals are available.(403) 678-2400

A stroll before dinner along the Fairmont Banff Springs terrace.

It's All in the Altitude

To have a true mountain experience, one must go up. There are people around to help us do just that and they'll feed us well too. Matthius Ahrens, mountain guide for the Chateau Lake Louise Mountain Heritage Program, knows his way around a peak or two.

"It's important to eat often," he says. "After an hour or two, start nibbling. I don't like commercial sports bars—in the winter it's like trying to eat a brick. Then, have lunch. Maybe Valbella's venison stick and some cheese." Salami and cheese, sustainers of the original Swiss guides, are both still classic mountain fare.

Your food needs to be lightweight, he says, with little waste and packaging: what goes up must come down. Matthius helped develop the boxed lunch that comes with the guided hikes. "It's not your typical tour bus boxed lunch," he says. "It's balanced and tasty with very little to dispose of." He makes his own trail mix with a variety of nuts, a little dried fruit, dates, apricots, ginger, sunflower and pumpkin seeds, plus his secret ingredient, M&Ms.

On long trips, like a hut-to-hut traverse, endurance is the key, "Drink constantly," Matthius advises. He likes peppermint tea with a little honey stirred in. For these trips, the food takes strategic planning. "What do you eat fresh, and have you planned for the last days?" he cautions. "It's not just what you feel like for dinner."

Matthius Ahrens
Tel: 403 678-2419
snowhow@expertcanmore.net

Chateau Lake Louise Guides' Granola

This was developed for the Chateau Lake Louise Mountain Heritage Program. It's a dense, chewy square that stands up well at the bottom of a backpack. It's also one of the three most popular snacks at the 24-hour Chateau Deli.

3 cups (750 mL) rolled oats
 (not instant)
¼ cup (50 mL) sunflower seeds
¾ cup (175 mL) pumpkin seeds
2 tbsps (30 mL) sesame seeds
1 cup (250 mL) wheat bran
¼ cup (50 mL) chopped cashews
¼ cup (50 mL) chopped pecans
¾ cup (175 mL) chopped walnuts
¾ cup (175 mL) sliced almonds
½ cup (125 mL) raisins
1 tsp (5 mL) cinnamon
¼ cup (50 mL) milk powder
¾ cup (175 mL) honey
¾ cup (175 mL) canola oil
2 tbsps fancy molasses

Preheat oven to 375 F. Mix oil, honey and molasses together in a heavy-bottomed saucepan. Bring to a boil. Remove from heat and cool.

Blend all the dry ingredients together in a large bowl. Pour liquid over dry ingredients and mix thoroughly. Put mixture on a shallow, rimmed baking sheet lined with baking paper or lightly oiled. Bake at 375 F for 12 min. Allow to cool, cut into squares and wrap with plastic wrap. It's a forgiving recipe, so cooks can incorporate their own favourite nuts and seeds, dried cranberries or finely chopped dates. Makes about 12 4-inch squares.

Yamnuska Mountain School Wilderness Food Catering

www.yamnuska.com
Yamnuska Mountain School, Canmore
Tel: (403) 678-4164

Liesl Addicott, an Australian who came to the mountains, fell in love, and stayed, is busy developing recipes, testing dehydrators and getting ready for the cold weather. She's the chef for Yamnuska Mountain School, a training and guiding facility near Canmore, responsible for the wilderness food catering program. On some days she'll prepare food for up to a dozen trips, plus whatever custom catering needs to be done.

This food program is a great convenience for back country travellers, it's no longer necessary to do your own dehydrating. You and your hardy mountaineering pals can ask Liesl to do your provisioning, whether your trip is for three days or a week.

"If you're sleeping in a snow cave and heating up food on a little stove, the food has to be lightweight, balanced, filling and nutritious," she says. "Everything takes more energy when you're high up in the cold."

Liesl's Yamnuska Spicy Coconut Curry Rice

This dish needs advance preparation, but when you're heading for a mountain top, it's worth organizing a few plastic bags. This is a hearty, warming supper.

STAGE 1
4 tsps (20 mL) curry powder
½ cup (125 mL) dehydrated vegetables
    (or vegetable soup flakes)
1 cup (250 mL) instant rice
1 tsp (5 mL) cumin
½ tsp (2 mL) ground coriander
¼ cup (50 mL) dehydrated corn
4 tbsps (60 mL) coconut
2 tbsps (30 mL) dried spaghetti sauce
1 tbsp (15 mL) chopped dried apricots
4 tbsps (60 mL) milk powder
Pack all ingredients in a plastic bag. Write water quantity on the bag (3 cups) so you don't forget.

STAGE 2: Choose 1 protein from below to add to the meal.
    ½ cup dehydrated ground beef
    or ½ cup dehydrated chicken
    or ½ cup TVP (textured vegetable protein)
Pack the protein in a separate bag and place both bags together so you know it's all one meal.

To rehydrate: Boil three cups water and add contents of both bags. Cover, reduce to a simmer for 3–4 minutes, turn off heat and allow the meal to sit for about 7–10 minutes to completely rehydrate. Serves 2.

NOTE: Rehydration time may vary depending on altitude. If needed, add more water.

In the past few years, we've seen a welcoming spirit return to Banff, an eagerness to share its history, its beauty and its glamour. Here are some of our favourite places.

BANFF PANTRY
WHERE GOOD COOKS SHOP

Barba Bill's

www.barbabills.com

23 Bear Street

Tel: (403) 762-0377

Open daily 11:00 AM–9:00 PM

CASH ONLY

Having a nosh at Barba Bill's.

This unassumming Greek souvlaki house makes a dynamite dressing, a blend of olive and canola oils with herbs, lemon and an exhilarating hit (or head-clearing jolt) of garlic. It's so good they plan to sell it throughout Alberta soon. But for now, saunter on down to Bear Street and while you're there, pick up a donair and an order of their awesome fries.

The Castle Pantry

Fairmont Banff Springs Hotel

Tel: (403) 762-6843

Open 24 hours

V, MC, AE, ENR, JCB, DEBIT

On the far side of the lobby, past the tour group check-in, you'll find the Castle Pantry complete with a juice and coffee bar, fruit, meals to go and picnic basket makings such as wine and beer, cheeses and breads. Of special note for intrepid food lovers is the extensive selection of gourmet Canadiana: organic maple syrup, wild smoked salmon from Bowen Island, caribou pâté from Nunavut, the Springs' own tea blends, condiments from Ontario company Wildly Delicious and Belgian chocolate from a Canmore chocolatier (the dark bar is called the Coal Mine) among the offerings.

Welch's Chocolate Shop
136 Banff Avenue (Mount Royal Hotel building)
Open daily 9:00 AM–9:00 PM (closed Christmas Day)
V, MC

www.banffcandy.com
Tel: (403) 762-3737

> The choices at Paulette Zarkos's candy store are dizzying. There are fudge and brittles, bearspaws, jawbreakers and all sorts of penny candy. Connoisseurs of liquorice will be in heaven as Paulette stocks over 40 varieties of black, brown, sweet and salty from Holland, Finland and England. Must haves: according to Paulette, happiness is walking down Banff Avenue with a bag of carmellos— marshmallows slathered in rich caramel.

DINING OUT IN BANFF
CAFÉS, BISTROS, DINERS
& NEIGHBOURHOOD JOINTS

$$ **Coyotes Deli & Grill**
206 Caribou Street
Open daily 7:30 AM–4:00 PM, 5:00 PM–11:00 PM
V, MC, ENR, AE, DEBIT

Tel: (403) 762-3963

> Coyotes serves casual food with a southwestern twist. Breakfast items include a selection of frittattas and huevos rancheros with blue corn tortillas—served all day, no less. This alone makes Coyotes dear to breakfast lovers. Check out the variety of pizzas, pastas, soups and salads, deli sandwiches, grilled sandwiches and burgers. The black bean chili is superb after skiing. Also try the seared Atlantic salmon with mango salsa, with maple sugar-crusted apple pie for dessert.

$ **Evelyn's Coffee Bar**
201 Banff Avenue
Open Monday–Saturday 7:00 AM–11:00 PM; Sunday 7:30 AM–11:00 PM
MC

Tel: (403) 762-0352

$ **Evelyn's II**
Wolf & Bear Street Mall
Open Monday–Saturday 7:00 AM–10:00 PM
　　　Sunday 9:00 AM–5:00 PM
CASH ONLY

Tel: (403) 762-0330

> Evelyn's roast chicken sandwich is the best chicken sandwich in the west, bar none. Lots of daily specials and delectable baked goods to choose from, especially the astonishing old-fashioned devil's food chocolate cake. Great mugs of cappuccino.

Giorgio's Trattoria

$$ (marker) **Giorgio's Trattoria**
219 Banff Avenue
Tel: (403) 762-5114 (R for 8 or more)
Open daily 5:00 PM–10:00 PM
V, MC

Giorgio's, an enduring Banff destination, is owned and operated by the Schwarz brothers of the Post Hotel. The menu, predominantly Italian, features pizza cooked in the wood-burning oven, essential for the authentic crisp crust. We like the tender little cappelletti al burro e salvia: pasta hats filled with spinach and fontina cheese, then tossed in Parmesan and sage butter. Another deliciously simple dish is the chicken, first marinated in olive oil and herbs, then grilled and served with asparagus.

Comfort food, Italian style.

$$$ **Maple Leaf Grille & Spirits**
137 Banff Avenue   Tel: (403) 760-7680 R
Open daily 11:00 AM–11:00 PM
V, MC, AE

The Maple Leaf wears its Canadian regional cuisine moniker proudly—the menu is a culinary geography lesson: PEI mussels, Nova Scotia lobster, Quebec foie gras, Bragg Creek bison, Alberta beef. Our hearts swell just reading the menu. All this emphasis on location goes over the top only once, with the back country bison. (Where else would those buffalo roam?) Maybe it's a brand name.

It's a big restaurant with seating for 325 on two levels, made more intimate through clever use of private rooms and a distinctly "Canadian rustic" look: lots of wood, rundle rock, antlers, moose heads, snowshoes and such. It's a big menu as well, with an emphasis on fish, seafood and grilled meats. Here's the best part: the food is terrific. Wild boar and prawn spring rolls with a slightly sweet dipping sauce were an inspired combo, the subtle gaminess of the meat offset by the briny sea taste of the prawns. The aforementioned bison was perfectly cooked, served simply with a potato-spinach tart.

The excellent wine cellar is ably managed by Samantha Rahm. Always ask her about those new offerings that haven't quite made their way onto the list— she'll have some goodies.

Shiki Japanese Restaurant

$

110 Banff Avenue (Clock Tower Mall)
Tel: (403) 762-0527
Open winter Monday–Sunday 11:00 AM–8:00 PM
Open summer Monday–Sunday 11:00 AM–9:00 PM
DEBIT

This is a soup house, period. Great big bowls of
fragrant noodle soup—that's reason enough to
stop at Shiki. Eat-in or takeout.

Sushi House

$$

304 Caribou Street
Tel: (403) 762-4353
Open daily 12:00 PM–11:00 PM
V, MC

We love the Sushi House, not just for the expert
sushi-making skills of the genial owner, Lou
Tabaki, but because of the scale model CPR
train that rolls around the counter, pulling its
load of freshly made California rolls. It just
makes it all the more fun.

Sushi engineer Lou Tabaki.

BIG NIGHTS, SPLURGES, CELEBRATIONS

Banffshire Club (Fairmont Banff Springs)

$$$

www.fairmont.com

405 Spray Avenue
Open Tuesday–Wednesday, 6:00 PM–9:00 PM
    Friday, Saturday 6:00 PM–10:00 PM
V, MC, ENR, AE, JCB

Tel: (403) 762-6860 R

Ask Banffshire Club chef Daniel Buss where he's getting his vegetables and you're
in for a long chat. He gets excited about things like that—different kinds of sal-
sify from the Fraser Valley, and Cinderella pumpkins with their deep red-orange
colour and delicate texture. "I found a source for fresh wasabi," he crows.

It's this attention to detail that we find exciting about the Banffshire Club. The
ornate room (carved chairs, lots of dark wood) seats 60 and has a dedicated kitchen
presided over by Daniel. His cooking style is wine-friendly, without a lot of sweetness or heavy salt. He prefers to cook simply, letting the ingredients speak for
themselves. Sourcing was at one time his biggest challenge.

Now his sous chef delights in tracking down rare regional treasures like fresh Quebec foie gras. The bar is set very high indeed. "We would like people to think of the Banffshire Club the way they think of Charlie Trotter or the French Laundry."

The food is luxurious, with foie gras, lobster and truffles in abundance. A recent tasting menu started with an exquisite lobster salad. The chestnut and celery soup with duck prosciutto and foie gras was finished with a light apple foam—the essence of autumn. Andrew Chalmers, maître d', chooses the wines for the tasting menus and has developed a list that suits the room, with lots of depth in Californian, French and Canadian VQA.

Rambling About the Castle

"Always the same" is the motto of Cornelius Van Horne emblazoned on the rug in the front hall. His vison lives on, not just on the rug, but in the sensitive environmental and historical restoration of this Scottish castle fantasy in the middle of the wilderness.

With all its rock and massive beams, and the sheer ruddy size of it (the population of a small Balkan village could set up camp and hardly be noticed), the Fairmont Banff Springs is still a welcoming presence.

Somehow, kids always "get" the Springs. They run about its quirky corridors, down the hidden staircases, past the suits of armour, all with Harry Potter-ish glee. It's their very own castle.

No matter if you're a backpack totin', peak baggin', granola-eatin' wilderness guru, let the Springs seduce you at least once. This baronial pile of rundle rock in the Bow Valley is timeless, unforgettable and worth a visit. ⬱

$$$ **Buffalo Mountain Lodge**   www.crmr.com
Tunnel Mountain Road   Tel: (403) 762-2400 R
Open daily winter 7:00 AM–11:00 AM, 12:00 PM–10:00 PM
Open daily summer 6:30 AM–11:00 AM, 12:00 PM–10:00 PM
V, MC, ENR, AE

Buffalo Mountain Lodge is one of those special restaurants that does more than simply feed the body. There's a rustic serenity here, an elegant simplicity in this setting that is reflected in the menu.

Executive chef Thomas Neukom is in charge of a strong kitchen. The signature appetizer is the Rocky Mountain game platter to share, with air-dried buffalo, smoked pepper duck, game pâté (you get the idea) paired with a tasty mustard melon compote and cranberry relish. Their own farmed elk is served as a pan-seared medallion in a veal reduction with port. Pears and dried cranberries are sautéed with a little white wine and onion to make the delicious compote.

For a decadent dessert, try the white chocolate and cranberry bread pudding, fragrant with cinnamon, served with a fresh orange cream.

Food and beverage manager Shelly Gordash has built a top-notch wine list. A three time winner of the *Wine Spectator* Award, the list has an excellent selection of Canadian VQA.

Don't miss the game hash at breakfast. It's a delicious beginning for a day of skiing.

Chef Thomas Neukom with hash.

Canadian Rocky Mountain Resorts Game Hash

8 oz (250 g) game meats cut in strips (venison, elk, caribou)
4 oz (125 g) smoked peppered duck breast
½ small red onion, sliced
1 clove garlic, finely chopped
4 medium Yukon gold potatoes
½ cup (125 mL) game reduction (see note)
small handful fresh chopped herbs (rosemary, thyme, oregano, chives)
8 cherry tomatoes, halved
½ cup (125 mL) corn kernels
8 poached eggs
salt and pepper
rosemary sprigs

Sear game meat in a very hot pan, then add onion, garlic and potatoes. Cook for a few minutes, add game reduction. Add herbs, tomatoes and corn and simmer until stew-like in consistency. Season with salt and pepper.

Serve hash in deep soup plates and garnish each serving with two poached eggs and a sprig of rosemary. Serves 4.

NOTE: 1 cup of good beef stock, reduced by half, may be substituted for the game reduction.

$$$ **Eden (Rimrock Resort Hotel)**   www.rimrockresort.com

Mountain Avenue   Tel: (403) 762-3356 R

Open daily 6:00 PM–10:00 PM

V, MC, ENR, AE, JCB

Diners are in for a suberb experience at Eden. "We're aiming for total decadence," says Blair Hunter, maître d' of Eden (formerly Classico) in the Rimrock. It's no exaggeration. Randy Luft is the Eden chef under the direction of executive chef Yoshi Chubachi, a Culinary Team Canada alumnus.

Eden tasting menus are a gastronomic experience not to be missed: Market Menu, Le Bois, Le Mer, Chef's and the Grand menu range in price from $75 to $110 per person—worth every penny. Each menu reflects a particular exploration of flavours, of ingredients, of style (six or eight courses) and of wines. The piece de resistance is the Menu du Paradis, a ten course degustation paired with stellar wines from the Rimrock's enviable cellar. The cost? A trifling $500 per person. La grande splurge, we say.

Eden's excellence extends to not one, but three certified sommeliers who are like puppies in their excitement about the award-winning, 850 label list.

Chowing Down at Banff Centre

Banff Centre   www.banffcentre.ca

1-800-884-7574

The Banff Centre, an arts and conference centre in a spectacular setting, is well known for its good food. Executive chef Beat Hegnauer manages to serve as many as 1000 people per meal during the high summer season, and still maintain his culinary standards.

"We host international conferences all the time," says Swiss-trained Hegnauer, who has done a guest-chef gig at the Canadian Embassy in Washington, promoting Alberta cuisine. "At the Centre, our numbers mean it's mostly buffet, and that's a challenge when you care about quality. We have to be super-organized." The upside of having 1000 to dinner? Very few leftovers. "With a turnover like that, our food is always fresh." ✎

$$$ **Le Beaujolais**   www.info-pages.com/beaujolais

2nd floor, corner Banff Avenue & Buffalo Street   Tel: (403) 762-2712 R

Open daily 6:00 PM–10:00 PM

V, MC

Albert Moser's Le Beaujolais offers classic cuisine, professionally rendered. The menu changes little over the years, and if it's not exactly trendy, that's because a good piece of salmon, baked to a turn and finished with a touch of pernod, doesn't get much better. The wine list continues the classic tradition of the dining room, offering an excellent selection of French bottlings, especially the Beaujolais region.

$$$ **The Pines, Rundlestone Lodge** www.pinesrestaurant.com
537 Banff Avenue Tel: (403) 760-6690 R
Open daily 7:00 AM–10:30 AM, 5:30 PM–9:30 PM
V, MC

> The Pines has developed an extensive regional menu with bison, venison, salmon and a creative use of root vegetables. Valbella Meats' bison carpaccio, smoked goose breast and air-dried venison sausage are paired with a tomato pear relish or combined in a salad with a blueberry lavender vinaigrette. We were partial to the yogourt and chive galette appetizer served with sweet and purple potatoes on a corn relish with watercress. The baked rack of venison with red cabbage, pears and blueberry spatzle exemplifies the Swiss influence. Another popular item is the salmon glazed with fireweed honey. The wine list displays a good selection of Canadian VQA bottlings.

$$$ **Samurai**
Main floor, Fairmont Banff Springs Hotel Tel: (403) 762-6860
Open daily 6:00 PM–10:00 PM
V, MC, ENR, AE, DEBIT

> Samurai offers a serious exploration of Japanese cuisine in a fine dining setting. Appetizers include sushi and sashimi, yaki nasu—grilled eggplant topped with ground ginger and dry tuna flakes—and those irresistible edamame: lightly steamed, salted soybeans. Tempura, bento, vegetarian table d'hôte dinners and Japanese-style fondue round out the possibilities. Save room for the sorbets, sake or plum wine, or the green tea ice cream.

OTHERS WE LIKE
Grizzly House, 207 Banff Avenue, 765-4055; **Saltlik Steakhouse**, 221 Bear Street, 760-7349; **Ticino**, 415 Banff Avenue, 762-3848.

◉ THINGS TO DO BETWEEN MEALS

Take a hike: Johnston's Canyon on the Bow Valley Parkway about 20 minutes from Banff.

Take a dip: Banff Upper Hot Springs, Mountain Avenue, (403) 762-1515.

Read a book: The Banff Book and Art Den, 94 Banff Avenue, (403) 762-3919.

Look at art: Whyte Museum of the Canadian Rockies, 111 Bear Street, (403) 762-2291; Canada House Gallery, 201 Bear Street, (403) 762–3757.

Lake Louise isn't really a town. What we have here is a shopping mall with a ski hill one way, and one of the world's most photographed lakes the other way. At first glance, the food lover may despair, but keep looking. Here's where to start.

DINING OUT IN LAKE LOUISE
CAFÉS, BISTROS, DINERS
AND NEIGHBOURHOOD JOINTS

$$ **Baker Creek Bistro** (Baker Creek Log Chalets)   www.bakercreek.com
Bow Valley Parkway   Tel: (403) 522-2182 R
Open daily summer 8:00 AM–9:30 PM
Open daily winter 5:00 PM–9:00 PM
V, MC

> The Bistro serves three meals a day in the summer and dinner only from December to mid-May. We liked the salmon with fresh cilantro and shallots, steamed in rice paper with a honey, soy and ginger glaze. Game is excellent here, as is the fondue. All desserts, including ice creams and sorbets, are made in-house.
>
> The generous fireplace in the lounge of this rustic 50-seat log and stone restaurant makes for comfortable après-ski lounging.

$ **Bill Peyto's Café**   www.hostelling.intl.ca/alberta
203 Village Road (Alpine Centre International Hostel)   Tel: (403) 522-2200
Open daily May–September 7:00 AM–9:00 PM
Open daily October–April 8:00 AM–8:00 PM
V, MC, DEBIT

> Peyto, a character of legend, is best remembered for once throwing a live cougar into the Cascade Bar in Banff. Things are a tad quieter at the café but the food is hearty and good. Look for big sandwiches, veggie wraps with hummus and lots of fresh vegetables, burgers and veggie burgers, veggie chili and quesadillas. For a big mountain-style breakfast, try the omelettes or the buttermilk pancakes made from scratch and served with real maple syrup.
>
> The atmosphere is casual. While you're at the hostel, check out the photo gallery of big moments in mountaineering history. It's fascinating.

$ **Laggan's Bakery**
Samson Mall Tel: (403) 522-2017
Open daily summer 6:00 AM–9:00 PM
Open daily winter 6:00 AM–7:00 PM
CASH ONLY

> Laggan is the original name of the train stop when there was just the lake, the mountains and the animals. This cheerful bakery/café serves breakfast, lunch, sandwiches and coffee and the incomparable health cookie—lunch in the round. No trip to Lake Louise is complete without a visit, and it's highway-handy.

BIG NIGHTS, SPLURGES, CELEBRATIONS

$$$ **Deer Lodge Dining Room** www.crmr.com
Deer Lodge, Canadian Rocky Mountain Resorts Tel: (403) 522-3747 R
109 Lake Louise Drive
Open daily summer 7:00 AM–11:00 AM, 6:00 PM–10:00 PM
Open daily winter 7:00 AM–11:00 AM, 6:00 PM–9:00 PM
V, MC, AE, ENR

> The original building, once a tea house built in the 20s, is a maze of corridors to guest and public rooms. It is rather like the home of a dotty old aunt, one with exquisite yet slightly eccentric taste, though no aunt of ours ever had a hot tub on the roof. And the food! The food is thoroughly up-to-date.
>
> Chef Kelly Strutt works within the vernacular of Rocky Mountain cuisine, using seasonal, local ingredients such as elk, venison and caribou, duck and pheasant, juniper and other wild berries and Bow Valley trout. Pickles, chutneys and relishes made from Alberta ingredients are a special treat.
>
> Not everything on the Strutt menu comes from outside the back door. Starters include duck confit on a spinach and radicchio salad with orange, fig and walnut vinaigrette, and a toothsome smoked chicken, mushroom and corn chowder. Choose among artichoke hearts with roasted peppers, asparagus and goat cheese, and the grilled ranch elk striploin with saskatoon berry glaze and potato hash. The well-organized and informational wine list has won the *Wine Spectator* award several times. At last visit, the Cipes Brut Summerhill VQA was available by the glass, just the thing for sipping in that rooftop hot tub.

Chef Kelly Strutt's Braised Lentils with Confit of Duck

CONFIT OF DUCK
1 duck leg
small handful fresh rosemary, chopped
small handful fresh thyme
1 tbsp (15 mL) coarse sea salt
2 cups (500 mL) rendered duck fat

Coat duck leg with herbs and salt. Cover and refrigerate for 48 hours. Rinse salt off duck, then lightly sauté in small saucepan until golden brown. Add duck fat and simmer on very low heat for 30 minutes or until tender. Let cool and flake meat off bone in large chunks.

BRAISED LENTILS
1 small shallot, diced finely
1 tsp (5 mL) canola oil
1/2 cup (125 mL) each red and green lentils, rinsed in hot water
3/4 cup (175 mL) chicken stock
1 tsp (5 mL) fresh thyme
pinch salt and pepper

In a medium saucepan sauté shallot in oil until glossy. Toss in remaining ingredients including flaked duck meat. Cook over medium heat until liquid is absorbed, about 10 minutes. Serve in a flat soup bowl with hot toast. Garnish with fresh thyme sprigs. Maybe a glass of Pinot Noir? Yum.

Chef Kelly Strutt behind the stove at Deer Lodge.

Fairmont Chateau Lake Louise

A Bavarian-cum-French fantasy on the shore of the exquisite turquoise lake, this wedding cake of a chateau is surrounded by poppies all summer long. In winter, ice carvings appear by the lake, which becomes a skating rink.

At Lake Louise, climbing mountains is still the best way to work up an appetite. In the early days, the Swiss guides helped guests over the steeper bits. The tradition continues today with the Chateau's excellent Mountain Heritage Program, recognized by Parks Canada and given the 2002 Heritage Tourism Strategy award for best interpretive practice.

$$$ **The Fairview Dining Room**   Tel: (403) 522-3511 R
Fairmont Chateau Lake Louise
Open daily 6:00 PM–9:00 PM
V, MC, ENR, AE, JCB

Executive chef Dominique Guyot displays an inventive use of regional Canadian ingredients: wild rosehip jelly, juniper berries, meats, fish and game, partnered with contemporary international accents.

It's a sophisticated, evolving menu, seasonal and luxurious. For starters, there's a tasting of foie gras presented three ways: a terrine with concord grape gelee; foie gras cappucino; and sautéed with a bit of cipollini onion. Wild salmon is poached in olive oil, sable fish is marinated in verjus. A black lentil ragout with green beans is napped in a yellow beet sauce and served with lobster and diver scallops. Alberta rack of lamb is rubbed with violet mustard, roasted and served with a goat cheese polenta, napped with a blackberry emulsion, the tartness of the blackberry balancing the richness of cheese and lamb. Quinoa, shredded Napa cabbage and grilled tofu rolls served in a miso lemongrass broth, are exquisite.

For dessert, a slice of fresh fig tart comes with a port reduction and cinnamon ice cream. A light and refreshing vanilla panna cotta, served in a strawberry and fennel soup is just the right finish to dinner in this elegant, romantic room with the heart-stopping view.

Torch-brûléeing at Chateau Lake Louise.

$$$ **Walliser Stube**
Fairmont Chateau Lake Louise   Tel: (403) 522-3511 R
Open daily, 6:00 PM–9:30 PM
V, MC, ENR, AE, JCB

The menu at the Walliser Stube evokes an earlier time. In 1899, Canadian Pacific Hotels introduced professional Swiss mountain guides to their guests. For 50

Director of Food and Beverage David MacGillivray

David MacGillivray was destined to come back to the mountains. After all, he practically invented the dishes that typify what was called the Grand Canadian Lodge experience at Jasper Park Lodge. (And then there's Mount MacGillivray—no relation.)

Legions of chefs we respect have worked with or for him, including David Garcelon, Mario Mathieu and Patrick McClary. But, with his move out of whites and into the executive offices, MacGillivray's role has changed.

"I have to have a bigger focus now. I loved being a chef, I still love cooking, but I wear a suit and tie now. And that's OK. It's where I want to be."

His style is restrained, refined decadence. "We're a grand dining room in a grand hotel. That means outstanding formal service, linens, silver, really excellent food that is luxurious, classic. We feature oysters, foie gras and truffles on the Fariview menu. We showcase straightforward, top-quality ingredients. Seasonality and regionality are a given on our menus. Of course there are challenges in January in the mountains, but we manage to make it work."

He sees his role as a mentor. A guiding hand to the youthful culinarians that work in the Chateau's kitchens. "I'm jazzed by these kids," he says, with real enthusiasm. "So they don't want to work 80 or 90 hours a week? Well, maybe they can teach us something about balance." ✎

Canadian Wine & Food Festival

Fairmont Chateau Lake Louise
Tel: (403) 522-3511
www.fairmont.com

Albertans may not grow wine, but we do love to drink it. For one weekend each May, the Chateau Lake Louise hosts the Canadian Wine and Food Festival. It's a great party in one of the world's most exquisite settings.

The Festival is a unique opportunity to mingle with some of Canada's best winemakers, taste new vintages and pair wines (and not just fine food but pizza and popcorn too) with food under the guidance of experts. Throughout the weekend, executive chef Dominique Guyot shares his philosophy on food preparation, including his ongoing search for regional ingredients that influence his contemporary Canadian cuisine.

It's a wine event with a difference. It attracts winemakers, principals and winery chefs in droves. There are over two dozen different seminars and great meals, including a lively reception, gala dinner and mountain brunch. For those inclined, there are hikes with the Chateau's Mountain Heritage Program guides as well. It's a great time to be in the mountains. ✎

years, these guides—Edward Feuz, Bruno Engler and others—made first ascents and taught thousands of people to climb in the Rockies. Their spirit lives on today, in the Swiss-influenced menu at the Walliser Stube.

With that kind of background, it seems appropriate to indulge in the classic-country Swiss cuisine offered at the Walliser. The warm Lehman Lake salad features a potato and Tyrolian bacon galette served with mixed greens tossed in a red wine vinaigrette with smoked duck and a little goat cheese crumbled over. Bruno Engler's Rocky Mountain Wurts is a plate of grilled caribou, debriziner and bratwurst sausages served with good mustards, sauerkraut cooked with pork hocks, a warm potato salad and a freshly baked pretzel. Sturdy stuff, all of it.

Fondue and raclette—timeless dishes—are ideal in this cozy room with the pine trees whispering outside the windows. Raclette is accompanied by the traditional baby potatoes boiled in their skins, smoked and aged thinly sliced beef, pickled vegetables, pearl onions and gherkins.

Desserts continue in the classic vein: Sachertorte, a plate of excellent Canadian artisan cheeses, apple strudel and, of course, chocolate fondue served with fresh fruit for dipping. Extensive wine selection, served by staff who know what they're talking about.

Walliser Stube Chocolate Fondue

3 100-gram bars of dark Toblerone chocolate (or use white Toblerone for winter white fondue)
1 pint (250 mL) heavy cream

Finely chop the chocolate and place in a mixing bowl. Bring the cream to a boil in a heavy saucepan and pour over the chocolate. Stir gently with a wooden spoon until the chocolate is melted and fully incorporated. Pour the mixture into a small ceramic fondue pot or other heatproof dish. If using a fondue pot, keep the candle/heat very low, as the chocolate might scorch. If you don't have a fondue pot, the small heatproof dish can be reheated for a few seconds in a microwave.

Executive chef Dominique Guyot serves the fondue with apple or pear slices, bananas, chunks of cantaloupe and honeydew melon along with whatever fresh berries are available (strawberries, large blueberries, cherries with stems). The white chocolate version goes particularly well with tropical fruit: banana, pineapple, passion fruit, mango slices.

"For extra indulgence, you can also serve a small bowl of plain or very lightly sweetened whipped cream alongside either fondue," says the chef. Serves 4–6.

$$$ **Post Hotel** www.posthotel.com

200 Pipestone Road Tel: (403) 522-3989 R

Open daily 7:00 AM–11.00 AM, 11:30 AM–2:00 PM, 5:00 PM–9:30 PM

Seasonal closing last weekend in October to first week of December

V, MC, AE

The brothers Schwarz, Andre and George, preside over this gracious pine-panelled dining room. The food, under the direction of chef Wolfgang Vogt, doesn't miss a beat. It's an international menu by any standards, but it also celebrates regional Canadian specialties like caribou, bison, fallow deer, duck and of course, beef.

For a light starter, there's a well-made buffalo consomme with barley vegetable ravioli. Or how about the house-made pheasant spring rolls on a pickled ginger sambal vinaigrette, or the pan-seared duck foie gras with a red wine reduction and confit of shallot? Classic, simple, elegant. You couldn't get more Canadian (or Albertan) than the grilled buffalo striploin with a blackberry and

maple syrup game reduction, finished with a little butter and served with a roasted corn potato fritter. The side dishes are outstanding.

There is a phenomenal wine list, with a cellar of 20,000 bottles. There's a page and a half of bubbly alone, including three Krug bottlings, and they have 34 red wines by the half-bottle. French and California are the best represented, especially Bordeaux (four pages!) and Burgundy. There's great depth here, with,

A visual feast at the lovely Post Hotel.

for example, vintages of the rare and wonderful Vega Sicilia Unico, dating back to 1970. Such a challenge, to gather these bottlings of a truly stellar Spanish wine. (See also page 238.)

POST HOTEL

Take a hike: On your own or with one of the Chateau's excellent interpretive guides.

Read a book: Woodruff and Blum Booksellers, Samson Mall, (403) 522-3842.

Have a massage: Temple Mountain Therapeutic Massage at the Louise Medical Clinic, 200 Hector Road (403) 522-3003.

View of Bow Lake from the Icefields Parkway.

TO JASPER

The most spectacular route to Jasper is Highway 93, AKA the Icefields Parkway. Check the forecast, fill up the tank, carry a safety kit with flares and blankets, and pack a lunch (the Chateau makes fabulous box lunches) as this is a good, but lonely, road.

Jasper is about four leisurely hours up the Parkway from Lake Louise, through some of the most stunning scenery in the world. This is a place to see wildlife, especially the majestic, curly-horned rams, whose imperious manner is enough to keep wise tourists safely in their vehicles.

You'll be ready for some good vittles. Jasper is another world from the hurly-burly of Banff. It reveals its charms slowly, and they're easy to miss if you're just passing through. It's a hiker's paradise. But first, to the Lodge!

But first, to the Lodge!
The Fairmont Jasper Park Lodge

In the whole world, this is one of our favourite places. It's like a summer camp for adults. We especially like it between seasons, for the aroma of pines and woodsmoke carried on the fresh, crisp air. The mist on Lac Beauvert in the stillness of the morning, Canada geese practising touch-and-goes on the water, an elk ambling past your window, the bellboy on bicycle delivering a chilled bottle of bubbly—this is the lodge we love. ⇐

Mountain-style comfort at the Jasper Park Lodge.

◎ DINING OUT IN JASPER
CAFÉS, BISTROS, DINERS
& NEIGHBOURHOOD JOINTS

$$$ **Andy's Bistro**
606 Patricia Street
Open summer Monday–Saturday 5:00 PM–10:00 PM
Open winter Tuesday–Saturday 5:00 PM–10:00 PM
V, MC

www.visitjasper.com
Tel: (780) 852-4559 R

Chef and owner Andy Allenbach's 40-seat bistro is popular with locals and visitors alike. You can sit at the bar for a chat with the genial staff or at one of the cozy tables. Swiss in ambiance and menu, the food leans towards the stick-to-the-ribs-glad-I-biked-for-miles fare—ample portions rich with cream and cheese. It's also a prime spot for dessert and a glass of grappa after a walk about town.

$ **Bear's Paw Bakery**
4 Cedar Avenue
Open Monday–Friday 7:00 AM–5:00 PM
Saturday–Sunday 7:00 AM–6:00 PM
DEBIT

Tel: (780) 852 3233

The Bear's Paw is known throughout these parts for its signature pastry called (you guessed it) the bear's paw. It's a bit like a cinnamon bun, only better, with lots of raisins baked in a buttery yeast dough. Sturdy, delicious stuff. The breads and rolls are hearty multigrain, suitable fuel for a day in the mountains. There are a few tables, or they'll make you an excellent boxed lunch to go.

$ **Coco's Café**
608 Patricia Street   Tel: (780) 852-4550
Open daily 7:00 AM–10:00 PM
V, DEBIT

> A compact, casual spot great for morning coffee, lunch or takeaway. Almost everything—soups, stews, sandwiches and wraps—is vegetarian. As well, there are many full vegan dishes. These people know what they're doing in the kitchen, everything we've had here has been tasty. You can make good use of your hostel membership, as Coco's offers a 15% discount.

$$ **Fiddle River Seafood Restaurant**
2nd floor, 620 Connaught Drive   Tel: (780) 852-3032 R
Open daily 5:00 PM–11:00 PM
V, MC, AE, DEBIT

> Owner Archie Krass takes a different approach to eating in the mountains: no elk, no venison, no caribou. It's all about fish. If you want simple grilled trout or crispy salmon firecracker rolls, he'll oblige. Think of salmon, seared rare, rolled in nori with wasabi, quickly deep fried and served with Thai noodles and a sweet chili dipping sauce.

$ **La Fiesta Tapas Restaurant**
504 Patricia Street   Tel: (780) 852-0404
Open Monday–Friday 12:00 PM–2:30 PM
    Saturday 12:00 PM–10:00 PM
V, MC, DEBIT

> Chef Ed Sodke trained on the west coast, apprenticing at Chateau Whistler and worked with trend-setting chefs Bernard Cassavant and Rodney Butters. After a stint cooking locally, developing his unique Jasper-meets-West coast-style, Ed opened La Fiesta, modeled after a favourite haunt at Chateau Whistler.
>
> "The ultimate idea is to come in with a group of friends and share some tapas with a pitcher of sangria, which we often used to do up in Whistler" says Ed.
>
> It's a flexible menu—order a few tapas: crab salad tortilla roll, mussels in a flavourful tequila-spiked broth with lime and smoky chipotle pepper, artichoke and goat cheese dip. Or, stick to appetizers and mains: a silky yam and cheddar soup, a toothsome burrito stuffed with lean beef, hefty chunks of spicy chorizo sausage and greens. Good, compact, well-priced wine list.

$$ **The Pines at Pyramid Lake Resort**   www.pyramidlakeresort.com
Pyramid Lake Road   Tel: (780) 852-4900
Open Monday–Thursday 7:30 AM–4:00 PM, 5:00 PM–9:00 PM
    Friday–Saturday 7:30 AM–4:00 PM, 5:00 PM–10:00 PM
    Sunday 7:30 AM–2:00 PM, 5:00 PM–9:00 PM
V, MC, AE, DEBIT

> The location is perfect for lunch or a snack after canoeing, hiking or skiing. Eclectic menu, ranging from bruschetta and spring rolls to pizza to chicken and fish. The kitchen does an excellent job with grilled meats: Alberta beef, buffalo and elk. We love the mountain pot pie—venison and caribou sausage in a rich red wine sauce fragrant with herbs and made hearty with lots of potatoes, onions and mushrooms. Don't miss the lavish Sunday brunch.

$ **Truffles & Trout**
Jasper Marketplace
Tel: (780) 852-9676
Open daily summer 8:00 AM–10:00 PM
Open daily winter 8:00 AM–8:00 PM
V

> No truffles and no trout, but we love the spinach and feta pizza with black olives and a touch of oregano. The crust is just right. This is a good spot to refuel after hiking, hiking or skiing.

Chef's Culinary Weekend at the Fairmont Jasper Park Lodge

Every February, food lovers gather at the Lodge to drink new wines, eat new dishes, meet new chefs and talk to winemakers. There are cooking demos, wine tastings, kitchen tours and gala dinners. A great-value midwinter getaway with a culinary twist. ✍

BIG NIGHTS, SPLURGES, CELEBRATIONS

$$$ **Edith Cavell Dining Room**   www.fairmont.com
Fairmont Jasper Park Lodge   Tel: (780) 852-3301 R
Open daily 6:00 PM–9:30 PM; Sunday brunch 10:30 AM–1:30 PM
V, MC, ENR, AE, JCB, DEBIT

> Executive chef Patrick McClary sources his ingredients locally and regionally. A recent menu started with one of their own classics—Alberta mushroom soup with a mix of prairie grain, including barley, splashed with fireweed honey. A salad of vine-ripened yellow and red tomatoes is served with a dressing made from cold-pressed local canola oil.
>
> The Lodge's own smoked salmon is partnered with a little gravlax-cured Arctic char and salmon tartare. The Alberta lamb rack with herbed mustard crust

Christmas In November at the Jasper Park Lodge

What started as a weekend to build off-season business has morphed into a culinary phenomenon, with cookbook authors, TV hosts, chefs and local personalities, all in their most entertaining frame of mind. Christmas in November attracts guests from all over the world.

The program changes every year, but it's always fun. Favourite presenters have included chef Jay Nutt and David MacGillivray who mix cocktails, measure (or not), cook (or not) and dispense holiday cheer. Michael Smith, the "Inn Chef" of television fame, stands on top of an Igloo to expound on the virtues of brining a turkey. The crantinis flow, the parties carry on into the night, old traditions are honoured, new ones made. Wives bring their husbands, daughters bring their mothers, friends bring more friends. The lavish gala dinner ends with a raucous carol sing. This is a don't-miss party. The 15th annual is in November 2003; book early. ⟨

The Cuisine of Memory

Mario Mathieu, Director,
Food and Beverage, Fairmont Jasper Park Lodge

Mario Mathieu's vision of regional food is based on fond memories of his apprenticeship in Burgundy. "I remember Mr. Megrot bringing us squabs so fresh they were still warm, and Mr. Lalime with his fine, fat ducks which contained that luscious foie gras," says Mathieu. "And then there was an elderly lady who brought her farm cheese to the kitchen every day at 8 AM, just as she'd been doing for 30 years." Every day he tries to get closer to that memory.

Mathieu's philosophy: local is better. A good chef can always make a great meal out of fresh, quality ingredients, but a great chef cannot do anything with second-rate ingredients, says Mathieu. As the director of food and beverage at the Fairmont Jasper Park Lodge, he gets excited about the growing number of Alberta producers.

"A canola grower said to me, 'Call me when you need canola oil. I'll press the seed, then I'll ship it.' —And this oil is amazing," he says. "It's so yellow, people ask me what it's coloured with. And it has a fresh, nutty flavour and aroma." In winter, he looks to locally grown root vegetables and meats: wild boar, milk-fed pork, bison, lamb and of course beef. "I'm still waiting for that call from someone who'll say, 'Mario, I found some fantastic foie gras somewhere in northern Alberta. Are you interested?'"

Mathieu is committed to local and regional products used in ever-expanding ways. "We have to support our regional cuisine as it evolves. Europe has hundreds of years of culinary history. Alberta's cuisine is in its infancy, and that's the exciting thing about it," he says. "Today's chefs have a responsibility, and an opportunity, to shape the next 25 years." ⟨

is roasted, and served with a barley and Oka cheese pilaf. McClary doesn't forget the other senses. Fresh berries are served on a slab of the local rundle rock in a pastry canoe that says JPL. You may be torn between eating it or trying to get it home in one piece.

The Cavell is a lovely room looking out onto tranquil Lac Beauvert. It's everything you would expect from a dining room of international stature: accomplished service, fine crystal and an extensive wine list with several good VQA selections, all served with loads of Jasper charm.

Edith Cavell dining room at Fairmont Jasper Park Lodge.

◉ THINGS TO DO BETWEEN MEALS

Take a hike: Maligne Canyon is spectacular, both summer and winter; do consider hiring a guide, especially for the fantastic ice walk. We like Murray, (780) 852-5595.

Take in the view: Ride the Jasper tramway up Whistlers mountain. Once at the top, you can dine, hike or just marvel at the awesome scenery (780) 852-3093.

Run the river: Take on the Sunwapta or the Athabasca rivers in a whitewater raft. Call the Jasper Adventure Centre 1-800-565-7547 to book with a variety of operators. www.JasperAdventureCentre.com.

EDMONTON

4

Edmonton is down-to earth, unpretentious. It's a comfortable city, easy to live in, close to its roots. It's blessed with a river valley that is a paradise for runners and golfers, and we're crazy about our sports teams. Make your way to the neighbourhoods: little India, Chinatown, little Saigon, little Italy to shop for ingredients and equipment for the most authentic food. When you're hungry and you want pho or French bistro cooking, Thai curry or the finest example of Alberta beef, you'll find it here.

⊙ EDMONTON PANTRY
WHERE GOOD COOKS SHOP

Grandma always said, "A cook is only as good as her (his!) ingredients." Some things never change, so here's the primer for the complete cook, everything from achiote seed to za'atar, from Chinatown to Little India and everything in between.

🖋 BAKING SUPPLIES

Bernard Callebaut Chocolaterie

10180 101st Street (Manulife Place)   Tel: (780) 423-3083
Open Monday–Wednesday, Friday, Saturday 10:00 AM–5:30 PM
  Thursday 10:00 AM–8:00 PM
V, MC, AE, DEBIT

Other locations: 11004 51st Avenue, 436-0908; 12325 102nd Avenue, 488-0690.

The Callebaut company has been making chocolate in Belgium since the 1800s. There are over 400 grades of Callebaut chocolate, but if you want your homemade truffles to taste almost as good as the ones you buy at the Bernard Callebaut stores, you must use his chocolate. While you're at it, you might as well indulge in a jar or two of the luscious caramel and chocolate sauces. And why not a few bonbons—looking elegant and irresistible in their chic little bronze coffrets.

Bosch Kitchen Centre

9766 51st Avenue

www.bosch-kitchen.com

Tel: (780) 437-3134

Open Monday–Wednesday, Friday 9:00 AM–5:00 PM; Thursday 9:00 AM–8:00 PM
      Saturday 10:00 AM–5:00 PM

V, MC, AE, DEBIT

You'll find a large selection of dried fruits, nuts and candy-making supplies displayed among the high-tech European kitchen appliances for serious cooks. Bosch also carries dried herbs and spices, grains and cereals.

CHEESE

Italian Centre Shop

10878 95th Street

Tel: (780) 424-4869

Open daily 9:00 AM–9:00 PM

V, MC, AE, DEBIT

The Italian Centre Shop specializes (to nobody's surprise) in Italian cheeses. For a change of flavour, check out the Portuguese and Spanish cheeses that are available, such as Manchego. If you don't know which cheese you want, ask for samples. Don't be shy; this shop respects a serious cook.

Paddy's International Cheese Market

10730 82nd (Whyte) Avenue

Tel: (780) 413-0367

Open Monday–Friday 9:00 AM–6:00 PM
      Saturday 8:30 AM–6:00 PM
      Sunday 10:00 AM–5:00 PM

V, MC

Paddy's concentrates on a broad selection of well-known international cheeses such as English Wensleydale and French Tomme de Savoie, Quebec and Ontario cheddars, and Oka. The original Paddy has moved on. The shop is now owned and operated by Fern Janzen who makes lovely gift baskets. Ask her to include the

tasty (and local) St. Maure from Natricia Dairy in Ponoka. She'll ask you when you plan to eat it and will select one of the correct ripeness.

Acquired Tastes Tea Company
12516 102nd Avenue

www.canadiantea.com

Tel: (780) 414-6041

Open Monday, Wednesday, Friday and Saturday 10:00 AM–6:00 PM

Thursday 10:00 AM–8:00 PM

V, MC, AE, DEBIT

Owner Colleen Murray is a tea expert and is always happy to talk tea. You can buy a wide variety of bagged and loose teas in this sunny shop, or have one blended to your taste. There are a number of unusual teas such as Genmaicha, a Japanese tea made from popped rice. If you're a tea lover, and curious, take a course at the store to find out what "fine silver tippy" really means. She also sells attractive and unique tea accessories.

Fanta Camara
Vitalyteas

Tel: (780) 461-3176

Fanta Camara sources tea and ingredients for blending from all over the world: Tanzania, India, China, the United States and South Africa. She hand blends eleven teas, using herbs, flowers, fruit and exotic ingredients such as rooibos, an African red bush whose leaves are full of vitamins and calcium. We love Orange Bliss, a fine black tea blended with dried orange zest. Or try Life is Beautiful, a blend of green tea, spearmint and peppermint. Her Canada Chai, made with aromatic spices and maple syrup, is available in 250 ml and one-litre sizes.

Gourmet Goodies To Go, Sunterra, Big Fresh, Planet Organics, Organic Roots and Upper Crust Café carry these products. Fanta also custom blends Voodoo tea for Louisiana Purchase, and makes a private label for the Hotel Macdonald and Jasper Park Lodge. Only in Edmonton you say? Calgarians will have to be patient a little longer; she plans to expand to the south of the province. ✍

Java Jive Coffee Factory
9929 77th Avenue

Tel: (780) 432-9148

Open Monday–Friday 9:00 AM–5:00 PM

Saturday 10:00 AM–4:00 PM

V, MC, AE, DEBIT

Michael Ould's company imports, roasts, wholesales and retails fine coffee. At one time, Ould and his brother had a little empire of coffee houses across the city. Since then, Michael has chosen to leave the selling of a cuppa joe to others. Only the campus locations remain, including the original in Hub Mall where generations of students were introduced to the wonders of a well-made cup of coffee from fresh-roasted and ground beans.

The factory is coffee central. Look for fairly traded estate coffee such as Café La Union and Mezzana Estate, which makes its way directly from farmer to retailer to consumer. There are organic and shade-grown coffees from Mexico and Peru, plus loose and bagged teas. His terrific staff can advise on roasting systems, discuss the relative merits of this espresso machine over that one and help you choose from a variety of coffee (and tea) related foods, drinks and things. There are mail order services and a frequent buyer's card.

From left: Georgina Welsh, John Traish, Michael Ould, and Cheryl Johnson.

FISH AND SEAFOOD

Billingsgate Seafood Market and Lighthouse Café   www.billingsgate.com
7331 104th Street   Tel: (780) 433-0091
Open Monday–Thursday 9:00 AM–9:00 PM
    Friday, Saturday 9:00 AM–10:00 PM; Sunday 11:00 AM 8:00 PM

5506 Tudor Glen Mall (St. Albert Trail)   Tel: (780) 460-2222
Open Monday–Thursday 9:00 AM–9:00 PM
    Friday and Saturday 9:00 AM 10:00 PM
V, MC, DEBIT

The Fallwell family has been in the fish business, both wholesale and retail, since 1907. Their recently renovated and expanded shop on Edmonton's south side, and their smaller St. Albert location, are the places for fresh catch. Look for monkfish, haddock, snapper, trout, salmon, halibut, Alberta whitefish, Boston bluefish—the works.

Shellfish arrives daily, everything in its season: live lobster, crab, clams, mussels, oysters. The annual two-day May lobster festival celebrates Newfie food and culture, and it's more like a down-home picnic than a commercial venture. Everybody has a good time. A hefty chunk of the proceeds goes to the University of Alberta Hospital burn unit.

Both have restaurants, with the southside location tarted up to look like a lighthouse. From clam chowder and fish 'n chips to more sophisticated fare, this is a good spot for a fish lunch. They'll also cook to order, and catering platters can be arranged.

Bryan Fallwell, Owner and President, Billingsgate Fish

Fallwell is the fourth generation of his family to be in the fish business, the same one that was started by his great-grandfather, Alfred "Bertie" Malthouse. Malthouse was a London tram driver whose last stop was the old Billingsgate Fish Market. When he arrived in Canada and found the fish business in Alberta sadly lacking in expertise and good fish, he took the plunge and started Billingsgate. He had seafood, including lobster, shipped from the east coast in ice and sawdust (it had to be watered down en route in Montreal and Winnipeg). He also bought and shipped fish and

Manager Chris MacKay checking out the catch of the day.

seafood from Vancouver and from northern freshwater lakes.

"It filled a gap for his customers, many of whom were also immigrants, missing all those English choices," says his great-grandson Bryan. Now he's president of the family firm, with three outlets, one each in St. Albert, Edmonton and Calgary.

"I love the challenges in the business. It's constantly changing—new seasons, new varieties coming on stream, old varieties lost. He worries about that loss of variety, the decline of Canadian fish stocks that have put both cod and salmon in peril. "There's a lot of politics in the fishery, especially now, when both our east and west coast fisheries have seen stocks drop so dramatically."

For Fallwell, there's no better eating than a good piece of fish well-prepared. "The worst mistake people make with fish? Overcooking." ✐

Fin's Seafood
278 Cree Road, Sherwood Park   Tel: (780) 449-3710
Open Monday–Thursday 10:00 AM-5:00 PM
     Friday 10:00 AM—6:00 PM
     Saturday 10:00 AM—5:00 PM
DEBIT

    Owner Doug Sauve is a former chef, as are many of the staff. They all know fish, and understand what chefs want for their customers. Fin's is a major wholesaler, supplying numerous area restaurants with oysters and shellfish, wild salmon in season, plus the exotics from warmer waters.

       There's a briny little retail storefront tucked into the complex off Baseline

Road, where you can buy any seagoing thing they have in stock, in season—mahi mahi, halibut steaks, many varieties of oysters and shrimps, the works. For instant entertaining, we like the dilled salmon pâté, the bacon-wrapped scallops and the Nanuk sliced sockeye. If you want a whole, impeccably fresh salmon for your barbecue, this is the place.

MEATS AND FOWL

A Cut Above Meat and Deli

12534 132nd Avenue   Tel: (780) 452-6890
Open Monday–Saturday 10:00 AM–6:00 PM
DEBIT

Owner Warren Smith calls himself the "alternative protein specialist," and he's right—this is all about specialties. Where else can you find a holiday display of confit duck legs, hot-smoked duck breast and chicken leg stuffed with brandied onions and cheddar? His charcuterie is distinctive, think of caribou and buffalo sausage. The fowl selection includes pheasant, rabbit, quail and guinea hen. Fresh fois gras from Quebec is available, on order, within two days.

This place sets a food lover's heart racing. He even stocks the delightful and hard-to-find Gourmet Sauvage line from Quebec—hand-gathered wild things such as milkweed pods and cedar gelee. You'll also find Aussie bush tucker: wattleseed, native pepperberry, bush tomatoes and lemon myrtle—all so delicious as a rub for any meat.

Cameron's Meat and Delicatessan

12729 50th Street   www.cameronsmeat.com
                                     Tel: (780) 476-3939
Open Monday–Saturday 9:00 AM–6:00 PM
V, MC, DEBIT

An old-fashioned butcher shop where Alberta beef is still dry-aged, a rare find these days—every ounce of shrink costs somebody money. Fresh custom cuts and freezer packs are their specialties. There is a lavish selection of fresh chicken, pork, lamb and holiday specialties by request, including free-range turkey and the noble haggis. As well, Cameron's makes a toothsome nitrate-free bacon on request. At any time, they'll have over a dozen fresh and about 50 smoked sausages on hand. The British tradition is honoured with bangers, black pudding and English bacon, and the Camerons' own meat pies. They also make all the European sausages—weisswurst, bratwurst, andouille, chorizo. Ukrainian (St. Michael's Baba's Own brand) and Polish specialties in the freezer case round out the selection.

Charcutaria Micaelense & Groceries

9574 118th Avenue   Tel: (780) 477-2802
Open Daily 8:00 AM–7:30 PM
V, DEBIT

> If your aim is to make the most authentic paella, you must visit this spotlessly clean shop. Freezers lining the wall hold a large selection of fish, including salt cod for bacalau. The house-made sausage, available in spicy and not-so-spicy, redolent of garlic and wine, is loaded with lean chunks of pork. There is a small restaurant in the back, and although it's mostly a gathering place for the local Portuguese community to play cards and watch football, you can actually eat here.

Delton Sausage House Company

12906 82nd Street   Tel: (780) 475-1769
Open Monday–Saturday 9:00 AM–6:00 PM
V, MC, AE, DEBIT

> The Delton Smoke House, as it is popularly known, specializes in traditionally made Polish sausage. They're no slouch with the other European varieties either. Try the spicy Hungarian paprika, the Ukrainian garlic smoked over applewood, or the mild yet flavourful chicken sausage. All sausages, both fresh and smoked, are made without filler and preservatives. Our favourite? The swojska, an old-fashioned smoked Polish sausage.

A selection of Chinese meats at United Grocers.

Hinse Poultry Farms

10173 97th Street (in the City Farmers Market)
Tel: (780) 429-3592
Open Saturday 7:00 AM–2:00 PM
CASH ONLY

> In the early days, Flora Hinse, the matriarch of this family, used to work her stall at the City Market with her baby daughter tucked into a cardboard box under the counter.
>
> As the family grew, so did the Hinse poultry business. These days, their chicken is available fresh at both the City and the Old Strathcona Farmers Markets, and at a number of local merchants including Sunterra in the Lendrum Shopping Centre. At Thanksgiving and Christmas, place your orders for fresh turkey early, as last-minute shoppers will be disappointed.

King of Kings BBQ

10623 97th Street

Open daily 10:00 AM–7:00 PM

CASH ONLY

Tel: (780) 420-0858

King of King's BBQ shares space with Pak's King Wonton and Noodle, and it wasn't until we looked closely that we discovered the store side of the business had a different name entirely. (Confused? Keep reading.) King of King's is a spotless butcher shop specializing in duck, chicken and pork. Fresh duckling is sold whole or by the leg or breast. Ready-to-go items include soy sauce chicken, steamed chicken, salted chicken, crispy skinned roast pork (sold by the piece), barbecued pork sausage and tantalizing barbecued duck (sold whole or by the piece). The freezer case has a selection of dim sum items, including pork or duck dumplings and spring rolls.

Mundare Sausage House

11401 50th Street

Open Monday–Saturday 8:30 AM–7:00 PM

V, MC, DEBIT

Tel: (780) 471-1010

The town of Mundare's ubiquitous Ukrainian garlic sausage (kubasa) has been immortalized in a 40 foot roadside statue. It also has pride of place on a pizza at the Grizzly Pub in Canmore, and has countless fans. This is the local outlet.

Old Country Meats

6328 106th Street

Open Tuesday–Saturday 10:00 AM–5:00 PM

DEBIT

Tel: (780) 415-5677

Peter and Linda Ross are experienced sausage makers. Their big specialty, apart from 17 varieties of fresh, additive-free sausage (no preservatives, no fillers) is the noble haggis. They sell it year round; order ahead if you want it during the Robbie Burns Day rush. They also offer steaks, roasts, cabbage rolls and pyrohy.

Omega Meats

Westlock

V, MC

www.omegameats.ca

Tel: (780) 349-5955

The Pfaeffli family raise Angus cattle on a specific diet resulting in beef that is lean and high in Omega 3 fatty acids—the good kind. Their freezer packs are designed with the smaller family in mind as well. Check out their web site for more information on purchasing.

Parkland Packers

4913 52nd Avenue, Stony Plain   Tel: (780) 963-2183
Open Monday–Friday 9:00 AM–6:00 PM; Saturday 9:00 AM–5:00 PM
V, MC, DEBIT

A local chef describes Herman Knupp as "the last of the master meat men." The immaculate storefront holds four tables, and on weekdays, there's always a hot lunch—soup, pork chops, steak sandwich. But the reason to seek out this shop is the European-style cuts of pork and beef, plus the excellent sausages, both smoked and fresh. Note the novel campfire item—the giant Swiss wiener is bacon-wrapped, cheese-stuffed and ready for the barbecue.

SUNTERRA QUALITY FOOD MARKETS INC.

Sunterra Markets

www.sunterramarket.com
Tel: (780) 426-3791
10150 Jasper Avenue (Commerce Place)
Open daily 9:00 AM–8:00 PM

5728 111th Street
(Lendrum Shopping Centre)
Tel: (780) 434-2610
Open daily 9:00 AM–8:00 PM
V, MC, DEBIT

Starting with a half section of land near Acme, the Price family has built an impressive farm-to-fork operation with six Alberta locations. Pork and beef remain the core of the business with products coming from their farms and processing plant Trochu Meats.

Trowlesworthy Farms

Mirror   Tel: (403) 788-2380
V

When Jim's grandfather homesteaded this land in 1895, little did he know that a century later, beef cattle would still be raised on the same land in much the same way. Today, Jim and Wilma Sturgeon produce and sell fresh and frozen hormone-free beef, grain finished and dry-aged for 10 to 17 days. The resulting meat is tender, juicy and full of flavour.

Quarters and halves are available. Just go to the Old Strathcona Farmers Market in Edmonton to see what's on offer this week.

Valleyview Buffalo Company

176 Whitemud Crossing

Tel: (780) 438-9202

Open Monday–Saturday 10:00 AM–6:00 PM

V,MC, AE, DEBIT

> This is the only shop in Alberta that is dedicated almost exclusively to North America's original red meat. Manager Heidi Lorraine carries deli items such as buffalo garlic sausage, pepperoni, jerky, bacon, ham and pastrami, plus all the fresh cuts of steaks and roasts. During barbecue season, they do a huge business in bison burgers. The meat comes from northern Alberta buffalo ranches, and deli items are locally smoked and cured. Lots of good information about bison—just ask.

SPECIALTY GROCERY
ASIAN

Canakor Food Company

3116 Parson's Road

Tel: (780) 463-5458

Open Monday–Saturday 10:00 AM–8:00 PM

Sunday and holidays 10:00 AM–6:00 PM

V,MC, DEBIT

> For the past 20 or so years, there's been a member of the Kim family in this store, reliably supplying restaurants and interested cooks with the essentials of good Korean and Japanese cooking. Chang Keun Kim emigrated from South Korea and took over the family business from his uncle Kyu Kim in 1990. Here you'll find imported dried foods, noodles, dried fish from Korea and rice flours. Kim points out that he sells only higher-quality California-grown rice. He stocks a good selection of rice cookers and grills ideal for Korean barbeque.

Chinese Superstore and Seafoods

7915 104th Street

Tel: (780) 437-7189

Open daily 9:30 AM–7:30 PM

V, MC, DEBIT

> Philip Wong has owned the Chinese Superstore since 1983, and he's still one of the largest importers of Asian products in the province. He carries a great variety of fish and seafood, both frozen and fresh. It's a good place to find fresh tilapia, buffalo fish, ling cod and rock cod. Friday is best for variety. The barbecue counter puts out scrumptious pork and duck. There's rice by the sack (several varieties and brands) plus all the accessories: steamers, rice cookers, woks, teapots, small China coffee pots and entire dinner services. Good selection of excellent Thai curry pastes.

"The hot item now is frozen dim sum," says Wong. "We carry so many different varieties, and so many kinds of noodle soup." He also stocks specialty items
like preserved lemons, sushi rice, nori, rice vinegars and mats for rolling the
sushi.

Fumiya Japanese Food Store

5926 104th Street   Tel: (780) 439-4201
Open Monday–Friday 10:30 AM–6:00 PM
    Saturday 10:00 AM–5:00 PM
V, DEBIT

Mark Fukushima's well-organized shop is the only strictly Japanese food shop in
town, and if you're making sushi this is the place to go. He has an excellent selection of dried items—mushrooms, rice, noodles, seaweed and wasabi in its various forms: powdered, in a tube or in a jar. Also green tea, sauces and soups and
frozen seafood for sushi and sashimi. Conveniently small packages of tuna, eel and
sea urchin are available along with sushi mats and lots of good advice. A great little shop.

Hiep Thanh Trading Ltd

10704 97th Street   Tel: (780) 424-6888
Open daily 8:00 AM–8:00 PM
DEBIT

Need a teapot, rice cooker or porcelain Kuan Yin for your shrine? How about a
big frozen durian? Durian ice cream? Durian candy? Durian drink? This market
on the west side of 97th Street caters to just about every Southeast Asian group
that has ever arrived in Edmonton.

It has a hefty selection of frozen seafood, canned tropical fruit (at least
seven brands of lychee), vinegars, sauces, pastries, dried fruit, mushrooms and
mysterious pickles. The produce section is small, but holds a selection of fresh,
perky-looking Vietnamese herbs and the essential Chinese vegetables. There's
frozen dim sum, fresh meat, the usual vintages of duck eggs, Chinese and
Vietnamese pastries, noodles and so forth.

Hoa Pinh Trading

10692 97th Street   Tel: (780) 426-1990
Open daily 9:00 AM–9:00 PM
V, MC, DEBIT

In everything but the worst of weather, this busy corner shop displays boxes of
fresh produce on the sidewalk. Once inside you'll find the narrow aisles to be a

treasure trove of the exotic and unusual, with a wide variety of Chinese teas for improved health, a slender figure, a sharper mind or a more exciting love life. You'll also find endless pickles and condiments, candy, dishes and cooking paraphanelia. In the back, there's a counter for fresh meat and fish, plus a small selection of produce and takeout items—leaf-wrapped dim sum items already cooked, needing only to be popped in a microwave for a minute or two. We come here in late fall just for the boxes and boxes of ripe and squishy persimmons.

L & K Oriental Foods and Imports

7743 85th Street   Tel: (780) 469-2770

Open Monday–Saturday 10:00 AM–8:00 PM

      Sunday 12:30 PM–6:00 PM

V, MC, DEBIT

Almost everything you'd need to stock a basic Korean or Japanese larder can be found here, and the owner is justifiably proud of the hard-to-find items for sushi, sashimi and other Japanese delicacies. Look for a wide variety of soy sauces, fermented rice vinegars, wasabi, kim chee, pickled and preserved ginger, special dried chilies (flaked, without the stems) and specialty rices. They also sell frozen fish.

Lucky 97 Oriental Market

10725 97th Street   Tel: (780) 424-8011

Open daily 9:00 AM–9:00 PM

V, MC, AE, DEBIT

The industrious Ba Tan Nguyen once owned a tiny shop across the avenue, then

built a larger store and finally took over the competition, turning a former IGA into his sprawling Lucky 97. It's still crowded, and it caters to a mixed clientele looking for fresh produce at good prices and a fortuitous blend of western and oriental products. Nguyen is a major importer of Oriental products, so the shop has a wide range of specialty items from all over Southeast Asia, including sauces, vinegars, dried and preserved fruit, fish and pickles.

In Chinatown

There are really two Chinatowns, known as the old and the new. Watch for the giant Friendship Gate into the smaller, older section running east from 97th Street, and the more contemporary red gate that takes you north along 97th Street.

Chinatown has grown into a busy, vital business area, with lots of small shops coming and going as fortunes rise and fall. The part of 107th Avenue between 95th Street and 114th Street, fondly known as Little Saigon, holds a growing number of Vietnamese grocery stores, restaurants and barbecue houses. No matter how many Asian shops open in other districts, Chinatown is always worth a visit, especially on Sunday for dim sum and shopping, and during the heady excitement of Chinese New Year.

Shun Fat Lucky 88

10638 100th Street Tel: (780) 421-8888

Open daily 9:00 AM– 9:00 PM

V, DEBIT

New, bright, busy, Shun Fat offers a hefty selection of pan-Asian groceries, both fresh and frozen. The seafood counter in the back of the store is a favourite source for live crab and other fish. We've bought huge, gorgeous rambutan here, as well as the usual fresh produce. Big selection of fish sauce—26 different varieties at last count!

T & T Supermarket

2580 West Edmonton Mall, 8882 170th Street

Tel: (780) 483-6638

V, MC, DEBIT

This is west coast Asian style on the prairies: huge, clean, bright, with convenient layout and a look of great abundance. The West Edmonton store (north end, second level) brings T&Ts cross-Canada total to 10.

East meets West in almost every aisle with dragon fruit and apples, lo bok and leaf lettuce. Need meat? Beside the tenderloins and rib-eyes, you'll find goat breast, oxtail and paper-thin slices of lamb for hot-pot. Fish tanks hold live lobster, mussels, crab and tilapia. Check frozen foods for quail, silkie chicken, squab and duck leg. There's a barbecue station by the mall entrance for takeout. A caféteria-style food court offers seating for the fresh fruit and salad bar, as well as hot food to eat in or take-out. The sushi display is attractive, with alternating black and red bento boxes holding individually wrapped sushi: spicy scallop, flying fish, tako (octopus), green onion tuna, jellyfish, California rolls, salmon lunch-to-go, and small boxes of tobiko (fish eggs) in various hues. The bakery specializes in Asian taro bread, many-flavoured sponge cakes, bean cake and croissants.

When T&T moved into Edmonton, there was consternation in Chinatown. No worries—it's an excellent grocery store with 12 checkouts, but this market, big and efficient as it is, doesn't replace a trip to Chinatown.

Tung-Lam Oriental Grocery

9660 107A Avenue   Tel: (780) 423-0967
Open daily 9:00 AM–9:00 PM
DEBIT

Thu Tran came here from Saigon several years ago and opened his small shop on the north side of busy 107A Avenue. An affable, approachable man, he's happy to share his extensive knowledge of Southeast Asian products.

Visit this shop for a wide variety of tinned, bottled and dried items from all over Southeast Asia: tamarind paste, chili paste, shrimp paste, vinegars, hot sauces and coconut cream. Fresh Chinese vegetables arrive on Friday nights, so weekend shopping is ideal. Tung-Lam also has a good selection of noodles and rice, including several varieties from Thailand.

On Friday We Have Everything

United Grocers Supermarket & Pharmacy
9516 102nd Avenue   Tel: (780) 425-8552
Open daily 9:00 AM–8:00 PM
V, MC, DEBIT

Every year as the Chinese New Year approaches, this store takes on the festive air of a small village getting ready for a party. People come and go from the Chinese Elders Mansion next door, and families arrive from all around town, coming in for tangerines with leaves attached, special red boxes of dried and candied fruit for the New Year, and maybe a nice fat fish from one of the tanks. If you counted all the tanks in the back of the store, as well as those in the storage room, there would be 16 tanks of live fish burbling away.

"I lose sleep over that sometimes," says Joanna Wong, picking up a small shark for our inspection. Her parents own the shop, and Joanna Wong is the ...

Nothing fishy about Joanna Wong.

pharmacist who can always be found in the back of the store, slipping easily from English to Cantonese as her customers come and go.

Handy to the City farmers' market and close to the Chinese Elders Mansion, the United is part department store (carrying kitchenware, and religious and festive trappings) and part social center for the elders who pop in to chat in their own language. It carries an amazing array of stock, including many varieties of dried mushrooms, vinegars, (fermented, sweet or dark), spices, soy and hot sauces, as well as the usual tinned and dried products from Taiwan, Hong Kong, the Philippines and Thailand. King-sized woks and steamers are available, too. This is a shop that caters to chefs as well as home cooks.

Owner Steven Wong brings fresh produce in on Thursdays. "On Friday we have everything." ⟨

SOUTH ASIAN

JB Cash and Carry India Supermarket
9324 34th Avenue   Tel: (780) 468-9455
Open Monday–Friday 10:00 AM–8:00 PM
    Saturday 10:00 AM–7:00 PM; Sunday 11:00 AM–6:00 PM
V, MC, AE, DEBIT

    A small store, but it has a good selection of naan, rice, flours, beans and lentils. There's a serviceable produce section. Check out the selection of cooking utensils and tiffin carriers, which are handy stacked metal boxes traditionally used for takeout lunches in India. We find them ideal for picnics.

Spice Centre
9280 34th Avenue   Tel: (780) 440-3334
Open Monday–Saturday 10:00 AM–8:00 PM
    Sunday 12:00 PM–6:00 PM
V, MC, DEBIT

    We love the bustle of the Spice Centre, the heady aroma of fresh spices that never have a chance to grow stale. Look for extra-long cinnamon sticks, black and green cardamom in the pod, star anise, resinous-smelling asafoetida, fenugreek, saffron, turmeric and other spices we've only read about in books.

        Wander down jam-packed aisles of lentils, beans and peas, numerous varieties of rice, East Indian snacks and bags and bags of nuts—fresh, dried, salted or plain. Check out the assortment of pickle, the East Indian condiment that is rather like a cross between green tomato relish and marmalade. In the produce section, you'll find taro roots, coconuts, and fresh vegetables in season—tiny green eggplants, fresh okra, pea shoots, big bunches of fresh herbs, garlic, hot peppers, kafir limes and curry leaf. Fresh and frozen paneer and ghee are in the dairy case. This place also has an intriguing selection of DVDs and tapes straight from Bollywood.

EUROPEAN

K & K Foodliners Meat & Deli

www.kandkimportdelis.com

9942 82nd (Whyte) Avenue
Tel: (780) 439-6913

Open Monday–Wednesday 9:00 AM–5:00 PM
    Thursday, Friday 9:00 AM–6:00 PM
    Saturday 8:00 AM–5:00 PM

9628 76th Avenue
Tel: (780) 431-1932

Open Tuesday–Friday 9:00 AM–6:00 PM
    Saturday 8:00 AM–5:00 PM

V, MC, AE, DEBIT

It's been a Whyte Avenue landmark for four decades, and it still carries a superb selection of German and Polish delicacies. You'll find fish—their smoked trout is excellent—plus condiments and jarred vegetables with fulsome choice in each category: five brands of marinated mushrooms, seven of sauerkraut, half a dozen different jars of marinated and pickled peppers.

Highlights in the meat department are Mennonite sausage, kasseler (smoked pork) and cold-smoked salmon. Cheese selections are from Germany, Denmark and Switzerland. This is the place to shop if your recipe calls for house-made schmaltz (a chicken fat concoction used in eastern European cooking) or sour cherries to make a lovely game or duck sauce. Check out the lavish sweets section for fruit lozenges, Dutch liquorice, Swiss chocolate and the entire line of the Ritter Sport chocolate bars–high quality bars from Germany.

LATIN AMERICAN & CARIBBEAN

118 Tropical Food Store and Restaurant

9715 118th Avenue
Tel: (780) 479-6756

Open Monday–Thursday 10:00 AM–9:00 PM; Friday 10:00 AM–12:00 AM
    Saturday 10:00 AM–10:00 PM; Sunday 10:00 AM–7:00 PM

V, DEBIT

This busy grocery store/lunch counter carries traditional Jamaican specialties like callaloo (a spinach-like green), yams, dried and canned pigeon peas, red kidney beans, and rice. There's also a freezer case full of other Caribbean essentials. Frozen oxtail, goat meat and even roti wrappers. A selection of Jamaican patties (spicy chicken, beef or vegetarian) share space with salt cod and snapper. The snapper could be fried and served with bulla cakes (spicy-sweet buns) and Tastee cheese (Jamaican processed cheddar), an Easter tradition.

Angie Brown does most of the cooking at the lunch counter. She'll show you how to use fresh ackee (available seasonally), rinse the salt cod or fry a plantain. Don't miss her curried goat served with rice and peas (actually red kidney beans) and steamed green cabbage.

Paraiso Tropical

9136 118th Avenue
Tel: (780) 479-6000
Open Monday–Saturday 9:30 AM–7:30 PM
Sunday 11:00 AM–5:00 PM
DEBIT

If you're looking for authentic Mexican and Central American ingredients, this is the place. The family store stocks queso blanco (fresh white cheese, similar to feta), red and green salsa caliente and a fine selection of dried chilies, all necessary for that south of the border flavour. You'll find adobe, mole and pipian sauces, cones of piloncillo (sugar cane sugar), masa flour, and both corn and flour tortillas. Try the Mexican chocolate, frozen Chilean chorizo sausage, fresh plantains and frozen vegetables such as yucca and green tomatoes. If you need a pinata for a party, you'll find it here. Check out the great selection of CDs to give your cooking a little Latin rhythm! There's a small lunchroom—nothing fancy—for homestyle cooking like fried fish, tamales, empanadas and, some days, excellent roast pork.

Gourmet products at Zenari's in Manulife.

Spice Island

www.spiceisland.ca

10058 163rd Street
Tel: (780) 489-2738
Open Monday 10:30 AM–6:00 PM; Wednesday–Saturday 10:30 AM–6:00 PM
Sunday and holidays 11:30 AM–5:00 PM; Closed Tuesday
V, MC, DEBIT

This is the home of Jamaica's island specialties. Look for ginger beer, jerk sauces, plantain, ackee, dried peas and beans. An interesting shop, and you can send money home to the islands by Western Union.

LUXE GROCERY

Le Gnome
1814 West Edmonton Mall
Tel: (780) 444-1137
Open Monday–Friday 10:00 AM–9:00 PM
    Saturday 10:00 AM–6:00 PM
    Sunday 12:00 PM–6:00 PM
V, MC, AE, DEBIT

Le Gnome's food section is where you'll find the newest condiment, the tastiest cookie or chip and that hard-to-find specialty item. Not expensive, but a well chosen selection of unique quality items, all tested or tasted by the owner herself.

Pnina Staav, owner of Le Gnome, in her store.

Urban Fare
9680 142nd Street (Crestwood Shopping Centre)   Tel: (780) 482-0021
Open daily 8:00 AM–10:00 PM
V, MC, DEBIT

Need a gift or a housewarming present that looks fabulous and tastes great? Lobster and duck liver paté, oils and vinegars, the most luscious dips, spreads, jewel-like jars of confiture, sauces, condiments—they're all here. Serious cooks will enjoy the selection of Palette Fine Foods' rubs and honeys, as well as the Dean and Deluca herbs and spices in their distinctive metal jars. To make a truly big splash, truffles, foie gras and caviar are available by special order. Celebrate!

Zenari's
10180 101st Street (Manulife Place)   Tel: (780) 423-5409
Open Monday–Wednesday 7:00 AM 6:30 PM; Thursday, Friday 7:00 AM–9:30 PM
    Saturday 9:00 AM–5:30 PM
V, MC, AE, DC

At the east door of this coffee bar/kitchen store/deli, you'll find a compact gourmet food section with an intriguing stock. Floor-to-ceiling displays feature vinegars including aged balsamics, a variety of olive and nut oils, sauces, jams (you can buy Dark Tickle blueberry preserves here), and seasonal items like marrons glace and pan forte.

Elsafadi Brothers Supermarket

11316 134th Avenue   Tel: (780) 424-4869
Open Monday–Friday 10:00 AM–10:00 PM
    Saturday, Sunday 10:00 AM–9:00 PM
V, MC, AE, DEBIT

Elsafadi is not just a great neighbourhood supermarket but a terrific source for Middle Eastern ingredients. The staff are helpful—quick to explain how to cook this vegetable or what to do with that spice. The extensive selection of Mediterranean groceries and staples includes herbs, spices, nuts, honeys, meats and cheeses, good seasonal local produce, Lebanese pomegranate molasses and Scarpone brand condiments, sauces and beans.

Hellas Food

12407 109th Avenue   Tel: (780) 455-8168
Open Monday–Friday 9:00 AM–8:00 PM
    Saturday 10:00 AM–6:00 PM
    Sunday 10:30 AM–4:00 PM
V, DEBIT

Hellas carries a useful selection from the entire Mediterranean basin, especially Greek: stuffed vine leaves, olive oils, pickled vegetables and filo pastry.

Italian Centre Shop

10878 95th Street   Tel: (780) 424-4869
Open daily 9:00 AM–9:00 PM
V, MC, AE, DEBIT

Ciao bella! This is the granddaddy of Mediterranean import shops in Edmonton. Enjoy browsing for Italian vegetables in season: fennel, baby artichokes, radicchio, eggplant. Pick up some fresh basil in a giant bag. Enjoy the good-natured bickering over olive preferences, or which cured meats go best with what, or whether or not the gorgonzola is Canadian or Italian. They carry almost every olive and red pepper condiment known to man. Check out some interesting honeys. Look in the freezer for quail and rabbit. In September, mountains of sweet

Sausage talk at the Italian Centre Shop.

and hot field peppers arrive—buy a big bag and go wild. It's also the season for wine grapes by the truckload. Order early and get in on the fun.

At the Italian Centre Shop, everybody's Italian.

Omonia Foods Import

10605 101st Street ·   Tel: (780) 426-6210

Open Monday–Saturday 9:00 AM–10:00 PM

    Sunday 10:00 AM–9:00 PM

DEBIT

Omonia is still *the* place to buy mizithra cheese (sharp, salty, essential for Greek cooking and tasty grated over hot pasta), canned vine leaves and other Greek and Turkish staples.

Frank Spinelli
The King of Little Italy

On September 1, 2000, Frank Spinelli's doctor gave him 10 days to live. He immediately had his passport renewed. It was a final, eloquent gesture by a man who was always a little larger than life.

Francesco Spinelli came to Alberta as a young man, from San Pietro al Tangro, in southern Italy. "It wasn't supposed to be forever. But you make friends, have obligations . . . your life is here."

In 1961 he opened a small confectionery store and quickly outgrew it. His next store was the Italian Centre Shop, which became one of the great passions of his life. Except for trips back to Italy, and three statutory holidays a year, he was in the store all day, every day, while the place known as Spinelli's became as much a community centre as a business.

He was the undisputed patriarch of Little Italy, and he never forgot how it felt to be the new kid in town, no money, no job, "and nobody would advance you a dime." Known for his big heart and open wallet, Frank's generosity extended well beyond the Italian community.

In the fall, there was always the wine. He made a medium-bodied Zinfandel, fresh, fruity, a hint of spice on the palate. In the old days, when Alberta was the Bible Belt, Frank (with juice stains on his immaculate white coat and a grin on his face) would deliver the California grapes, merrily sneaking them into cronies' basements in the middle of the night.

His devotion to the shop on the corner of 95th Street never wavered. He insisted on spending time there, walking from the cheese counter to the bulk olives, the fresh peppers and figs to the pasta aisle, and up the stairs to his office, overlooking the whole store. He did it every day until he was no longer able to make the short trip across the street from his home. Today, his daughter, Teresa, has her office upstairs. Downstairs, Rina, Frank's widow, still runs a cash register three days a week. ✎

Saccomanno's Pizza, Pasta and Deli

www.saccomannos.com

10208 127th Avenue

Tel: (780) 478-2381

Open Monday–Saturday 9:00 AM–9:00 PM; Sunday 9:00 AM–6:00 PM

V, MC, DEBIT

Saccomanno's specializes in fresh pasta. They also carry Italian staples such as dried pasta, cheeses, deli meats and vegetables in a friendly, small-store atmosphere. Saccomanno's brings in lovely figs and green almonds in season, plus wine grapes. There is a little café adjoining, popular with the ràil yard workers down the street. The food? Simple and hearty.

ORGANIC FOODS AND FRESH MARKETS

Produce guru Bobby Gibb and owner Shelley Robertson.

The Big Fresh

12120 Jasper Avenue

Tel: (780) 433-7374

Open   Monday–Friday 10:00 AM–8:00 PM

Saturday, Sunday 10:00 AM–6:00 PM

V, MC, DEBIT

The new-age design surrounds an extensive selection of bulk goods, fresh vegetables, frozen products, meats and chicken, even pet food. For health-minded cooks in a hurry, there is a selection of microwave ready soups and homemade dips. This store has been a runaway success. Maybe it's the location, maybe it's being in the right place at the right time. We like the emphasis on local products, the (almost) obsessive attention paid to the fresh produce and the tastings and cooking demonstrations that happen regularly.

Excel Food Market

6523 111th Street

Tel: (780) 434-1020

Open Monday–Friday 9:00 AM–8:00 PM

Saturday 9:00 AM–6:00 PM; Sunday 12:00 PM–6:00 PM

V, MC, DEBIT

It looks like a typical neighbourhood grocery store, but it's far from average. Almost every product in this store, including some of the usual snack foods like chips and candy, is organic. Customers can order ahead and pick up a box of fresh produce weekly or have it delivered. Owner Tina Park was a pioneer, the first to offer such a selection of organic products and services.

Organic Roots Food Market

8225 112nd Street (College Plaza)   Tel: (780) 413-1730

Open Monday–Friday 7:00 AM–10:00 PM

    Saturday 8:00 AM–9:00 PM; Sunday 9:00 AM–7:00 PM

V, MC, DEBIT

    Almost as much restaurant as food store, one side is a cheerful, Movenpik-style 24-table caféteria, while the other side is given over to fresh produce, organic meats, bulk groceries, and a hefty stock of dietary supplements.

Planet Organic Fresh Market

7917 Calgary Trail South (Strathcona Town Centre)   Tel: (780) 433-6807

Open Monday–Friday 9:30 AM–8:00 PM

    Saturday 9:30 AM–6:00 PM; Sunday 12:00 PM–5:00 PM

V, MC, DEBIT

    Planet Organic is the old Terra with a better location and more selection. We love the good-for-you yet hedonistic mix. Excellent selection: in-house bakery, bulk bins of grains and pulses, candies, nuts, dried fruit, baking supplies, all the natural and organic product and supplements anybody could ever want. There is a fine selection of Japanese products including many dried seaweeds and the artisan miso made on Denman island, Shinmeido. They carry Bles Wold yogourt, all sizes and flavours. It may not be organic, but it's made in Lacombe and it's fantastic. The pristine, seasonal produce is sourced locally and from BC—not just the standard California offerings.

    Planet Organic completes a little bit of foodie heaven in what is now called the Strathcona Town Centre: Greenwoods' Books (for cookbooks), the Chinese Superstore, an IGA, a Save-On and the Old Strathcona Farmers Market just a few blocks away. Brilliant!

Urban Fare

9680 142nd Street (Crestwood Shopping Centre)   Tel: (780) 482-0021

Open daily 8:00 AM–10:00 PM

V, MC, DEBIT

    We're impressed with recent improvements at this high-end version of Save-On— the meat counter with Winter's turkeys, a lavish produce display and knowledgeable and helpful staff ready to search the aisles for whatever your heart desires.

Bread, the great comforter. The staff of life. With nothing but flour, water and a little salt, bakers who are committed to their art still craft this indispensable food. Our favourite bakers are part talented artists, part knowledgeable craftspeople. In Edmonton, many have their roots in Eastern Europe. We look to them for hearty peasant loaves, seeded breads, Polish ryes, and those chewy, sustaining dark breads we love so much.

Bagel Bin Bakery & Bistro

226–6655 178th Street   Tel: (780) 481-5721
Open Tuesday–Friday 7:00 AM–7:00 PM
        Saturday 7:00 AM–6:00 PM; Sunday 9:00 AM–5:00 PM
V, MC, DEBIT

The bins behind the counter at Diane and Michael Alkalay's west-end shop are chock full of tasty Eastern European specialties, crisp-crusted caraway rye, dark

breads, plus all the Jewish holiday favourites. And, of course, bagels. Bagel Bin was the first place in town for decent boiled bagels. People no longer had to bring them back from Montreal or Toronto. The selection is completed by tortes, cookies, sweet rolls, cakes and squares.

Check out the cooler filled with gourmet condiments and such: Zinter Brown products, Experience Gastronomique smoked salmon, flavoured cream cheeses. The small lunch spot is a meeting place for coffee and a nosh of soups, sandwiches and a spot of something sweet. We love the convenient Sunday hours as well. That good, crusty bread you love at French Meadow? It came from the Bagel Bin.

The Bee-Bell Health Bakery

10416 80th Avenue   Tel: (780) 439-3247
Open Monday–Friday 9:00 AM–5:30 PM; Saturday 8:00 AM–5:30 PM
CASH ONLY

The venerable Bee-Bell has been a part of Old Strathcona since Edwin Strimer, the original owner, turned out the first loaf of healthy multi-grain bread one fine day in 1956. Their honey-sweetened seven-grain bread is famous, but they have some 300 other items ranging from biscotti and bagels, to pies, pastries and tortes, plus the best carrot cake in town. Saturday mornings when the nearby farmers' market is in full swing, the Bee-Bell is always chock-a-block with eager fans lined up for their favourite cookie or loaf.

Bon Ton Bakery

8720 149th Street   Tel: (780) 489-7717
Open Monday–Friday 7:00 AM–6:00 PM
    Saturday 7:00 AM–5:30 PM
V, MC, DEBIT

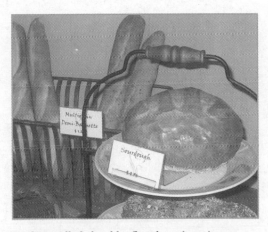

When Hilton and Michelle Dinner took over after baker Eugene Edelmann's retirement, they kept the long-serving staff, the tradition of quality baking and a number of recipes that remain unchanged— the onion bun made with delicious caramelized onions, the light Polish rye with caraway and the delicious multi-grain, high-protein bread.

    On the pastry side of the business, they've expanded considerably. Try the small, fudge like flourless chocolate cake, the turtle tarts, the almond-filled croissants. The white chocolate version of pain au chocolat brings out the child in everybody.

Cay's Bakery

15053 Stony Plain Road   Tel: (780) 489-9740
Open Tuesday–Friday 9:00 AM–6:00 PM
    Saturday 9:00 AM–5:00 PM
CASH ONLY

Cay Bastian specializes in French pastries, tiny mouthfuls that are exquisite examples of the art of patisserie. Terrific Danish too, like walnut, cream cheese, fruit. Bastian makes good bread, including his own schinkenbrot, a sour rye with whole-grain organic kernels that are first sprouted, then dried. When baked into the bread, they open up and give the loaf a delightfully chewy texture. The Dutch raisin currant bread is also a big favourite.

ESM Bakery

9413 118th Avenue   Tel: (780) 477-3987
Open Tuesday to Saturday 8:00 AM–5:00 PM
CASH ONLY

> Here's the place to buy toss, an anise-flavoured toast to dunk in a cup of good Indian tea. The ESM specializes in it, and ships it to customers around the continent. They make Indian sweets and breads, cookies and specialty meat pies as well.

Kinnikinnick Foods

10940 120th Street   Tel: (780) 424-2900
Open Tuesday, Wednesday, Friday 11:00 AM–5:00 PM
      Thursday 11:00 AM–6:00 PM
      Saturday 10:00 AM–4:00 PM
V, MC, DEBIT

> No gluten ever darkens this door.
>
> Ted Wolff, North America's most forward-thinking entrepreneur of gluten-free baking, believes in going "gate to plate." He and his business partner, Jerry Bigam, personally visit every mill they deal with to be sure every ingredient comes from dedicated lines (used for gluten-free grains only). "Avoiding any form of cross-contamination is critical for people with severe allergies," says the genial baker.
>
> Wolff's extensive research pays off in superior flavour, texture and convenience—they have a phenomenal line of all-purpose baking mixes for breads and cakes. Theirs is a small, crowded shop where they sell in-house baked goods—English muffins, bagels, doughnuts, breads, cookies, pizza crusts—plus pasta, cereals and other products that meet their strict criteria. They ship all over North America and are expanding into the European market. Look here for dairy-free and egg-free products as well.

La Favorite

11401 95th Street   Tel: (780) 477-2084
Open Tuesday–Saturday 10:00 AM–5:00 PM
V, MC, DEBIT

> Other locations: 12431–102nd Avenue (on the High Street), Tel: (780) 482-7024; 70–19 Bellerose Drive, St. Albert, Tel: (780) 459-4583.
>
> Max Morpurgo is from Trieste, but he's Swiss trained, and he's predictably lavish with cream and chocolate. Mousse cakes, especially the exquisite raspberry and white chocolate version, are part of his signature, as is the fabulous tiramisu.

Semi-freddo (that delectable frozen Italian almost-ice cream dessert) and tortes are fresh daily, and the house-made truffles melt in your mouth.

At Christmas, Max goes wild: look for delicate, beautiful cookies, chocolate treasure chests and panforte, small disks of rich, dark boiled-honey Christmas cake crammed with fruit and nuts. "The recipe dates back to the 15th century," says Max.

Paradiso Bakery

11318 134th Avenue (next door to Elsafadi Bros Supermarket)   Tel: (780) 448-7292
Open Monday–Friday 10:00 AM–10:00 PM
   Saturday 10:00 AM–9:00PM; Sunday 10:00–6:00 PM
V, MC, DEBIT

This bright and airy pastry shop specializes in Middle Eastern pastry, generally of the honey-drenched filo variety. Both the cashew and pistachio baklava are top-notch. People line up for the delicious breakfast pastry called konassee—a mild white cheese, covered in shredded filo, then baked, soaked in honey and served in a bun—it's a honey and cheese sandwich. Paradiso is a great source for rose-water and other flavoured syrups as well.

Sherbrooke Bakery

13232 118th Avenue   Tel: (780) 455-2323
Open Tuesday–Friday 9:00 AM–5:30 PM; Saturday 8:00 AM–5:00 PM
V, MC, AE, DEBIT

Peter Huppelschoten has been in business for more than 30 years, producing his trademark fluffy raisin buns, and the Dutch raisin bread enriched with raisins, currants and almond paste. His famous almond pie is made fresh daily. There's an in-house deli with soups and sandwiches, imported cheeses and lunch meats.

Tree Stone Bakery

8612 99th Street   Tel: (780) 433-5924
Open Tuesday–Friday 10:00 AM–6:00 PM; Saturday 8:00 AM–4:30 PM
Debit

Tree Stone breads are made by a centuries-old method called pain au levain, which employs a "mother" made from wild yeast rather than the conventional brewer's yeast. These breads take a long time to develop and require a cool, slow rising. The result? Incomparable textures, layers of flavour, and a bread with long-keeping qualities.

Among the favourites at this bakery are the rye, the whole wheat with sprouted kernels, and a rye raisin walnut loaf. The baguettes are wonderful—

crisp-crusted, great aroma and flavour, a pleasure to eat. And the pizza dough is top notch. Tuesday and Thursday baker Nancy Rubuliak bakes potato bread; Wednesday it's her coarse country loaf; Friday and Saturday she makes the basket-raised maslin, based on an old English peasant loaf and made with equal portions of rye and whole wheat. Weighing in at one kilogram, it's a hefty loaf.

Orange currant cookies are always available. On Friday and Saturday there's sweet butter brioche—ask for the brioche with brandy-soaked raisins. At Christmas and Easter, Nancy bakes the special festive breads of the season: panettone, hot cross buns, stollen.

Nancy Rubuliak
Tree Stone Bakery

Nancy Rubuliak is an ex-social worker who loves good food and finds tremendous satisfaction in the hands-on aspect of the baker's craft.

"I use all my senses, and I enjoy that. I also love the physicality of baking," she says. "The smell of the yeast, the feel of the dough against my hand. It's important to me to work in traditional ways. I've always felt a strong connection to the land, and as a baker I create food that nourishes people. At one level, baking bread is so functional, such an ordinary thing to do. But at some other level, it's an exquisite thing."

A strong supporter of local producers, Nancy buys some of her organic grains from a local farmer and grinds them at the bakery. All the other flours come from Alberta mills because of the high quality of the grains. "Ultimately, I just want to make the best bread I can."

Nancy's loyal customers would like to nominate her for sainthood. "Her bread changed our lives," insists one of the regulars. "It's healthy, it's delicious; the way bread should be!". ⇐

◉ DINING OUT IN EDMONTON
COFFEE SHOPS & TEA HOUSES

Sure, you can go to a Starbucks anywhere. But, for the true flavour of a city check out its coffee shops and tea houses, each with a personality that's all their own.

Café La Gare

10308A 81st Avenue   Tel: (780) 988-2400
Open daily 8:00 AM–12:00 AM
DEBIT

La Gare is a little artsy-fartsy, befitting a café with a French spirit close to the historic railway station (which incidentally, is now a bar). It's full of bonhomie, which takes us beyond the simple menu and standard coffee and tea offerings. Choices on the chalkboard reflect the Euro-sensiblilty: macchiato, bibi café, espresso. The food is homey: giant chocolate chip cookies, bagels and coffee cake, soup in a crockpot and a surprisingly large choice of omelettes for breakfast. Unfortunately, La Gare is another victim of the crazy-making smoking regulations—kids and non-smokers outside!

Cargo and James

10634 82nd (Whyte) Avenue, Old Strathcona   Tel: (780) 433-8152
Open Sunday–Thursday 9:00 AM–10:00 PM
    Friday, Saturday 9:00 AM–11:00 PM
V, MC, AE, DEBIT

Lower level, City Centre West   Tel: (780) 425-3330
Open Monday–Friday 6:30 AM–5:00 PM
    Saturday 10:00 AM–5:30 PM; Sunday 12:00 AM–5:00 PM
V, MC, AE, DEBIT

There was a time when tea rooms were cozy places with ruffles, lots of baked sweets and a dozen tea bag flavours. We still love the retro comforts, but there's a fresh wind blowing through the tea house trade, and new tea rooms are ruffle-free zones that specialize in multi-varieties of loose tea, whether black, green, medicinal, herbal, exotic, or rare.

There's a sleek, open look in the City Centre location and a clubbier feel to the Whyte Avenue spot. Ask about specialty teas (Hawaiian cocktail, Mongolian delight, safari sunset, samurai rooibos) and rare teas (golden heaven Yunnan, jasmine dragon tears, organic makaibari), plus a bevy of chai teas, tea slushes like the maple blend, and herbal infusions. How about that CJ Love Potion?

Friends of Rutherford House Tea Room

11153 Saskatchewan Drive   Tel: (780) 422-2697 R
Open Tuesday–Sunday 11:30 AM–4:00 PM
V, MC, DEBIT

Jill Dixon is the manager and cook at this graciously restored 1911 heritage home, once the official residence of Dr. Rutherford, a former Premier of

Alberta. The freshly baked scones, served with house-made preserves, are delicious. So are the homemade tea breads, the small sandwiches and the scrumptiously fattening desserts. Lunch is also a major part of the Rutherford day, and they now include vegetarian items on their menu. Rutherford House is a spectacular setting for private parties. It can accommodate up to 35 guests seated for dinner, or up to 80 for cocktails. "Remember, this house was built for entertaining," Dixon says.

Kennedy's Coffee House

220–590 Baseline Road, Sherwood Park   Tel: (780) 449-4966
Open daily Tuesday–Friday 7:00 AM–10:00 PM
    Saturday 9:00–10:00 PM
    Sunday 9:00 AM–5:00 PM
CASH ONLY

Audrey Dolinski knows most of her regular clients by name, and her place is as comfortable as your sister's kitchen. Kennedy's is a mixed bag, offering 45 varieties of fresh whole-bean coffee and a couple of dozen varieties of bulk tea, plus 11 flavours of the newly-trendy rooibos. Audrey always has delicious baking on hand: cheese or berry-studded scones, loaves, big muffins, killer butter tarts, biscotti, as well as healthy lunch options like soups, salads and her specialty, a big chicken sandwich, made with the real thing, freshly roasted.

La Tienda

8426 109th Street   Tel:(780) 439-5108
Open Monday–Saturday 11:00 AM–9:00 PM; Closed Sunday
V, MC, DEBIT

The best place to buy cigars in Edmonton also happens to be a great place for a cup of Cuban coffee: rich, dark and with enough caffeine to fuel your day.

Muddy Waters Cappuccino Bar

8211 111th Street   Tel: (780) 433-4390
Open Monday–Friday 7:30 AM–12:00 PM
    Saturday 9:30 AM–12:00 PM
    Sunday 10:00 AM–12:00 PM
V, MC, AE, DEBIT

Another favourite University area haunt was opened eight years ago by Denny and Marilyn Kay—"So our kids would have a place to work during school," says Danny. Well, the kids have graduated and moved on with their lives and Muddy Waters is still going strong. Among the several coffee and tea options, a good selection of beers, breakfast burritos, sandwiches, quesadillas, great tasting crumbles, squares and pies and a few salads are offered. Jenn, the soup diva, makes profound soups daily—her carrot with dill and feta cheese is amazing. Edmonton's bizarre smoking laws (hiss, boo) have caused much consternation for some small café owners. Muddy Waters tried the non-smoking route, business dived. Now it's a smoking establishment. Danny installed a HEPA air filter so the smoke is negligible but you still can't have lunch with your kids. The patio outside solves this dilemma in good weather.

The Pomegranate

8614 99th Street   Tel: (780) 433-8933
Open Tuesday–Friday 8:30 AM–6:00 PM
    Saturday 8:00 AM 4:30 PM
DEBIT

Next door to the impossibly good Tree Stone Bakery is The Pomegranate, recently opened by baker Nancy Rubiliak. The menu is modest, with assorted Tree Stone baked goods, brioche, and rustic baguette available with some cheese, jam or the café's own aromatic pomegranate spread. On offer are Italian sodas and loose teas along with good drip coffee, espresso and such. With just a few tables and chairs, it's a perfect, tiny café.

Steeps The Urban Tea House

12411 Stony Plain Road   Tel: (780) 488-1505
Open Monday–Thursday 10:00 AM–11:00 PM
    Friday 10:00 AM 12:00 AM
    Saturday 11:00 AM–12:00 AM
    Sunday 11:00 AM–10:00 PM
V, MC, AE, DEBIT

Brendan Waye and his brother Paul, known in some circles as "those two tea guys," have a passion for good tea. Brendan, inveterate traveller and mountain climber, has sipped his way around the globe. While drinking chai on one of his excursions, he decided to take it home—literally. Now, his own chai mix figures prominently on the menu. Along with traditional chai, vanilla green chai and an herbal chai, Steeps offers more than 160 varieties of loose teas, including 30 varieties of rooibos and their newly hatched rooibos chai. Sweets with your tea? Pastries, pies, cakes and cookies are available. Their tea houses, both here and in Calgary, are comfortable, conversational spots, rather like being in the living room of a slightly funky, somewhat worldly, socially responsible party-type friend. People come for tea and stay for hours.

The Strathcona Tea House

Wye Road at RR 221, Ardrossan   Tel: (780) 922-6963

Open Tuesday–Thursday 9:00 AM–3:00 PM

     Friday–Saturday 9:00 AM–9:00 PM; Sunday 10:00 AM–7 :00 PM

V, MC, AE, DEBIT

Country-style cooking is the order of the day in this old bank adjacent to an antique shop, the Treasure Chest. Owner Marlene Lothian offers a full menu for lunch and early tea, with dinner served on weekends. Expect roast chicken, turkey, pork, bison and ostrich, all locally grown. Eggs and cream are supplied by a neighbouring farmer. Freshly baked anadama bread is a house specialty. It's one of the few cornmeal breads made with yeast and molasses. Children's tea parties have been a big hit here. Marlene serves sandwich wedges with dips and relishes and throws in an etiquette lesson "suited to their ages."

Sugar Bowl Coffee and Juice Bar

10922 88th Avenue   Tel: (780) 433-8369

Open Monday–Friday 7:00 AM–12:00 PM

     Saturday, Sunday 8:00 AM–12:00 PM

V, MC, AE, DEBIT

Expect poetry, angst and existentialism. And chess! The Sugarbowl is a thriving hotbed of chess playing. There are New York Times chess columns (explaining nifty moves, we presume) and e-mail addresses of those looking for a game—sort of a chess ladder—along with a list of good stations on Sugarbowl's DMX system.

If there are beatniks in this century they'll eventually turn up at The Sugarbowl. The gorgeous old brass Rancilio that takes up half the counter dispenses espresso in all its forms. The food is the usual student staples: panini,

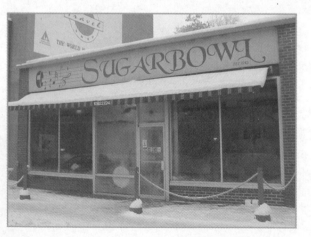

spanokopita, and spicy Jamaican patties. If you're craving sweet, try owner Abel Shiferaw's tiramisu. New this year is table service and tapas in the evening.

The timeless atmosphere is heightened by the brick walls, local art, funky music (often live in the evenings) and the thick pall of cigarette smoke that hangs in the air. But on Saturday mornings the air is clear, classical music pours forth and the half-cinnamon bun and cup of joe are the best deal in town at $2.50. A few tables outside (placed to catch rays most mornings, even in winter) are a refuge for nonsmokers.

Tea Cottage

10588 100th Street

Tel: (780) 425-6404

Open Sunday–Thursday 11:30 AM–10:00 PM

Friday, Saturday 11:30 AM–12:00 AM

CASH ONLY

If big sago balls (think tapioca) rolling around in the bottom of a liquid refreshment (think milkshake) doesn't sound like your cup of tea, try it on a hot summer day. Although the name for this rather peculiar beverage varies from city to city, in Edmonton it's known as bubble tea, and at Danny Yiu's small café, the tapioca treats are called sago pearls. Among the 61 versions of available sago bubble drinks are milk teas—two-flavour, fresh fruit and coconut (available with herb jelly, red or green beans, coconut chunks), plus a roster of special slushes and bubble milk drinks—watermelon, papaya, mango (our favourite), green apple, taro, chocolate, sesame, barley, or red or green tea sago. If bubble tea isn't your thing, you can eat here too—fast sandwiches, plus baked potatoes and loaded waffles.

Timothy's World Coffee

8137 104th Street

Tel: (780) 433-8758

Open Sunday–Thursday 7:00 AM–12:00 PM

Friday, Saturday 7:00 AM–1:00 AM

V, DEBIT

Though in general we don't think a chain can crystallize the coffee shop experience, we do make an exception for the Whyte Avenue Timothy's, because of the people: warm, friendly and quick with the coffee. The staff could give seminars in customer service. The muffins are made by Zenari's and the lattes are perfect, not too milky, not too bitter, with lots of good coffee flavour.

Tea at the Harvest Room

www.fairmont.com

10065 100th Street

(Hotel Macdonald)

Tel: (780) 424-5181

High tea is served in the summer only: May through Labour Day, Sunday 3:00 PM–5:00 PM

V, MC, AE, ENR, DEBIT

When the venerable Mac rolls out its high tea, it's a real treat: finger sandwiches (cucumber, smoked salmon, that sort of thing), petit fours, dainty afternoon pastries, scones, housemade strawberry compote with real Devonshire cream, and of course the tea of your choice. It's a delicious tea, elegantly served in a formally appointed dining room with a beautiful garden terrace and a river view. Sadly, it's only once a week, and you have to plan ahead. ✎

Tra A Mici Café & Bar

10850 95th Street   Tel: (780) 424-8259
Open Monday–Friday 7:30 AM–11:00 PM
    Saturday, Sunday 8:30 AM–11:00 PM
V

When Bar Italia closed, the whole city mourned, but it was felt most keenly by
Italian males. Where to go for midmorning cards? Where to shout insults at a television referee, or commiserate with fellow fans when the team tanks? Never
mind, now there's Tra A Mici. Don't let the contemporary design fool you, this
is the quintessential Italian bar. Have a panini, espresso, maybe a caffe corretto—
morning espresso with a restorative shot of grappa. The menu is chalked on the
board, television blares Italian programs, and handsome Stan Cerra keeps the coffee and the news flowing.

The St. Thomas Coffee House

44 St. Thomas Street, St. Albert   Tel: (780) 458-8225
Open Monday–Thursday, Saturday 8:00 AM–11:00 PM
    Friday 8:00 AM–12:00 AM; Sunday 10:00 AM–10:00 PM
V, AE

Margeurite Nelson's coffee shop-cum-restaurant sits at the western edge of St.
Albert's glorious farmers' market. Summer Saturdays it's crazy-busy, and seats on
the patio are at a premium. The best seller among the 25 or so whole bean coffees is the St. Thomas Encore, their special blend secret recipe. They're also
known for their pies and cheesecakes—try the raspberry rhubarb pie, the turtle
cheesecake or the white chocolate cherry cheesecake.

Victorian Affair (formerly Victorian Tea House)

Golden Spike Road, Spruce Grove   Tel: (780) 962-3177
Open Tuesday–Saturday 11:00 AM–9:00 PM; Sunday 11:00 AM–4:00 PM
V, MC, DEBIT

Cory and Anna Penner took over this wonderful old farmhouse in September of
2002, and although it's no longer strictly a tea house, they do serve a scrumptious
high tea Tuesday through Sunday. It arrives on a three-tiered tray, with homemade
scones, lemon curd, jam and Devonshire cream on the bottom, dainty sandwiches
on the middle tier and delicious desserts on the top tier. The sweets, always our
main reason for ordering high tea, vary from day to day, with cookies, small
cakes, even baklava. Anna offers a choice of 47 different varieties of bagged tea.

    To get here, turn south at Zender Ford on Golden Spike Road. It's on your
right, two kilometres south.

$$$ **Blue Pear** www.bluepear.com
10643 123rd Street Tel: (780) 482-7178 R
Open Wednesday–Saturday 6:00 PM–10:00PM
V, MC, AE, DEBIT

Price fixe dining returns to Edmonton with the Blue Pear, creation of Darcy and Jessie Radies. The couple bought the restaurant L'Anjou from Phillippe and Heather Bourigault, freshened the look and opened for business about two years ago. Darcy, a former chef at Jack's Grill with extensive European experience, possesses a cooking style that is subtle with a deft touch. His cooking is developing a regional bent, using (and highlighting on Blue Pear's web site) local producers' meats, cheeses and vegetables.

L'Anjou and the Bourigeaults had many fans and the food honours this heritage in a modern eclectic fashion. The glorious ragouts, casseroles and confits that made L'Anjou a welcoming haven for many years can still sometimes be found on the seasonal menus, in the Blue Pear style.

$$$ **Characters**
10257 105th Street Tel: (780) 421-4100 R
Open Monday 11:00 AM–2:00 PM
Tuesday–Friday 11:30 AM–2:00 PM, 5:00 PM–10:00 PM
Saturday 5:00 PM–10:00 PM
V, MC, AE, ENR, DEBIT

Chef and owner Shonn Oborowsky is a bit of an iconoclast — the chef people love to talk about as much for what he says as for what he's cooking. But we'll concentrate on what's on the plate. A stint cooking in the Far East created his avid East/West sensibility. Current offerings include tastes of this and that, often grouped in threes. The soya braised bison rib with a veal loin and a small Barrhead Nouvella Dolca pork rack, all uniquely sauced, was delicious.

Leave room for dessert at this restaurant. "I love making desserts!" says Shonn. There is the Callebaut chocolate trio: warm molten cake with a milk chocolate mousse, finished with a luscious white coffee ice cream. Another favourite is a grouping of three exquisite crème brûlée presented in sake cups: one coconut, one macadamia, the third a sprightly passion fruit. The room is modern with clean lines, blonde woods, and an open kitchen. If you're feeling really flush, order a wee dram of the 1937 Rare Collection Glenfiddich. At $1500 a shot—pocket change.

$$$ **Crowne Plaza Chateau Lacombe's La Ronde**   www.chateaulacombe.com

10111 Bellamy Hill   Tel: (780) 428-6611 R

Open Monday–Saturday 5:30 PM–10:30 PM

    Sunday 10:30 AM–2:00 PM, 5:30–10:00 PM

V, MC, AE, ENR, DEBIT

Extensive renovations have given beloved maître d' Hans Voegeli a much-needed new look to showcase the graceful service and the extensive regional cuisine this room is noted for. Chef Jasmin Kobajica has become the poster chef for regional cuisine, and rightly so. He has nurtured strong relationships with local suppliers and builds menus around their products. Carpaccio becomes peppered wapiti (elk) with a drizzling of Highwood Crossing's cold pressed flax oil. On a cold winter night the organic Paddle River rabbit with smoked wild boar bacon ragout was perfect. There are two tasting menus and the menu changes seasonally.

$$$ **Hardware Grill**   www.hardwaregrill.com

9698 Jasper Avenue   Tel: (780) 423-0969 R

Open Monday–Thursday 11:30 AM–2:00 PM, 5:00 PM–9:30 PM

    Friday 11:30 AM–2:00 PM, 5:00 PM–10:00 PM; Saturday 5:00 PM–10:00 PM

V, MC, AE, DC

It took guts to turn an old hardware store at the wrong end of Jasper Avenue into a first-class restaurant, but Larry and Melinda Stewart have pulled it off in spades. This menu celebrates regional Canadian cooking with inventive touches.

Larry and Melinda Stewart.

However, the Stewarts are happy to use other ingredients too. Note the baked blue potato with truffles and foie gras, and the roast organic chicken with asparagus mushroom ragout scented with white truffle oil. Albertans love beef and the Hardware menu offers a beef tenderloin in goat cheese crust, and a "really big" Sterling Silver AAA Alberta beef strip. Then there's the deliciously smoky planked salmon, the bison meatloaf with ale sauce and the truffled potato pyrohy.

The wine list has won the *Wine Spectator* magazine award four years running. Big plus: a dozen wines are available by the glass at any given time and it's not your standard plonk. The Stewarts use their by-the-glass program to try out new wines, so expect an ever-changing selection. The wine list also includes numerous verticals—multiple vintages of the same wine.

Robust Country Cooking
Hardware Grill

Melinda and Larry Stewart own and operate the Hardware Grill, an upscale 100-seat eatery in downtown Edmonton. People return to the Hardware Grill because of its consistency, and for the toothsome dishes in Alberta-sized portions. Larry describes his cooking style as robust country cooking. "It's from my heart and soul," he says. "I grew up on a farm. I think that translates into my cooking."

He's a man of strong opinions, and regarding Canadian cuisine, it's all about being open to new ideas. "Do you need maple syrup and wild rice to call it Canadian? That's nonsense."

Consistency of supply of local ingredients is still a problem but Larry has seen big improvements since opening the restaurant. He feels it's a learning process for the smaller suppliers. He also worries about contemporary attitudes toward food in general. "I have a fear that people have forgotten what real food is. Everything is pre-packaged, pre-made," he says. "We're losing some basic cooking skills that used to be handed down through the generations."

A large team of cooks prepares lunch and dinner using the principles of classic French cuisine. All stocks are made from scratch. Sourdough breads are made with a natural starter. A customer looking for catsup is out of luck; nothing at the Hardware Grill comes out of a bottle or from a mix.

"We look to Alberta first for our ingredients but we are getting high quality fowl and foie gras from Quebec," he says. "We had to take pork off the menu for a while because we couldn't find a supplier to raise and cut to our specifications. Now we are really happy with the pork from Barrhead. It's exactly what we wanted." ✉

Mike Buckley, executive sous chef of Hardware Grill, preparing the appetizer feta-terranean.

Maple Pork with Tangle Ridge Whisky Molasses Glaze and Sweet Corn Sauce

MARINADE
½ cup (125 mL) maple syrup
½ cup (125 mL) apple cider vinegar
2 tbsps (30 mL) soy sauce
½ cup (125 mL) canola oil
1 tbsp (15 mL) Dijon mustard

Whisk all ingredients well. Place 4 pork tenderloins (approximately 8 oz [224 g] each) in marinade and refrigerate overnight.

SWEET CORN SAUCE
¼ cup (50 mL) diced onion
1 tbsp (15 mL) butter
1 tsp (5 mL) salt
½ tsp (2 mL) black pepper
¼ tsp (1 mL) nutmeg
2 cups (500 mL) peaches and cream corn kernels
½ cup (125 mL) chicken boullion
½ cup (125 mL) whipping cream

Put onion, butter and seasoning in small pot and sweat over low heat until onion is soft. Add remaining ingredients and simmer for 20 minutes. Purée with hand blender or food processor. Keep warm until ready to serve.

TANGLE RIDGE MOLASSES GLAZE
1 cup (250 mL) fancy molasses
¼ cup (50 mL) Tangle Ridge Canadian Whisky
2 tbsps (30 mL) Dijon mustard
2 tbsps (30 mL) apple cider vinegar

Place all ingredients in pot and simmer on low for 30 minutes until slightly thickened, stirring occasionally. Remove pork from marinade and pat dry. Brown in a hot pan. Generously brush glaze over pork. Roast at 400 F (200 C) for 10-12 minutes, or until a meat thermometer registers 160 F (70 C) Do not overcook. Slice each tenderloin into four pieces on the diagonal and place over the corn sauce. Serve with braised red cabbage and whipped potatoes. Serves 4.

$$$

Harvest Room, Fairmont Hotel Macdonald

10065 100th Street   Tel: (780) 429-6424 R

Open Monday–Friday 6:30 AM–2:00 PM, 5:30 PM–10:00 PM

Saturday, Sunday and holidays 7:00 AM–10:00 PM

V, MC, AE, ENR, DEBIT

We like this room best in summer, when you can have a glass of champagne on the terrace with its tinkling fountain and superb view. It's lovely in winter too, with snow falling beyond the tall windows and lights twinkling across the river.

Executive chef Roary MacPherson is originally from Newfoundland. He celebrates Canadian ingredients and goes to considerable trouble to use and promote local and regional products. Expect to taste dishes like rack of Pembina milk-fed pork, quickly grilled and served with a cassoulet of great northern beans, wild boar bacon and root vegetables. Canola-fed chicken is served with a soft corn polenta, and there's a tenderloin of Alberta beef glazed with Natricia Dairy's St. Maure cheese, accompanied by a galette of Yukon gold potato, charbroiled portobello mushrooms, roasted onions, all with au jus laced with Pinot Noir.

The Mac's Roary MacPherson with production chef Dori Dubetz.

It's also a good place to try specialties from farther north, like the Yukon Arctic char served with all-blue baby potatoes, or the Nunavut caribou medallion with caramelized sweet potato casserole and jus of Alberta Springs Whisky. The Harvest Room offers a couple of toothsome vegetarian dishes every day. We love the roasted vegetable layered pasta with pickled peppers and tomatoes.

For dessert the baked Anjou pear and French toast brûlée with cranberry ice cream was extraordinary. But it's hard to ignore the sticky date and fig pudding with whisky sauce.

$$$ Hy's Steak Loft

10013 101A Avenue, Rice Howard Way   Tel: (780) 424-4444 R

Open Monday–Friday 11:30 AM–2:00 PM, 5:00 PM–10:00 PM

    Saturday 5:00 PM–10:00 PM; Sunday and holidays 5:00 PM–9:00 PM

V, MC, AE, DC

> Hy's has a '70s retro feel about it. From the tuxedoed waiters to the garlicy, anchovy-laden Caesar salad (boldly flavoured, and not tall enough on the plate to be trendy), it's a trip back in time. But in these parts, a great steak is the stuff of icons, and Hy's does do a great steak. Other highlights are the mesquite-grilled chops, the lamb rack and the aforementioned Caesar salad. The street-front bar is popular with movers and shakers of the oilpatch persuasion.

$$$ Il Portico

10012 107th Street   Tel: (780) 424-0707 R

Open Monday–Thursday 11:30 AM–2:30 PM, 5:30 PM–10:30 PM

    Friday 11:30 AM–2:30 PM, 5:30 PM–11:00 PM

    Saturday 5:30 PM–11:00 PM

V, MC, AE, DC

> Chef Kevin Lendrum has a deft touch with fresh produce, which he uses lavishly as the seasons change. Even his salads are celebrations—Italian greens (arugula, radicchio) spiked with brandied figs and grilled portobellos. Try the mozzarella-stuffed, prosciutto-wrapped grilled radicchio. For main courses, there's a Tuscan lamb medley: lamb chops, oven-roasted striploin and braised lamb shanks served over baked cannellini beans with pancetta, or a lamb chop simply grilled with fresh herbs.
>
>   We love the warm sienna tones in this dining room, and the outdoor patio is

serene and lovely on summer evenings. Manager Patrick Saurette is justifiably proud of Il Portico's cellar, large and carefully chosen, with its generous selection of wines under $30. It has received the *Wine Spectator*'s blessing for an outstanding wine list several times. Watch for the splendid winemaker's dinners—multiple courses served Italian family-style, downstairs in a convivial atmosphere with outstanding vintages poured by visiting winemakers.

Jack's Grill

5842 111th Street (Lendrum Plaza)   Tel: (780) 434-1113 R
Open Sunday–Thursday 5:00 PM–9:00 PM
    Friday, Saturday 5:00 PM–10:00 PM
V, MC, AE, ENR, DEBIT

Chef and owner Peter Jackson has segued from California fresh-and-casual to classic French bistro in his small, consistently fine restaurant. Most dishes change with the season. The chef treats vegetables with respect and makes use of local produce and meats whenever he can, although he refuses to be tied to any one supplier.

Try the salt-cured foie gras on cornbread with sautéed apples, or the confit of small Monterey squid prepared in Provençal olive oil with roasted tomatoes and garlic. Go on to the osso bucco on sun-dried tomato pasta with baby green beans and preserved lemons. Steak lovers will enjoy the T-bone steak, pan-seared bistro-style, au jus with shallots and red wine vinegar, finished with butter. It's topped with real, honest-to-bistro pommes frites. The rack of lamb is slow-roasted and served over a cassoulet of lamb with beans and tomatoes, finished with balsamic vinegar. There is an extensive wine list that keeps its eye on value for money and a well-chosen selection of Canadian VQA, including some limited production wines.

For dessert, the warm berry gratin is deceptively light, served as it is with whipped cream folded into a champagne sabayon. Decadent!

Peter Jackson behind the bar.

Return of the Bistro
Peter Jackson of Jack's Grill

Peter Jackson's food career goes back to California, where he worked in a number of restaurants in the wine country, developing his love of quality ingredients and good California wines. By the time he arrived in Edmonton, he was eager to pursue his own vision: the best food and a good wine list in a casual atmosphere.

"When I got here in '86, nobody was doing what I wanted to do," he recalls. In one of North America's colder cities, he tried to replicate that warm California feeling at a reasonable cost. Word got around, and soon he had a full house almost every night. But times change, and Peter likes to stay one step ahead of the trend. His new passion is French bistro cooking. "Everybody is grilling everything, but I'm backing off. I like French bistro now," he says. "Bistro cooking isn't …

new. It looks really simple, but simple isn't easy. The flavour combinations are brilliant, but they do take longer to develop. You don't do a salt-cured foie gras in an hour. Or a good confit."

His new style also reflects his concern with keeping prices in line. "It costs a fortune to put a naturally raised veal chop on a plate, or a rack of lamb. I'm looking at something more creative as well as cost-effective—part of a rack, served on a cassoulet of beans and lamb," he says. "To survive in this business, we have to be very flexible, very frugal. But I use as much organic food as I can—oddly, the cost of high-quality organic ingredients doesn't fluctuate as much as ordinary produce."

"This restaurant gives me a great sense of fulfillment. Sometimes I walk around the dining room midway through an evening, and there are good smells coming from the kitchen, good food on the plates, all my guests are enjoying themselves—it's my own party. It's terrific. I never know what to expect. I guess that's what I love about this business." ✎

Peter Jackson's Berry Gratin with Champagne Sabayon

4 cups (1 L) mixed berries
4 tbsps (60 mL) Grand Marnier
2 tbsps (30 mL) granulated sugar
1 egg yolk, extra large
¼ cup (50 mL) champagne or sparkling wine
¼ cup (50 mL) whipping cream, whipped

Toss berries with Grand Marnier. Divide among four heatproof bowls and reserve.

Whisk sugar and egg yolk together in stainless steel bowl until pale yellow. Whisk in champagne. Over hot, but not boiling, water, whisk until thick and glossy (about 5 minutes). Remove bowl from heat and whisk over ice until cool and thick. Fold into whipped cream. Spoon over berries and run under broiler just until golden and bubbling. Serves 4.

$$$ **Madison's Grill**   www.unionbankinn.com
10053 Jasper Avenue (Union Bank Inn)   Tel: (780) 421-7171 R
Open Monday–Thursday 7:00 AM–10:00 AM, 11:00 AM–2:00 PM, 5:00 PM–10:00 PM
        Friday 7:00 AM–10:00 AM, 11:00 AM–2:00 PM, 5:00 PM–11:00 PM
        Saturday 8:00 AM–11:00 AM, 5:00 PM–11:00 PM
        Sunday 8:00 AM–11:00 AM, 5:00 PM–8:00 PM
V, MC, AE, ENR, DEBIT

The Grill is the dining room for a smart little boutique hotel owned by Diane Buchanan. Besides being the breakfast room for hotel guests and offering a good speedy lunch for the downtown crowd, Madison's has a fine evening menu executed with creativity and confidence by Chef Brian Leadbetter. Although it's not a steak house, they do treat their AAA beef with respect. Check out the intimate, book-lined lounge with fireplace, a good spot for morning coffee or cocktails before dinner.

$$$ **Northern Alberta Institute of Technology (NAIT)**
11762 106th Street   Tel: (780) 471-8678 R
Open September–June, Tuesday–Friday 6:00 PM–10:00 PM
V, MC

> The recently renovated room, ably managed by the affable Phillippe Bourigault, and operated by students from NAIT's professional culinary arts program has become so popular that weekend dining is booked several months in advance. Of special note is the pastry repertoire of award-winning pastry genius Vinod Varshney's students. Considering the high quality of food and service in this dining room, it represents an excellent value.

$$$ **Pradera**
10035 100th Street, Westin Hotel   Tel: (780) 426-3636 R
Open Monday–Friday 11:00 AM–2:00 PM, 5:00 PM–10:00 PM
Saturday–Sunday 7:00 AM–2:00 PM, 5:00 PM–10:00 PM
V, MC, AE, ENR, DEBIT

> We love the chefs who know the farms where their ingredients are grown. Chef Ross Munro has sought out producers across the country, and put his own stamp on the food with regional and local ingredients. Consider: Edsland bison carpaccio with shaved Leoni Grana cheese, red onions vinaigrette made with Highwood Crossing cold pressed canola oil. And that's just the beginning. He bumps it up a level with the same farm's bison in a great, peasanty dish—a choucroute with bison brisket, fennel bison sausage and cabbage. He's one of the few Edmonton chefs to have both Galloway (Angus) and Wagyu (Kobe-style) beef on his menu. The wine list is compact, listed from light to heavy—a boon for the busy diner.

$$$ **Sorrentino's Bistro Bar**   www.sorrentinos.com
10162 100th Street   Tel: (780) 424-7500 R
Open Monday–Friday 11:30 AM–12:00 AM; Saturday 5:00 PM–12:00 AM
V, MC, AE, ENR, DEBIT

> There are now six versions of Carmelo and Stella Rago's Italian restaurants. Sorrentino's Bistro Bar is the flagship, slightly more upmarket than the others, and home base for their annual festivals: Festa Regionale with visiting Italian chefs in winter; the garlic festival in April; and the mushroom festival in September.

Chef Sonny Sung's signature dish is rack of lamb, oven-roasted in a crust of goat cheese and almonds, and served rare. On a cold winter night, the house-made gnocchi with a red wine ragout of wild duck, bison and venison is a warming dish. It's also unusual—the meats are ground and cooked together for a tremendous wallop of flavour, a perfect foil for the gentle gnocchi. The wine list has great Italian selections, but also Chilean and Australian, with some real finds.

Carmelo Rago

Carmelo Rago didn't plan to own a dozen restaurants. On the other hand, these things don't just happen. Born in the southern Italian town of Zunguli, he went to an American university and had an eight-year teaching career before he decided to be a restaurateur. "I had no experience," he says, reflecting on his entry into the hospitality business. "I guess I was naive." But he credits his grandfather, a flour miller back in Zunguli, with giving him a serious work ethic and an abiding interest in food. "Maybe it was the flour. Maybe I had it in my veins."

Today Carmelo has an even dozen restaurants, most of them called Sorrentino's. He and his wife, Stella, divide their time among all twelve, including one each in Calgary, St. Albert and Sherwood Park.

Sorrentino's is also known for their festivals celebrating Italian food. "I wanted to show people that Italian restaurants, even southern Italian restaurants, could be more than just chianti bottles and spaghetti." Every spring, Sorrentino's holds a month-long garlic festival with special events, imported talent, contests and cooking classes. Every fall they do the whole thing over again with a mushroom festival. Both festivals help support Sorrentino's Compassion House, a resource centre and refuge for breast cancer patients from northern Alberta who have come to Edmonton for treatment. "We're in business, we have to make a dollar," he says. "But after that, we need to give something back to the community." ✑

$$$ **unheardof**   www.unheardof.com
9602 82nd (Whyte) Avenue   Tel: (780) 432-0480 R
Open Tuesday–Thursday 5:30 PM–9:00 PM
        Friday, Saturday 5:30 PM–9:30 PM
        Sunday 5:30 PM–9:00 PM
CV, MC, AE, ENR, DEBIT

The Heard family (Lynn cooks, David and Claudia serve) have created this landmark at the eastern end of Old Strathcona. The decor is homey, the cooking is earthy and we love the fresh local produce that appears here during the summer. On this ever-evolving menu, watch for rack of lamb with fresh herbs; beef tenderloin rolled in crushed peppercorns, finished with a three peppercorn red wine reduction; pork tenderloin medallions, pan-seared, finished with Marsala and garnished with fresh apple coulis; and stuffed portobello mushrooms—one of the restaurant's best dishes.

Desserts are always terrific. We love the white chocolate lemon mousse, and there are often wonderful homemade pies. If you're on a special diet (gluten-free, vegetarian, low-fat) let the kitchen know in advance and they'll cook just for you. There's a lengthy wine list, with up to a dozen premium house wines available by the glass reflecting Lynn's extensive knowledge and passion for the grape.

Indulgence
A Canadian Epic of Food and Wine

Imagine ten fabulous, inventive chefs. Put them together with local food producers of grain-fed pork, wild boar, grass fed beef, artisan cheeses, unique condiments, lamb, rabbit, saskatoon berries. Pair this with Canada's best VQA wineries. Mix in a band, a lively auction and 300 guests in an elegant ballroom. That's the recipe for Indulgence.

It's organized by the local chapter of Cuisine Canada to showcase and build awareness of the excellent local food products, talented Edmonton chefs and top-notch wine Canada is producing. Here's an ideal opportunity to taste great food, sample wines, chat with the people who grew and prepared it, and support a good cause (it's a fundraiser for the Junior League). It's a rocking good time. Check it out at www.cuisinecanada.ca. ⟨

CAFÉS, BISTROS, DINERS
AND NEIGHBOURHOOD JOINTS

$
Back Home Fish and Chips
11544 104th Avenue (Oliver Square)   Tel: (780) 428-8331
Open Tuesday–Saturday 11:00 AM–8:00 PM

12323 Stony Plain Road   Tel: (780) 451-7871
Open Monday–Saturday 9:00 AM–10:00 PM
    Sunday 12:00 PM–8:00 PM
V, MC, DEBIT

This is what fresh does for cod and skinny French fries—real homestyle fish and chips so good the mouth waters. Side orders of creamy coleslaw or bread dressing with gravy (it's a Newfie thing) are part of the experience, and there's unlimited homemade tartar sauce. At the Stony Plain Road location there are often long lineups, but it's worth the wait.

Block 1912

$

10361 82nd (Whyte) Avenue   Tel: (780) 433-6575

Open Monday–Thursday 9:00 AM–11:00 PM; Friday–Sunday 9:00 AM–12:00 AM

V, MC, AE, DEBIT

> The Naidoo family has transformed the bottom floor of this Whyte Avenue land-
> mark into a gracious high-ceilinged café. Mrs. Naidoo is a truly talented cook.
> Her blueberry scones melt in the mouth—get them when they're just out of the
> oven, still butter-meltingly warm. The chicken curry is outstanding, layers of
> flavour with a sweet hot bite. The noodle salads, daily soups and assorted grilled
> sandwiches are of the same high standard, as are the lovely pastries, especially the
> fruit-filled. There is a phenomenal selection of gelati. Try the coffee, the pistachio
> or the mango, which tastes like nothing less than a squashed, dead-ripe mango,
> always a thing of beauty. Bonus: the selection of Sunday newspapers from around
> the world.

Blue Iguana Grill

$$

11304 104th Avenue   Tel: (780) 424-7222 R

Open Monday–Friday 11:30 AM–2:00 PM, 5:00 PM–10:00 PM

Saturday 11:00 AM–3:00 PM, 5:00 PM–10:00 PM

Sunday 11:00 AM–3:00 PM, 5:00 PM–8:30 PM

V, MC, AE, DEBIT

> Brother and sister duo Lyle and Tamara Beaugard have opened this 104th Avenue
> eatery dedicated to the charms of American southwest cooking using local ingre-
> dients—judicious amounts of heat with grilled and roasted meats and vegetable

> preparations often based on corn and peppers. Tamara
> runs the kitchen and Lyle, one of Edmonton's few certi-
> fied sommeliers, has built an intriguing and well-priced
> wine list for this wine friendly cuisine. On it you'll find
> splurges like '91 Caymus Special Selection. New Mexico
> is ably represented by a pinot noir, chardonnay and a very
> fine bubbly from Gruet Winery.
>
> Standouts: the rustic, deep-flavoured soups, the
> pork on white corn polenta, and the desserts by pastry
> chef Jennifer Binns. Must trys are the chili-laced warm
> chocolate cake (go on, try it, the chili is there for the
> flavour) and the pecan macadamia nut tart.

Blue Iguana's pastry chef Jennifer Binns applies finishing touches.

Bua Thai Restaurant

$$

10049 113th Street   Tel: (780) 482-2277

Open Monday–Friday 11:00 AM–2:00 PM, 5:00 PM 9:30 PM; Saturday 5:00 PM–9:30 PM

V, MC, AE

A chef we know says he could eat Bua Thai's Panang beef curry daily. It's that good and that memorable. The beef, cooked with red and green bell peppers and onions, is fragrant with kaffir lime leaves and yellow curry. This simple, elegant restaurant's coconut rice is splendid, as is the fried tofu with Thai chilies and basil.

Churros King

$

10152A 82nd (Whyte) Avenue   Tel:(780) 989-1083

Open Tuesday–Thursday 2:00 PM–9:00 PM

Friday, Saturday 11:30 AM–9:00 PM; Sunday 1:00 PM–7:00 PM

CASH ONLY

Churros, a Latin American street food staple, are deep-fried sweet dough fingers sprinkled with icing sugar. But churros are not the only reason to go to the Churros King. The pulled pork sandwich, slow-roasted pork with a piquant sauce, is a thing of beauty. It's a nice spot, run by nice people. Hours are unusual—if you go during the week, plan for a late lunch or go before the show. NOTE: The King is currently expanding. Watch for reopening.

Col Mustard's Sandwich Canteen and Catering

$

12321 107th Avenue   Tel: (780) 448-1590

Open Monday–Friday 9:00 AM–7:00 PM; Saturday 9:00 AM 5:00 PM

V, MC, DEBIT

Col Mustards makes the best sandwiches in town. Owners Brad and Carla Pipella roast their turkey and make all the pantry items from scratch: tomato jam, tara-masalata, hummus, tapenade, plus daily soups. Check the special sandwiches such as the Samman, named after their son, Sam—a heap of deli meats on rye, a real jaw stretcher. Other not to be missed sandwiches are the Cobb, a combination of blue cheese, bacon and turkey on French loaf, and the Mediterranean, with oven-dried tomatoes, bocconcini and lots of fresh basil. Nobody makes a sandwich as fast as Brad. Carla knows. She's timed him, and he's got it down to under 30 seconds.

The Creperie

$$

www.thecreperie.com

10220 103rd Street   Tel: (780) 420-6656 R

Open Monday–Friday 11:30 AM–9:00 PM; Saturday, Sunday 5:00 PM–10:00 PM

V, MC, AE, ENR, DEBIT

Hans Kuhnel's comfortable basement restaurant has aged gracefully from the days when he first brought the crepe to town. It also has something of a reputation as a romantic spot, and if walls could talk, this place could keep us entertained for hours. The crepes are still the thing, with savoury or sweet fillings, including a ratatouille crepe for vegetarians, plus chicken, shrimp or beef in a variety of sauces. Or you can have an Alberta beef striploin with wild mushroom glaze spiked with peppercorns, and delicious coconut shrimp cakes served with a zingy sauce that breathes chili and ginger from the plate, but doesn't bite your tongue. For dessert, return to the crepes.

$$ Furusato Japanese Restaurant
10012 82nd (Whyte) Avenue   Tel: (780) 439-1335 R
Open Tuesday–Thursday 5:00 PM–9:30 PM
    Friday, Saturday 5:00 PM–10:00 PM
    Sunday 5:00 PM–9:00 PM

V, MC, AE, DEBIT

The fish is pristine. Mackerel so fresh the blue/black skin glistens. Among the cooked dishes, tender barbecued unagi (eel) is presented on a cushion of rice, barely slicked with wasabi. Alaskan black cod is cooked just until the fish flakes, glazed with a soy-based sauce with ginger that is never overwhelming. Pickled daikon and pickled eggplant make bright counterpoints, providing small explosions of flavour that work so well with the gentler themes of rice and fish.

The tempura is light as air and made with seasonal vegetables, this time with squash and pumpkin, next time sweet potato, broccoli, onion, even mushrooms. You'll eat well at Furasato.

$$ The Highlevel Diner
10912 88th Avenue   Tel: (780) 433-0993
Open Monday–Thursday 8:00 AM–11:00 PM
    Friday 8:00 AM–12:00 AM
    Saturday 9:00 AM–12:00 PM
    Sunday 9:00 AM–11:00 PM

V, MC, AE, ENR, DEBIT

In the University district and not far from two cinemas, The Highlevel Diner is something of an institution. Mornings, go for the big yeasty cinnamon buns. There are people who can't start their day without one, especially on weekends; day-olds become their incredible bread-pud with a brown sugar bourbon sauce and a hit of whipped cream. We also love the egg dishes—try the eggs benny. After the movie, there's a jumbo platter of appetizers, with generous servings of tabbouleh, hummus, tzatziki, chicken kabobs and pita bread.

$$ **Hoang Long**

10715 98th Street   Tel: (780) 414-0877

Open Monday–Thursday 11:00 AM–9:00 PM
    Friday and Saturday 11:00 AM–10:00 PM

V, MC, DEBIT

> Cecilia Hoang and David Vu's restaurant is a bit off the beaten track, but it's well worth the search. The menu is huge and mixed: Vietnamese, Chinese, Japanese. They make the best salad rolls in town, served with Hoang's homemade sauce, made with judicious amounts of vinegar, sugar, hoisin, roasted peanuts, carrot and hot chilies. We also love the huge, meal-sized vermicelli bowls with steamed noodles, fresh lettuce, bean sprouts and basil. Other dishes to try are the Thai chicken or beef salad and the curried chicken, a green curry tamed with coconut milk.

$$$ **The King and I**

8208 107th Street   Tel: (780) 433-2222 R

Open Monday–Thursday 11:30 AM–10:30 PM
    Friday 11:30 AM–11:30 PM
    Saturday 4:30 PM–11:30 PM

V, MC, ENR, AE

> Eric Wah has an uncanny ability to roll with the punches. When his restaurant in a former location burned to the ground, he found a bottle of Dom Perignon in the rubble and took it as a sign of better things to come.
>
> Eric Wah's passion for Thai cuisine began during a trip to Thailand in the early '80s. The hot and spicy mushrooms with chives and the Panang curry with chicken are both toothsome dishes. Among our current favourites are chu chu kai (tenderloin of chicken with oyster sauce and chili flakes) and pad kung karee (jumbo stir-fried prawns with a yellow curry, cashews and asparagus). There are several vegetarian choices on the menu, and if you ask for a vegetarian salad roll they'll make it for you.

$$ **Lemongrass Café**

10417 51st Avenue   Tel: (780) 413-0088

Open Tuesday–Thursday 11:00 AM–2:00 PM, 5:00 PM–9:00 PM
    Friday 11:00 AM–2:00 PM, 5:00 PM–10:00 PM
    Saturday 5:00 PM–10:00 PM

V, MC

> Tanya Dang's intimate southside eatery is a haven for seekers of good, traditional Vietnamese food with a delicate balance of flavour and texture. Add to that some

delicious things for vegetarians and you'll taste why we love this place. The traditional autumn salad, a bowl of thinly sliced vegetables dipped in the lightest of all batters, deep-fried, sprinkled with sesame seeds and drizzled with hot sauce, is delectable. We also enjoy the chicken, with mango and apples sweetening the spicy red curry sauce; and the filet of salmon with lemongrass and spices, grilled in banana leaves. The surprise here is dessert—chocolate pecan spring roll with run-laced caramel sauce or the gingery apple spring roll with a cinnamon caramel sauce. Of special note is the well-chosen wine list with many possibilities that would enhance Vietnamese dishes.

$ **Marco's Famous Burgers**
10526 82nd (Whyte) Avenue   Tel: (780) 436-1814
Open daily 10:00 AM–3:00 AM
DEBIT

> The secret to a fine burger in our books? A juicy grilled patty, a warm toasted bun, tomato and lettuce that is cool and crisp, not limp and soggy. The sauce? Just enough so it's not mushy and drippy. Marco's burgers have the basics and then some. They're definitely two-handers, not a scrawny little burger to be eaten with one hand while driving. No sir! The six-ounce patties, made by a local butcher, are amazingly flavourful and juicy. Marco's tasty combinations range from a classic cheeseburger to the innovative. Try the Salisbury, single or double, topped with crispy seasoned (with a soy sauce blend) onions and mushroom sauce.

$$ **Maurya Palace**   www.mauryapalace.com
9266 34th Avenue   Tel: (780) 468-9500
Open Monday–Thursday 11:30 AM–2:30 PM, 5:00 PM–10:00 PM
    Friday–Sunday 11:30 AM–10:00 PM

10220 103rd Street   Tel: (780) 421-8100
Open Monday–Friday 11:30 AM–2:30 PM, 5:00 PM–9:00 PM
V, MC, AE, DEBIT

> Although palace is a bit of a stretch for this understated room, the lunch buffet and the Sunday brunch are both excellent value. Signature dishes are the chicken tikka—boneless chicken marinated in yogourt and cooked in the tandoor oven—and the freshly baked Indian breads, especially the delicious naan with paneer and onions. There's a good selection of vegetarian dishes, including baby okra and onions, and the buttery dal with red kidney beans and fresh herbs. Heavenly curried eggplant, and a lovely version of rice pudding for dessert. The downtown location seats 200, and the menu has fewer curries but more dry dishes (grills and tandoories).

Living the Cuisine: Raj Sharma at Maurya Palace

Raj Sharma's Maurya Palace restaurant sits in the heart of Edmonton's Little India. "We are very much a part of the Indian community," he says. "When we cater weddings, this lady or that grandmother will come to us and say, 'This is my mother's recipe. Could you please cook it?' Of course we always say yes."

Indian cooking is a cuisine of many regions, many styles. "We are always experimenting and changing. The food's authenticity is important to a restaurant like ours, because 70 per cent of our clientele is Indian, and they want the genuine article." In order to supply it, Raj travels to India to find his cooks. Once they get here, they have to deal with adjustments and challenges in India, the

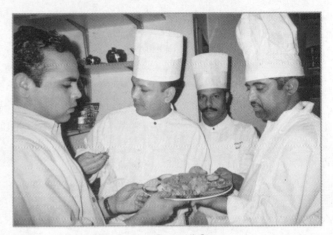

"They live their cuisine" — Raj Sharma (left).

ingredients are different. So is the equipment, but it's worth the extra time and trouble to train these people because of their unique cooking skills."

The cooks understand the subtle nuances of the complex Indian cuisine as nobody else could. "They've lived it," says Raj. ✍

$$$ **Normand's**   www.normands.com

11639A Jasper Avenue   Tel: (780) 482-2600 R

Open Monday–Thursday 11:30 AM–10:30 PM; Friday 11:30 AM–12:00 AM

Saturday 5:00 PM–12:00 AM; Sunday 5:00 PM–10:00 PM

V, MC, AE, ENR, DEBIT

Norm Campbell has always made the most of Alberta game, and his annual November game menu features specialty wild meats, adding even more depth to the possibilities for dedicated carnivores. Think of bison, musk-ox, caribou, ostrich, wild boar. There's fresh fish daily, and Normand's version of bouillabaisse is a celebration. They start with house-made fish stock laced with saffron, and a fine dice of red bell peppers. The fish varies: always shellfish—often squid—plus whatever fish they have in the kitchen that day. The secret to this big, big soup: the chef sautées the fish in oil and garlic before it hits the broth.

$$$ **Packrat Louie Kitchen & Bar**
10335 83rd Avenue   Tel: (780) 433-0123 R
Open Tuesday–Saturday 11:30 AM–11:00 PM
V, MC, AE

> We've always loved the lemon pizza, a thin-crusted white pizza with fontina or
> mozzarella and fresh thyme, with lemon on the side to drizzle over the molten
> cheese. Try the chicken salad made with Jerry Kitt's organic chicken, featuring suc-
> culent leg meat in a soy-honey glaze. Delicious. When it's available, the grilled
> salmon on greens is a lovely dish, sometimes in honey soy, sometimes rubbed with
> chili spice, with roast potatoes, served on mesclun. The roast rack of Barrhead pork
> is served on a sesame-spiced risotto. For dessert, the chocolate pudding, made
> with Callebaut chocolate and served with black currant sauce is deeply, darkly deli-
> cious. Owner Peter Johner is also a chocolatier; he makes fabulous truffles.

$$ **Parkallen Restaurant**   www.parkallen.com
7018 109th Street   Tel: (780) 436-8080
Open Monday–Thursday 11:00 AM–11:00 PM
> Friday 11:00 AM–12:00 AM
> Saturday 4:00 PM–12:00 AM
V, MC, AE, ENR, DEBIT

> This friendly neighbourhood restaurant owned by the Rustom family has been
> renovated and expanded, but what really counts is the delicious Lebanese cooking.
> Nahia Rustom uses her culinary skills to great advantage preparing traditional
> dishes. Here's a woman who understands that fresh parsley is not just a bit of
> greenery hanging off a plate. And we love her generous use of fresh herbs and cit-
> rus. Try the fatouche: bits of crisped pita with tomatoes, green onion, radishes,
> parsley and romaine, spiked with sumac leaf and lots of fresh chopped mint. The
> baba ghanoush melts on the tongue. In the tabbouleh, the lemon and olive oil do
> wonderful things for the bulgur wheat, leaving it soft and pillowy served with
> small romaine leaves for scooping. There's a variety of traditional kabobs, sizzling,
> grilled to perfection.

$$$ **Red Ox Inn**
9420 91st Street   Tel: (780) 465-5727 R
Open Tuesday–Sunday 5:00 PM–10:00 PM
V, MC, AE, DC

> Everybody likes Frank Olson's solid, unpretentious cooking in this cozy spot in
> Edmonton's Francophone district. The corn soup (available only in season) is a
> true Alberta experience. He scrapes the corn off the cobs, simmers both kernels

and cobs in chicken stock, and finishes it with whipping cream. It's garnished with thinly sliced shiitake mushrooms, fried golden. If it's available, try the salmon glazed with Moroccan-spiced barbecue sauce, served with mango salsa. We loved the pan-seared coconut-crusted scallops served on a julienne of sweet pepper and leek, drizzled with zesty chili lime oil, or the beef tenderloin with a southwestern demiglace, pico de gallo and grilled Bermuda onions.

$$ **Rigoletto's Café**
10068 108th Street   Tel: (780) 429 0701
Open Monday–Friday 11:00 AM–2:00 AM
       Saturday 5:00 PM–2:00 AM; Sunday 5:00 PM–1:00 AM
V, MC, AE, ENR, DEBIT

The regulars cried buckets when this popular café left its downtown spot, but they've followed it the few blocks to its new digs and it's as busy as ever. Chef Sergio Turlione's specials are always a good bet. We like the crisp, golden-skinned roast chicken, cooked high up in a hot oven. The stir-fry of fresh vegetables is quickly tossed with angel hair pasta and a soy-based sauce spiked with lime juice. It's a good choice when there's fresh asparagus available. Try the Arctic char in maple pecan butter sauce, and Turlione does well with beef.

$$ **Sakura**
10518 101st Street   Tel: (780) 428-8883
Open Monday–Thursday 11:30 AM–10:00 PM
       Friday, Saturday 11:30 AM–11:00 PM
       Sunday 4:30 PM–10:00 PM

Sakura II
Bourbon Street, West Edmonton Mall   Tel: (780) 481-3786
Open daily 11:30 AM–10:00 PM
V, MC, AE, ENR, DEBIT

The West Edmonton Mall outlet is a kaiten: sushi by conveyor belt. It's all great fun, but the important thing is the food—quality ingredients handled with skill, artfully presented. When you tire of raw fish as a main ingredient, try the deep-fried soft-shell crab in season.

$$ **Savoy Lounge**
10401 82nd (Whyte) Avenue   Tel: (780) 438-0373
Open daily 4:00 PM–10:00 PM for dinner, tapas from 10:00 PM–1:00 AM
V, MC, AE, ENR, DEBIT

Brad Lazarenko, formerly of Pack Rat Louie, is making tasty and innovative food ideally suited to the hip lounge vibe of Savoy: grilled scallops with lavender, Pine Terra grass-fed beef with a gorgonzola mole, curried mussels, really good pommes frites. Check the theme dinners with menus based on wines from visiting winemakers or bottle-conditioned beers. Great value. Have dinner and stay to party into the night . . . there are guest DJs Wednesday through Sunday.

Cool cocktails: Co-owner Ed Donszelmann and friend Miriam Berg.

$$ **Sicilian Pasta Kitchen**

11239 Jasper Avenue   Tel: (780) 488-3838

Open Monday–Thursday 11:00 AM–11:00 PM

Friday, Saturday 11:00 AM–12:00 AM

Sunday 11:00 AM–10:30 PM

V, MC, AE, ENR, DEBIT

Owners Frank Mannarino and Joe Viana know how to make their guests feel at home. On Sunday mornings when the church bells are ringing, we close our eyes and pretend we're on the Via Jasper, complete with palm trees and the requisite vintage Vespa. This is cooking from Italy's southern island. The chilled seafood salad is a refreshing summer lunch. For pastas, try the angnolotti served in a simple tomato sauce. But the cooking is more than basic. Mussels in a zesty gorgonzola sauce? Outstanding, mopped up with great hunks of bread. Spaghetti alla Norma is rich with roasted eggplant, garlic and ricotta cheese. Then there's the luxurious penne al diavola: baby lobster, grilled chicken and diced tomatoes in a decadent cayenne cream sauce.

$$ **Singapore Baba**

10121 151st Street   Tel: (780) 415-5656

Open Tuesday–Sunday 11:30 AM–2:00 PM

Summer 5:00 PM–9:00 PM

V, MC, DEBIT

> Daniel Quek and Winnie Teo are from a Singaporean culture known as Paranakan, a happy combination of Malaysian and Chinese. Their food reflects the Baba (father) version of that cuisine. They offer an extensive menu of dishes you won't find anywhere else in Edmonton. Beef fans should try the beef jerky appetizer — sliced paper-thin, marinated with soy, sugar and spices, and quickly grilled over charcoal. We also like the definitive chili crab: Dungeness crab, cut up and fast-fried in the wok with garlic, ginger and chili paste until a deliciously spicy sauce forms. Then there's the Fatty-style fish, named after a famous Singapore restaurant. The fish is first deep-fried, then bathed in a sweet and sour sauce with lychee fruit. Delicious tofu dishes; also mee goreng, a traditional vermicelli noodle platter cooked to the degree of spiciness you want.

$$ **Tasty Tomato Italian Eatery**

14233 Stony Plain Road   Tel: (780) 452-3594

Open Monday–Thursday 11:30 PM–2:00 PM, 5:00 PM–9:00 PM

Friday 11:30 PM 2:00 PM, 5:00 PM–10.00 PM

Saturday 5:00 PM–10:00 PM

V, MC

> "Nothing fancy, just good home cooking," says Mirella Amendola, the woman behind the stove. Mirella, husband Angelo and son Joe own and operate this cozy west end restaurant that has 'em lined up on weekends—for Mirella's veal canelloni, ricotta manicotti, veal limone and the excellent pescatore. The simple potato gnocchi is baked in a tomato cream sauce and of course there is tiramisu. Arrive hungry; the food is filling . . . and it's tasty!

$$ **Tasty Tom's**

9965 82nd (Whyte) Avenue   Tel: (780) 437-5761

Open Tuesday–Thursday 11:00 AM–8:00 PM

Friday and Saturday 11:00 AM–10:00 PM

Sunday 10:00 AM–5:00 PM

V, MC, AE, DEBIT

> Talk about your global village. Here we have a couple of German guys from Berlin, Christian and Tom Hennig, making terrific yaki-yaki shrimp. You get eight grilled tiger shrimp in a chili-laced tomato basil broth with toasted

baguette slices for sopping up the last drop. But the Hennigs' greatest contribution to the indigenous cuisine of Old Strathcona is the pocket dog. Using their special machine, they make a hole in a half baguette, lengthwise, and toast the darned thing on the inside. Then they add sauerkraut, mustard, cheese, onions, their homemade catsup and the pièce de résistance, a big, juicy bratwurst. Behold the dripless hotdog, the perfect walkaway lunch for hikers, bikers and window shoppers.

$$ **Upper Crust Café & Caterers**
10909 86th Avenue   Tel: (780) 433-0810
Open Monday–Wednesday 11:00 AM–9:00 PM
  Thursday, Friday 11:00 AM–10:00 PM
  Saturday 9:30 AM–10:00 PM
V, MC, ENR, AE, DEBIT

This is a bustling, happy place. Nothing cutting-edge, but everything they do is very well executed, from soups to sweets, and they make the best chicken salad sandwich in town. There's also an outstanding salad of mesclun with baked goat cheese, nut-crusted, still warm. The baked goods are to die for: oatmeal cookies, lemon squares, the morning glory muffins. And their holiday fruitcake is stellar—this is one cake that won't end up as a doorstopper.

$ **Zenari's**
10180 101st Street (Manulife Place)   Tel: (780) 423-5409
Open Monday–Wednesday 7:00 AM–6:30 PM
  Thursday, Friday 7:00 AM–9:30 PM
  Saturday 9:00 AM–5:30 PM
V, MC, ENR, AE

Adriano Zenari's beloved deli/kitchen shop/wine bar is a downtown institution. Tables spill out into the mall to the tiny wine bar, and it's tough to find a seat at lunch. Zenari's makes great muffins, and if they look familiar, it's probably because he supplies several good cafés. The lunch fare—crostoni, chicken salad on greens, a stuffed baked loaf, pasta specials—is outstanding.

Every Thursday night, Zenari's stays open late. The food gets a bit more complex, the atmosphere is convivial, tables are shared with total strangers, toasts are made, new friendships are born, and all of this before 9:00 PM. If you're a stranger in town, drop in. It's a good gig.

$$

Tony's Pizza and Italian Restaurant

9603 111th Avenue   Tel: (780) 424-8769

Open Monday–Thursday 11:30 AM–2:30 PM, 4:30 PM–11:00 PM
      Friday 11:30 AM–2:30 PM, 4:30 PM–1:00 AM
      Saturday 2:00 PM–1:00 AM; Sunday 4:30 PM–11:00 PM

V, MC, AE

If you're lucky, you'll be here on one of those rare evenings when Tony, Tony Jr and brother Sal are all in the kitchen, and they have the big white disks of dough in the air, spinning like three saucers. Meanwhile, hungry fans are clapping and making side bets on who quits first. Feels like a party!

It's a happy story: two kids watched their dad build a business from nothing, and now all three are merrily up to their ears in pizza dough. The dough is key to the quality of this pizza. "Always fresh, never dough from yesterday," says Tony Jr. They take their baking seriously too. No soggy crust, no burned cheese. "We're specialists," he says.

They do all the North American favourites, but try a more Italian version: capicolla and prosciutto on a marinated tomato base topped with melting lumps of soft white boccocini. If you aren't in a pizza mood, there's a hefty pepperonata,

Keeping the dough in the air at Tony's.

a fry-up of sausage, veal, green peppers and mushrooms in a red wine sauce. It's huge. You won't need to eat again for a week. ✐

Fat Franks: Gotta Get a Dog!

There is no better sign of fair weather than the smell of sizzling hotdogs wafting from one of the Fat Franks hotdog stands. They pop up in various spots—on Rice Howard Way, outside Canadian Tire Stores, or on Whyte Avenue. These are terrific hotdogs—meaty, all-beef dogs, spurting juice with every bite, complemented by a smorgasbord of condiments in a fresh roll —are as good as it gets for hot dog aficionados. ✐

Just a Little Something After Church
Sergio Re at the Santa Maria Goretti Community Centre

11050 90th Street   Tel: (780) 426-5026
Open Sunday 11:00 AM–2:00 PM
CASH ONLY

Every Sunday at 11:00 AM, Chef Sergio Re flings open the doors of Santa Maria Goretti Community Centre and starts dishing up the first course of a seven course brunch. Nobody goes home hungry. Re wants his Sunday brunch to be like the trattorias he remembers in northern Italy, where the customers sit down and wait for whatever surprise the chef happens to be cooking. "We try to do some unusual dishes, especially for the first antipasto, which is always cold. Maybe vitello tonnato—veal in tuna sauce, something you don't often see here."

His next course will be a hot antipasto. "Possibly polenta with escargot, or eggplant parmigiana. Something light, not too filling." Then to the pasta. "You know Italians. We cannot do without pasta, and there's no end to the possibilities." Indeed there is not. Rigatoni, linguine, spaghetti, manicotti, cannelloni—there are dozens, even hundreds of possibilities for the shape alone. And the sauces? Endless choices.

The salad will be light, a few green leaves dressed with oil and vinegar, just something to refresh the palate. "For the first main course, a scaloppine is always good. Or fried peppers with steak, capers, a few anchovies," Sergio says. "In this town, the only way you can get people to eat anchovies is to disguise them with something else." There's always a second main course. "You're already full, so it's just something to make you say, 'Wow, look at this' . . . Again, something light, rabbit in wine sauce, or sausages with fried peppers."

The dessert isn't much, he says. Peaches stuffed with crushed amaretti and broiled, maybe. Or a semi-freddo, or . . . The Centre welcomes all comers. No reservations are necessary. ✎

$ **Zenari's on First**   www.zenaris.com
10117 101st Street (Manulife Place)   Tel: (780) 425-6151
Open Monday–Thursday 8:00 AM–10:00 PM
         Friday 8:00 AM–12:00 AM
         Saturday 12:00 PM–10:00 PM
V, MC, ENR, AE, DEBIT

This is one of our favourite spots for lunch downtown, always busy, and the servers actually like their jobs. It's a good bet for daily soup specials (try the mulligatawny if it's available), salads, crostini with generous toppings, and a terrific grilled vegetable sandwich, the muffaleta, with articoke hearts, hot and sweet peppers, tomatoes, greens and cheese. You'll find a tempting array of tortes and pies in the cooler. On Friday nights there's live jazz from 8:00 PM to midnight, with a small cover charge in effect.

Bach Dang Noodle House, 7908 104th Street, 448-0288; **Café De Ville**, 10137 124th Street, 488-9188; **Café at Holts'**, 10180 101st Street, 525-5300; **Charles Smart Donair**, 8952 82nd Avenue, 468-2099; **French Meadow**, 10736 82nd Avnue, 413-8045; **Funky Pickle Pizza**, 10441 82nd Avenue, 433-3865; **Golden Bird**, 10544 97th Street, 420-1612; **Jaipur Palace**, 3065 66th Street, 414-1600; **Kyoto** 10128 109th Street, 420-1720; 8701 109th Street, 414-6055; **New Experience Bistro**, 10610 105th Street, 423-6614; **Red Goose Restaurant**, 9625 66th Avenue (Hazeldean Shopping Centre), 435-8661; **Pagolac**, 10566 97th Street, 425-1591; **Pizza Boys**, 8110 82nd Avenue, 414-0500; **Smoky Joes**, 15135 Stony Plain Road, 413-3379; **Spago,** 12433 97th Street, 479-0328; **Three Musketeers French Creperie**, 10416 82nd Avenue, 437-4239. **Note:** Two of our favourite culinary duos, Judy and Wilson Wu and Patrizio Sachetto and Flora Corazzo, are currently without stoves. Watch for new locations for Polo's Café and Via Vai on the Boulevard.

IN SEARCH OF THE DEFINITIVE PYROHY

Alice's Adventures in Pyrohyland

Edmonton has a long tradition of good Ukrainian food, including the ubiquitous pyrohy. For the uninitiated, a pyrohy/pyrogy/perogy is a simple dish: a half-moon shaped dumpling, made with thinly rolled dough, filled with potatoes, cheese, sauerkraut or various combinations thereof. To prepare your pyrohy, boil up a huge pot of water and slide in the fresh or frozen dumplings. When they float to the top, they're ready to be fried in butter with a dollop of bacon grease and a chopped onion. Serve them hot, with a big spoonful of sour cream. Yum. Bacon or sausage and a little fresh or fried onion are appropriate garnishes.

Regarding the spelling of the definitive Ukrainian potato dumpling, AKA perogy, or perohy, or pyrohy, we went to the experts. (It's a contentious issue!) For the sake of consistency, we've chosen pyrohy, which is the choice of Savella Stechishin in her wonderful book, *Traditional Ukrainian Cookery*. The root of the word is *pyr*, meaning a banquet. Spellings for other Ukrainian specialties are also taken from her book. Notwithstanding, we're leaving proper names—the Pyrogy House, Pyrogy Drive, Pyrogy Park and Cheemo Perogies—strictly alone.

Most Albertans, at least those with children to feed, will confess to having a bag of Joe and Walter Makoweki's Cheemo Perogies in the freezer. Five varieties: cheddar, onion, cottage . . . cheese, herb and roasted garlic, bacon and romano cheese. Now hear this, trivia buffs: if all the pyrohys in a Cheemo production year were laid end to end, they'd circle the entire globe. ✎

St. Basil's Cultural Centre

10819 71st Avenue   Tel: (780) 434-4288

Edmonton

On the food lover's trail, the search for the definitive pyrohy begins at a lovely old church on Edmonton's south side. The people of St. Basil's Parish will make, serve and sell approximately 10,000 dozen pyrohy this year. That's 120,000 dumplings. So says Kay Knibs, who manages the Cultural Centre next door to the church. Her army of cooks is made up entirely of volunteers. The babas are still the resident experts, but these days their children and grandchildren work beside them. According to Kay, all sorts of people hold celebrations here, including the occasional East Indian wedding, where chutneys and curries share plate space with pyrohy and cabbage rolls.

St. Basil's supplies the food concession at the Ukrainian Cultural Village and also to the public, available frozen, in bags of two or five dozen. There are five varieties: cottage cheese, potato and cheddar cheese, potato and cottage cheese, potato and onion, and plain sauerkraut. As well, you can buy cabbage rolls, pyrizhky (buns filled with cottage cheese and potato), nalysnyky (crepes), pampushky (prune buns, made only at Christmas) and chicken Kiev. Festive braided breads are available on a limited basis. Call ahead to order.

St. Michael's Pyrohy Festival

Northgate Lion's Centre   Tel: (780) 473-5621

7524 139th Avenue, Edmonton

The St. Michael's Health Group holds an all-you-can-eat annual pyrohy festival on the second weekend of September. For $11, you can have pyrohy filled with cottage cheese, potato and cheddar, cheese and bacon, sauerkraut, or the oddly delicious pizza flavour, made with pepperoni, mozzarella, and tomato sauce. St. Michael's operates Baba's Own Food Products, producers of several varieties of pyrohy. The most popular are the fruit-filled—blueberry or cherry—dessert pyrohy. If you can't make it to the festival, they're available at IGA stores, Cameron's Meat and at their extended care facility at 7404 139th Avenue.

Pyrohy Pizza? Believe it.

At the Old Strathcona Farmers Market, you can have a Ukrainian pizza, topped with bits of bacon, rough-chopped pyrohy and green onion. Available by the slice or whole. ⬓

Posh Pyrohy at the Hardware Grill: Truffled Potato Dumplings

At Edmonton's Hardware Grill, chef and owner Larry Stewart makes a pyrohy that would have had Catherine the Great swooning at his feet. His truffle-studded potato dumplings, scented with white truffle oil and served with house-smoked salmon and crème fraîche, go like this:

DOUGH

1 cup (250 mL) all-purpose flour
1 cup (250 mL) sour cream
Mix flour and sour cream together until smooth dough forms, adding more flour or cream as necessary to make a soft dough. Wrap in plastic and refrigerate 4 hours or overnight.

FILLING

2 lbs (1 kg) red or white skin-on potatoes, quartered
6 tbsps (90 mL) butter, melted
6 tbsps (90 mL) sour cream
1 tsp (5 mL) salt
½ tsp (2 mL) pepper
6 tbsps (90 mL) whipping cream
1 tsp (5 mL) white truffle oil (see note)
1 tbsp (15 mL) truffle shavings, coarsely chopped (see note)

Put potatoes in pot and cover with water. Cook 30 minutes or until soft. Drain thoroughly. Mash. Add remaining ingredients except truffle oil and truffle shavings. Blend thoroughly. Refrigerate until very cold. Fold in truffle oil and shavings.

To assemble, roll dough on well-floured surface to 1/8 inch thick. Let dough relax for 2 to 3 minutes, then cut into 2 ½ inch (6.4 cm) circles. Place a tablespoon of filling in center of each circle and fold over to form a crescent. Pinch edges firmly. Place on tray and freeze overnight.

To serve, boil dumplings in large pot of water for 4 to 5 minutes, stirring gently so they don't stick. Rinse in cold water. Place in hot pan with butter and cook to golden brown on both sides. Serve with smoked salmon and red beet salad, and crème fraîche or horseradish cream. Makes approximately 36.

NOTE: Truffle shavings and white truffle oil are available at Urban Fare and G Dennis and Co in Edmonton, and The Cookbook Co Cooks in Calgary.

Maria's Place

$

11739 83rd Street   Tel: (780) 474-4059

Open Monday–Saturday 8:00 AM–8:00 PM
  Sunday 8:00 AM–3:00 PM

V, MC, DEBIT

> There's no Maria, but there is a Joe and he makes the lightest pyrohy going. Ethereal, more like an Asian pot sticker, furthering our theory that every food culture has its own dumpling. A pyrohy by any other name . . .

Pyrogy House

$$

12510 118th Avenue   Tel: (780) 454-7880

Open Monday–Thursday 11:00 AM–9:00 PM
  Friday 11:00 AM–9:45 PM
  Saturday 4:00 PM–9:30 PM
  Sunday 4:00 PM–8:30 PM

V, MC, AE, DEBIT

> This is where people go when their baba is out of town. Best bet on the menu is the Ukrainian plate—borscht or cabbage soup, cabbage rolls, sausage and pyrohy plus dessert. Save room for the fantastic poppy seed cake.

So far on the Pyrohy Trail, we've found terrific dumplings in Edmonton. Next? North to Kalyna Country.

FRANK L'ECUYER

KALYNA COUNTRY

5

There's a story of grit and determination that starts east and north of Edmonton, along the North Saskatchewan river basin, and runs all the way to the Saskatchewan border. It's the tale of Ukrainian immigrants: the homesteaders, their beautiful onion-domed churches, their communities and their food.

Kalyna is a Slavic term for the bright red high-bush cranberries that grew wild in this part of the province. Native people used the berries along with saskatoons to flavour pemmican. Early settlers used them in bannock, syrups and jams, and as a flavouring for vodka. (Kalyna Country: home of the original crantini.)

All summer long, Kalyna Country celebrates its origins in a series of community picnics, agricultural fairs, rodeos, church suppers and cultural days. There's good food: kielbasa (hefty Ukrainian garlic sausage, affectionately known as a kuby), pyrohy, cabbage rolls and barbecued beef.

www.kalynacountry.ab.ca
www.strathcona.ab.ca

Because most of these events rely on volunteers, dates and times are subject to change, so we suggest you check the web sites above for current details and call ahead to confirm.

◉ HITTING THE PYROHY TRAIL

Our search for authentic foodstuffs led us to the pyrohy capital of Alberta and possibly the world: the village of Glendon. In Pyrogy Park on Pyrogy Drive stands the world's largest pyrohy, a steel and fibreglass dumpling on a fork, erected in 1991 to celebrate the 100th anniversary of Ukrainian settlement in Canada.

Although the original Pyrogy House is (sadly) closed, travellers can eat their fill of dumplings at the Pyrogy Park Café. If you're staying over, Glendon even has the Pyroghy Motel.

$ **Alberta Hotel**

5134 50th Street, Vegreville   Tel: (780) 632-3528

Open daily 7:00 AM to 6:00 PM

V, MC

> Dan Kobylnuk owns this hotel, and he's proud of his pyrohy. He says it's all in the
> way you make the dough. "Those (commercial varieties) are too hard," he says.
> "Our pyrohys are softer, more pliable, and they taste better." He's ready to stack
> his up against all comers. Friday is pyrohy-making day, and the Ukrainian plate
> special at Friday lunch goes for $7.25.

$ **Baba's Bistro (Rosenbary Mohawk Service Station)**

Junction of highways 28 and 63, south of Radway   Tel: (780) 736-3752

Open daily 7:00 PM–11:00 PM

V, MC, ENR, AE, DEBIT

> Rose Lyle calls her café "just a meat and potatoes place." This is home cooking, all
> from scratch, including daily soups, cream pies and fruit pies. Her Ukrainian spe-
> cialties are top notch: sweet and sour cabbage rolls, nalysnyky (tiny crepes filled
> with dill and cottage cheese), pyrizhky (small, dilly, cheese-filled yeast buns) in a
> rich cream sauce, and local garlic sausage.
>
>   "Can I whine a little? Ukrainian food is really labour-intensive," she says. "I'd
> love to be able to use commercial products, but the quality just isn't there, so I
> keep on making my own." Apart from running a café and gas station 364 days a
> year (they do close on Christmas Day), the Lyles also cater.

$ **Country Memories Tea House and Gifts**

One Block East of Main Street, Radway   Tel: (780) 736-3900 R

Open Monday–Friday 9:00 AM–5:00 PM; Saturday 9:00 AM–5:00 PM

Open July–August Monday–Friday 9:00 AM–8:00 PM

V, MC, DEBIT

> Jackie Lessard is chef and owner of this comfortable café and tea shop in a for-
> mer general store, circa 1919. The store has been restored, and the former living
> quarters now serve as the more formal dining area while the tea shop occupies
> the front of the building.
>
>   In summer, there's afternoon tea by reservation. Breads and pastries are all
> homemade, with bake sales every Friday. Year round, lunches run to good home
> cooking: meatballs and mashed potatoes, roasts, hearty sandwiches. On Fridays
> they serve breaded codfish and robust Ukrainian food.

D & R Family Restaurant

5106 48th Avenue, Vegreville   Tel: (780) 632-3233
Open daily 6:00 AM–8:00 PM
V, MC, AE, DEBIT

Dianne and Ron Humeniuk's busy restaurant offers the usual café fare, but it's the Ukrainian food that brings people back for seconds. Cabbage rolls and pyrohy with garlic sausage aren't hard to find in this part of Alberta, but Dianne goes beyond the standard dishes. You'll find nalysnyky (crepes filled with cottage cheese), pyrizhky (small buns filled with cheese and dill, served hot with a topping of butter-fried onions or cream) and kulesha (a fluffy cornmeal dish lightened with eggs).

During the Christmas season, she makes kutya, the boiled wheat with honey that is traditionally eaten on Ukrainian Christmas Eve. "We do the whole dinner on Ukrainian Christmas Eve," Dianne says. "There are 12 meatless dishes—beet borscht, jellied fish, pickled herring . . . the poppyseed bread, too, with stewed fruit and, of course, the kutya." There's a big lunch buffet weekdays, a dinner buffet Friday and Saturday, and Sunday brunch.

Maple Tree Grill

Waskatenau, west side of Highway 831(near Smoky Lake)   Tel: (780) 358-2882
Open Monday–Thursday 11:00 AM 8:00 PM; Friday–Sunday 11:00 AM–9:00 PM
V, MC, DEBIT

Bob and Arlene Herrick started with a burger stand and takeout window, and became known for their fresh-cut French fries. They still go through a ton of fresh spuds every week. The room at the front is totally casual, with Bob going from table to table, pouring coffee and visiting. The dining room has a more formal look, but all the food comes from the same kitchen, run by chef Jocelyn Robinson. Their steaks are cut from Alberta beef, their salmon is fresh, and they serve an oddity—Danish pork ribs, from extremely lean pigs.

The Pyrogy Park Café

Glendon   Tel: (780) 635-3040
Open Wednesday–Monday 10:00 AM–8:00 PM
V, MC, DEBIT

Ah, the global village. Tanner Ngo and family operate this café, where they have two specialties—Chinese food, and pyrohys. The dumplings, made by two local experts, Iris and Rosemary, are a model of their kind, whether filled with cheddar, cottage cheese, sauerkraut or potatoes. They're served with fried bacon, fried onions and full-fat sour cream.

GETTING THERE: from Smoky Lake take Highway 28 east to Ashmont, then take 28A to the Glendon turnoff.

❀ CELEBRATIONS AND FESTIVALS

The Great White North Pumpkin Fair and Weigh-Off
Smoky Lake   Tel: (780) 656-3674

It's the first weekend in October and outside the agricultural complex in Smoky Lake, four men are wrestling a giant pumpkin off the back of a half-ton truck and carefully, carefully loading it onto a tarp so it can be pushed, pulled, dragged or lifted onto a scale. Local pumpkins are up against heavies from Lloydminster, Warspite, Fort St. John and Kelowna.

John Lobay and one of his award-winning pumpkins.

The bleachers fill as townsfolk and pumpkin aficionados gather to ogle the giants and discuss the politics of pumpkins: is it fair to pit pumpkins from southern BC against those grown in the wild-and-wooly seasons of Smoky Lake? Tension mounts in the stands. Favourites are picked as the weigh-in continues, and a dedicated phone line is opened to World Pumpkin Headquarters in New York so the results will reach them without delay.

When the final announcement is made, the applause is thunderous. The great pumpkins never fail to entertain and astonish. The previous town record—for a 751-pound monster grown by John Lobay of the famously successful Lobay pumpkin-growing family—was broken in 2001, with Archie Lingl's great 903.5 pound Kelowna-grown pumpkin. Other giants have included Archie's 465.5 pound squash and a 66-pound watermelon, grown by Robert Lobay.

In a typical year, some 4,000 people pay admission to watch the weigh-off. If you have a giant pumpkin and would like to enter it, call for information.

During the Great White North Pumpkin Fair and Weigh-Off in Smoky Lake, the Old Fashioned Bread Bakery goes pumpkin crazy. "We have pumpkin soup, pumpkin doughnuts, cinnamon buns with a brown sugar and pumpkin filling, pumpkin cheesecake and wonderful pumpkin cookies," says Berangere.

Our cookies were adapted from Berangere's original (huge) recipe. Ours is somewhat smaller, but still produces a good mitful of cookie.

Bread and Soup: The Old Fashioned Bread Bakery

White Earth Street, Smoky Lake   Tel: (780) 656-3780

If you're in Smoky Lake at lunchtime, you aren't far from The Old Fashioned Bread Bakery and a piece of good bread, with a bowl of Berangere Brousseau's delicious homemade soup. "To make chicken soup, start with a whole chicken and fried onions," she says. "Keep adding the vegetables as they come—celery, carrots, red peppers, cabbage, whatever you have. The most important thing is the onions. They have to be fried."

When the weather is right, Ernie Brousseau fires up their traditional Ukrainian outdoor oven—the peeche oven, the outdoor mud brick ovens built by Ukrainian settlers. The originals were built by settlers, and the Brousseaus decided to build one in the tiny park they established next to their bakery. In the summer, on long weekends and during the pumpkin festival, the oven makes the best bread in the world.

"I don't know anything else that smells as good as that bread when it comes out of the oven," she says. "After that we put a roast in, and it cooks all day."

The town's favourite loaf is a traditional Ukrainian bread stuffed with cottage cheese and dill, and baked on a big cabbage leaf. When the oven is going, the residents from the seniors lodge next door come out to watch, to smell the bread, to remember.

Great Pumpkin Cookies

1 cup (500 mL) butter or shortening
1 cup (500 mL) granulated sugar
1 cup (250 mL) cooked pumpkin
1 large egg
2 tsps (10 mL) vanilla
1 1/2 cups (375 mL) sifted flour
1/2 cup (125 mL) rolled oats
1 tsp (5 mL) baking powder
1/2 tsp each (2 mL each) soda and salt
1 tsp each (5 mL each) cinnamon and ginger
1/2 tsp each (2 mL each) allspice and nutmeg
1/2 cup each (125 mL each) chopped walnuts
    and sunflower seeds
1/2 cup (125 mL) chocolate chips
1 cup (250 mL) raisins

Cream butter or shortening and sugar. Beat in pumpkin, egg and vanilla. Mix all dry ingredients together. Add to pumpkin mixture in two batches to form stiff batter. Drop by rounded teaspoons onto a sprayed cookie sheet. Bake at 375 F about 15 minutes. Makes about 60 cookies.

Josephsburg Chicken Supper

Josephsburg   Tel: (780) 998-3159

Every June for more than 90 years, there's been a fried chicken supper in Josephburg. What began as a church supper in a farmer's field is now a whopping big supper put on by the local agricultural society.

Every year, 200 volunteers roll up their sleeves and fall in step to fry the chicken, make the coleslaw, bake the pies, and mix the potato salad, with a mustard-laced boiled dressing from a recipe in the original Ladies Aid church cookbook. For anybody who doesn't love fried chicken, they also serve ham and baked beans. "We ran out of beans one year," says Trudy Kadatz, their longtime treasurer. "We won't do that again."

What They Ate

We love lists! The grocery list for 2,176 chicken dinners, the average number served each year, goes something like this:

528 lbs (240 kg) chicken breasts
176 lbs (80 kg) drumsticks
572 lbs (260 kg) thighs
160 lbs (73 kg) crumbs for breading
390 lbs (177 kg) peeled potatoes
11 gallons (42 L) homemade potato salad dressing
185 lbs (84 kg) coleslaw
160 lb (73 kg) ham
50 gallons (189 L) baked beans
500 pies

The meal is served in the arena, the only place in town big enough to hold the crowd. The entire community helps, including a crew of trusted inmates from the Fort Saskatchewan Correctional Institution, who set up tables and chairs. Dinner is served by legions of volunteers: the hockey team, firefighters, RCMP, seniors, 4-H gymkhana and a variety of celebrity servers. Some 890 people at a time sit down to finger lickin' good chicken and all the trimmings.

"Ralph Klein was here, but he didn't serve any food," Trudy confides. "He just visited."

Bonnie Mohr prepares pies for Josephburg's community dinner.

Ukrainian Pysanka Folk Festival

Vegreville

Tel: (780) 632-2777

Vegreville, home of the world's largest Ukrainian Easter egg, celebrates its roots every summer when the local Agricultural Society hosts the annual pysanka festival. There's ample opportunity to sample Ukrainian fare: cabbage rolls, garlic sausage in a bun, the redoubtable pyrohy with sour cream, bacon and fried onions on the side. The society also puts on a wonderful country fair and an annual threshing bee.

Ukrainian Cultural Heritage Village

25 minutes east of Edmonton on Highway 16

Tel: (780) 662-3640

Open daily May 15–Labour Day 10:00 AM–6:00 PM

Labour Day–Thanksgiving 10:00 AM–4:00 PM

V, MC, DEBIT

In the village, guides in costume and in character greet visitors to the churches and homes, recreating early Ukrainian life, and handing out samples of freshly baked bread if you're there at the right moment. Ukrainian food items are available in the main building, and pyrohy dinners are held during major cultural events such as the spring festival and The Harvest Festival.

The Harvest Festival is one of those country folk/city folk events that make an autumn weekend special. A bison barbecue heads the list of culinary distractions. After that there are the food kiosks, cooking demonstrations, regional product displays. It's a chance to sample homemade jams and preserves, shop at the farmers' market, enjoy the live entertainment or watch a threshing demonstration among friendly people in an old-time country setting.

The Andrew Garlic Festival

www.lamontcounty.com

Andrew

Tel: (780) 365-2005

"We already have the big duck in Andrew, but it's a wild duck," says Roberta Ropchan, one of the Friends of the Andrew Garlic Festival. "The garlic festival celebrates the harvest. Something we grow right here."

In the spring, the Friends give free garlic plants to anyone who wants to grow their own garlic. On a weekend in mid-October, they celebrate the harvest with a garlic-themed dinner. Two accomplished Ukrainian cooks, Helen and Gerry Tymchyshyn, do most of the cooking. The big favourite is studenetz—jellied pork hocks. There'll be beef or chicken too, heavy on the garlic. In the past they've included Caesar salad, some garlicy pasta dishes, and mashed white beans with garlic. They've also had baked garlic heads, and slivered beets with garlic. Think pineapple upside down cake with garlic is too wild? Not in Andrew. "She put one clove of garlic in each pineapple ring," says Roberta. "It was subtle." ✑

In many parts of the world, public art means contorted sculptures of rusting steel. In Kalyna Country, public art has gone a more colourful, and yes, more meaningful route.

Glendon's Giant Pyrogy

It's the $60,000 pyrohy: 6000 pounds of fibreglass and steel dumpling on a fork, standing three storeys tall on Pyrogy Drive, in Pyrogy Park. A small town with deep Ukrainian roots, Glendon has a long tradition of a pyrohy in every pot, and they take good cooking seriously. Sadly, they've been turned down for a spot on the $2 coin. "Maybe we were too big," muses mayor Johnny Doonanco, who is hoping for a shot at the $5 coin.

ALSO WORTH A VISIT

Pyrohy souvenirs (hats, T-shirts, various memorabilia) are available at Glendon Hardware. If you're hungry, stop into the café, where they do a dynamite version of locally-made pyrohy.

Vilna's King-Size Mushrooms

Three king-size mushrooms dominate the Vilna landscape. Erected nearly a decade ago, standing 20 feet high with a 15-foot diameter, the mushrooms weigh more than 18,000 pounds and balance delicately on stems made of 18-inch steel pipe. The faux mushrooms were constructed and painted by local artists at a cost of around $28,000, and sunk eight feet into the ground so they won't topple over. People love to have their pictures taken beneath the umbrella-like tops.

Mushroom hunting has been a tradition since the first Ukrainian settlers arrived. Almost anybody in town can identify this particular species, the locally abundant tricholoma uspale, which is either dried or cooked into traditional Ukrainian dishes.

ALSO WORTH A VISIT

If you're here on Saturday, the local farmers' market runs from 1:00 PM to 3:00 PM in the Agriplex. Vilna boasts the oldest pool hall in Alberta, circa 1920. On a hilltop not far from town stands the historic onion-domed Dickiebush Church.

Vegreville's Huge Pysanka

Vegreville's Ukrainian Easter egg, the Pysanka, draws visitors from all over the world, including Queen Elizabeth II and Prince Philip. The enormous egg with the colourful anodized aluminum shell towers 31 feet from top-of-egg to earth, and the intricate star patterns represent prosperity, life, good fortune and eternity. The computer-designed structure was funded by a number of grants, for a total cost that approached $300,000.

The design and fabrication took 12,000 hours over a two-year period, and required a full month to erect. If you add the shell, the internal structure and the base, the egg weighs 32,000 pounds. Yet it turns smoothly in the wind like a weathervane. That's a whole lotta egg!

ALSO WORTH A VISIT:
The Lakusta Heritage Museum and the Vegreville Regional Museum are both of historic interest. If you're looking for an authentic Ukrainian meal, the D and R Family Restaurant or the Alberta Hotel will fix you up. (See also pages 146 and 147.)

Andrew's Enormous Mallard
The town of Andrew, with a 160-acre wetland nearby, sits beneath one of the world's busiest flyways. Mallard ducks by the thousands visit every year. The biggest duck in town is their 5000-pound mallard, with a 25-foot wingspan, standing on a 10-foot pedestal. Fabricated from steel-framed fibreglass, the duck rises skyward toward Whitford Lake. It was built in Kelowna by the same people who built the great Glendon pyrohy.

ALSO WORTH A VISIT
On summer weekends, Koko's Bakery and Num Num Shop bakes duck-shaped dough-nuts. The Duckie Restaurant on Main Street serves Ukrainian food on Friday. Wildlife viewing sites at Whitford Lake Nature Complex and Wetland Preserve have boardwalks and elevated viewing platforms.

The Great Smoky Lake Pumpkin
Each October the town of Smoky Lake holds the Great White North Pumpkin Fair and Weigh-Off (see page 148). At press time, the great pumpkin was at Ed's Auto Body, undergoing a few cosmetic repairs, but it will soon be the focal point of a small park which is even now being called the Pumpkin Patch.

ALSO WORTH A VISIT
Smoky Lake has seven Eastern Rite churches in and around the town, each one with a beautiful onion dome. Also check out the Old Fashioned Bread Bakery on page 149.

Mundare's Big Sausage
The world's biggest sausage, six tons of steel-framed fibreglass, stands in a park on the north end of Mundare, where Mayor Ed Stawnichy is also known as "the sausage king."

"The minute you mention Mundare, people think of sausage," says Stawnichy. "Ours is 42 feet (13 metres) tall and weighs six tonnes."

It sits at a rakish tilt in a park at the end of Mundare's Main Street, just off highway 855, surrounded by four flags flapping in the breeze, including the official Stawnichy flag, a stylized SMP in white on a sausage-coloured oval. "Why not?" muses Mayor Stawnichy, who's mulling over other souvenirs of a sausage nature, including commemorative licence plates.

ALSO WORTH A VISIT

The Basilian Fathers Museum attracts history buffs from all over Canada. Stawnichy's Meat Processing offers tours of the sausage factory Tuesday, Wednesday and Thursday.

World's largest sausage, bar none.

PEACE COUNTRY

6

You could call it the land of meat and honey. The rich, wild place we call the Peace Country has always had its share of traditional agriculture in cattle, hogs and oilseed crops. It has also produced a steady golden stream of honey.

Beekeepers in the Peace number their hives in the thousands, and their bees are inspired to even greater activity by the long hours of summer daylight and a wide variety of floral sources. In small towns like Falher and Girouxville, honey flows like a river during the extraction season. Small fruits, primarily saskatoons, thrive in the Peace. In the past decade, the more exotic side of food and agriculture has also beaten a trail through the Peace Country, with bison and elk ranches and even a few wild boar producers. Here's a small sample of what we found along the Peace Country Trail.

CHERYL VANDERAEGEN

The Berry Basket   Tel: (780) 567-2495

Arnie and Susan Meyer, Clairmont

If Arnie and Susan Meyer had a favourite rock band it would have to be Deep Purple. Saskatoons may be the small stuff of the fruit business, but when you're handling and freezing 8,000 to 10,000 pounds of the famously delicious berries a day during the harvest season, there's nothing small about it.

Meyer's Berry Basket is the biggest commercial saskatoon orchard in the Peace, with 10 acres in production now and another 16 planned for 2004. To ensure the best quality berries, everything has to be picked, cleaned with a blower, de-stemmed, washed, and poured onto the inspection table within a few hours, then onto trays in a walk-in freezer. In six to eight hours they're frozen.

The Meyers hope to expand into products like fruit leather, and there are murmurings around Peace Country about a jam and jelly industry, and even farm-gate fruit wineries. But Arnie wonders about that: "We're already in the orchard all spring and summer," he says. "When would we have time to make wine?"

Peace Country Saskatoon Banana Bread

¾ cup (175 mL) sugar
1 ½ cups (750 mL) all-purpose flour
¼ tsp (2 mL) salt
2 tsps (10 mL) baking powder
¾ cup (175 mL) quick-cooking oats
⅓ cup vegetable oil
2 lightly beaten eggs
2 large mashed bananas
1 cup fresh or frozen saskatoons

Preheat oven to 350 F (180 C). Sift together sugar, flour, salt and baking powder. Stir in oats. Add oil, eggs, mashed bananas and saskatoons. Mix just until ingredients are blended. Pour into a greased and floured 9" x 5" inch loaf pan.

Bake about 1 hour, or until loaf is firm and tests done with a toothpick. Cool 10 minutes in pan before removing to a rack. Let cool completely before slicing. Freezes well. Makes one 9" x 5" loaf.

Shadow Ranch Wild Boars

Ronda and Rene Desaulniers, FalherTel: (780) 837-8272

If you happen to be driving the Peace Country backroads, and a cute, bristly critter with four short legs, stripes on its back, pointy little ears and a short, straight tail crosses your path, you're probably looking at a juvenile version of a wild boar.

Ronda and Rene Desaulniers of Falher own a herd of purebred Kaldens at Shadow Ranch Wild Boars, one of about a dozen wild boar farms in the Peace. "Those stripes on the little guys are quality markers," she says. "The longer they retain the stripes, the higher the quality of the animal."

Boar meat is low in cholesterol and saturated fat. Although Shadow Ridge boars live in a natural wooded habitat, they're fed wheat, barley, alfalfa and peas because it improves the quality of the meat. It also cuts down on runaways—why

Lorraine Desaulniers' Beehive, Falher

Lorraine Desaulniers' shop, called the Beehive, doesn't look like one of those high-domed fairytale hives. It's square and boxy, like the 1000 hives she and her husband, Luc Desaulniers, manage in their honey operation. Lorraine sells her own honey as Wardes

Honey, which begins as golden unpasteurized liquid and gradually hardens, becoming firm and white. She also offers locally made chocolates and caramels made with Peace Country honey. Her shop is within sight of a giant honey bee sculpture, appropriate public art for the town that calls itself the Honey Capital of Canada.

BEEMAID HONEY LTD

The buzz starts in the spring, when the bees are collecting pollen from dandelions and pussy willow catkins. They leave it in the hive for the bees, who feed on early spring pollen. "By July or August all the other flowers are in bloom," she explains. "The honey flow runs from two to six weeks."

Honey from the Peace is world-renowned for its mild flavour and white colour. Long summer days encourage hard working bees. Flowers from alfalfa, canola, various clovers and wild flowers like the gorgeous red fireweed are abundant. Lorraine feels that their cool nights make a difference in the quality and flavour of the honey. "Some of the Peace producers have over 4000 hives," she says. "Luc and I are smaller, but that lets us pay a lot of attention to our bees, check the health of the queen and the colony, watch for diseases, that sort of thing."

The first frost kills the flowers, ending production, but beginning the extraction, a sticky procedure yielding anywhere from 150 to 300 pounds of honey from each of the hives. ⬳

Peace Country Honey Tarts

2 eggs
½ cup (125 mL) honey
½ cup (125 mL) raisins
2 tbsps (30 mL) softened butter
2 tbsps (30 mL) cream
1 tsp (5 mL) vanilla
tart shells

Stir together eggs, honey, raisins, soft butter, cream and vanilla. Spoon into tart shells and bake in 350 F oven for 10 minutes. Reduce heat to 325 F and bake another 10 to 15 minutes or until filling is set. Makes 2 dozen small tarts.

bother to forage when the grub is so good at home? Shadow Ranch boar meat is available frozen, in chops, farmers' sausage, bacon and ham, ribs, cutlets, roast, ground meat and hocks.

Hog Wild Specialties

www.hogwild.ab.ca

Debbie and Earl Hagman

1-888-668-9453 (WILD)

Box 1209, Mayerthorpe

Debbie and Earl Hagman maintain a small herd of about 300 European-Russian wild boars on their ranch just outside Mayerthorpe. They also market the meat for five other boar ranches, to places like Urban Fare and Ital Canadian Meats in Edmonton. "We'll custom cut, wrap and deliver, fresh or frozen, anywhere in Alberta," Debbie says. Try a full-flavoured, herb-spiked paté or some smoky wild boar bacon, one of Debbie's favourites. She also likes to marinate a shoulder roast in herb-infused oil and vinegar, and oven-roast it at about 275 F. When it's almost ready, she glazes it with cranberry orange sauce.

For a special occasion, Hog Wild Specialties will pull their travelling rotisserie up to your house and barbecue a whole wild boar to perfection. It'll serve 100 guests, and the aroma wafting through the poplars is guaranteed to have the neighbours lining up at the fence.

❂ DINGING OUT IN PEACE COUNTRY
CAFÉS, BISTROS, DINERS
AND NEIGHBOURHOOD JOINTS

$$ **Rochfort Bridge Trading Post**

Rochfort Bridge, Highway 43 (near Mayerthorpe)   Tel: (780) 785-3467

Open daily 9:00 AM–9:00 PM

V, MC, DEBIT

This is a charming spot. To get to the restaurant, go through the store—knick-knacks, oddities and donkey food for the herd of friendly donkeys just up the road.

The Trading Post's claim to fame is the Bridge Burger—a table-sized burger on a house-made sourdough bun, served with curly fries and all the condiments we know and love. First, we marvel at the burger's size, then we marvel that the cook was able to get it on the platter in one piece. We marvel all the more because it's a darn good burger. If you can finish it in twenty minutes, it's free! Check the wall of fame for snaps of people who have managed the feat, sometimes more than once. There's a full menu of breakfast items and diner classics including liver and onions, veal cutlets and assorted sandwiches. Hold your fork, there's pie.

Central Alberta's artisan cheesemakers burst on the scene several years ago with the opening of the state-of-the-art Natricia Dairy and Sylvan Star's big win at the national cheese awards. A trip to any one of these operations is a terrific diversion to break the monotony of the Calgary Edmonton run. Call first. Or, make a day of it and have lunch at one of our favourite eateries, listed on the next page.

Leoni–Grana
Camrose
www.leonigrana.com
Tel: (780) 672-1698

Emmanuela Leoni makes a delicious Parmesan-like cheese in the style of her birthplace in Italy's Po Valley. A recent move to the intersection of Highway 13 West and Highway 21 (actually, 500 metres north on Highway 21 toward Edmonton) makes this cheese much more accessible. Look for the big sign. Call first, as this is a new move and the hours are still being finalized. Check the web site for more information.

Natricia Dairy
5710 49th Street, Ponoka
Tel: (403) 783-8945
Open Monday–Friday 9:00 AM–5:00 PM

Saturdays 10:00 AM–2:00 PM to sample and buy cheese.
For tours, call ahead to arrange and reserve.

CASH ONLY

Virginia Saputo's goat cheese is in demand worldwide, and you can sample and purchase the fine handmade goat cheeses of varying styles and ripeness at the dairy about ten minutes off Highway 2. The fresh cheese, mild in flavour and creamy in texture, is available only at the dairy. Try it for breakfast with a little maple syrup and you may never go back to cornflakes in the morning.

Chevre artisan Virgina Saputo conducts a tasting.

Sylvan Star Cheese

RR 1, Red Deer Tel: (780) 340-1560

West on Highway 11A from Highway 2. You'll see the sign on the highway.

Open Monday–Saturday, but call first

CASH ONLY

John and Janny Schalkwyk make amazing cheese. We're partial to the aged gouda with it's winey aromas and a texture perfect for grating or eating out of hand. You can pick up their younger cheeses at the little shop on the property, as well as their spiced gouda and the excellent Bles Wold Dairy yogourt.

DINING OUT IN CENTRAL ALBERTA
CAFÉS, BISTROS, DINERS
AND NEIGHBOURHOOD JOINTS

$$ **Bricco Ristorante Italiano**

Calmar Tel: (780) 985-4528 R

Open Wednesday–Saturday 5:00 PM–10:00 PM

Sunday 11:00 AM–2:00 PM, 5:00 PM–10:00 PM

V, MC, DEBIT

Town councillor Kirk Popik ("I was tired of eating pizza") has turned a lifelong interest in food and cooking into a great little restaurant. Expect Italian favourites such as tomato and onion salad, fettucini alfredo, chicken parmigiana or risotto and steaks, often from Lauriston Farm's Highland beef. The menu changes frequently depending on the season, what looks good at the market and what Kirk feels like.

An excellent Sunday brunch gives purpose to a drive in the country.

$ **Burger Barn**

5003 47th Avenue, Millet Tel: (780) 387-4776

Open Monday–Wednesday 11:00 AM–7:45 PM

Thursday–Saturday 11:00 AM–8:00 PM

Sunday 12:00 AM–7:00 PM

Summer hours are longer

V, MC, DEBIT

You can have one patty or three (they've even made a five patty stack) with fresh or fried onions, bacon, cheese, all the condiments and then some. Excellent crispy fries and real hard ice cream milkshakes as well. There are 15 different burgers (including a salmon filet and two chicken burgers), soon to be 16 when

"A good burger takes more than 30 seconds."

they finish developing their veggie burger. Nothing is pre-formed, pre-cooked, pre-anything.

Carmen Rahner and her husband bought the Burger Barn two years ago. "You don't buy a niche place to turn it into something like something else. But ya gotta unprogram the McDonalds right out of them," she says emphatically.

$$ | **Footloose Caboose Lodge**

www.footloosecaboose.com

20324 Township Road 502

Tel: (780) 662-2372 R

RR 2, Kingman (just off Highway 14 East about an hour from Edmonton)

Open May–Christmas Thursday, Friday 5:00 PM–8:00 PM

Saturday, Sunday 9:00 AM–2:00 PM, 5:00 PM–8:00 PM

V, MC

Eva and Ray Loranger have gone to considerable trouble to restore an antique CP railcar (the Mt.Lefroy) into a dining car offering a lovely seat from which to take in the scenery.

Eva's cooking is simple and good, using fresh, seasonal ingredients. Breakfast is hearty: omelettes, crispy filled crepes, eggs Benedict—no one will leave hungry. Dinner is four courses with several choices in the mains, and menus change frequently.

Dining in these rolling hills of mixed forest and grassland is especially beautiful in the fall, when the aspens turn bright gold against the bluest blue sky. The plan is to turn all the railway cars scattered about the property into guest suites. For now, visitors will have to content themselves with a good meal and a visit to the barbed wire museum.

$$ **Kavaccinos**

5028 51st Street, Lacombe

Tel: (403) 782 7844

Open summer Monday–Thursday 7:30 AM–11:00 PM

Friday 7:30 AM–12:00 AM; Saturday 8:30 AM–11:00 PM

Open winter Monday–Thursday 7:30 AM–11:00 PM

Friday 7:30 AM–12:00 AM; Saturday 8:30 AM–6:00 PM

V, MC, DEBIT

Everybody likes Jenny Bakker's herb tomato soup and her signature hearty

German potato bake, a casserole of mashed potatoes with bacon and sauerkraut. Expect two or three specials at lunch, including many vegetarian choices, and go early. With its large patio, Kavaccino's is a favourite for light meals and coffee.

$$ **Leto's Steak & Seafood**
4944 Highway 2A, Lacombe   Tel: (403) 782-4647
Open daily 11:00 AM–12:00 AM
V, MC, AE, DEBIT

> If you're on a date in Lacombe, this is the place to go. It's an elegant looking room and the food is prepared with a light touch. The Greek salad and the baked salmon are always a good bet, and they're justly proud of their steaks. There's an extensive lunch buffet, including good pyrohy.

$ **Pete's at the Beach**
4711 Lakeshore Drive, Sylvan Lake   Tel: (403) 887-4747
Open Winter Monday–Saturday 8:00 AM–10:00 PM
        Sunday 8:00 AM–9:00 PM
Open Summer Monday–Thursday 8:00 AM–10:00 PM
        Friday–Sunday 8:00 AM–12:00 AM
V, MC, DEBIT

> Beach food is seldom wonderful, but so many people raved about Pete's that we had to check it out. This is a big place, with seating for more than 100 on the patio alone, and they do several things very well: eggs Benedict, gourmet pizzas, and burgers, which come amply filled and garnished. We like the Surf Burger with sautéed onions, mushrooms, mozza and tomatoes on a toasted bun. Their hashbrowns and French fries are made from potatoes in-house and the fish (for fish and chips) is Alaska cod in a beer batter.

◉ DINING OUT IN RED DEER
COFFEE SHOPS AND TEA HOUSES

$ **Caroline's Cappuccino Café**
1–255 Davison Drive   Tel: (403) 347-5545
Open daily 8:00 AM–10:00 PM
V, MC, AE, DEBIT

> It's a coffee house, and Caroline's food menu isn't extensive, but the sandwiches are a local favourite. The egg salad with green onion is an especially tasty version of the old standard. Housemade cheesecake comes in many flavours, and is avail-

able by the slice or whole. This is a great place for a fast, informal meal or for takeout.

$

City Roast Coffee

4940 Ross Street   Tel: (403) 347-0893

Open Monday–Friday 7:00 AM–6:00 PM

    Saturday 8:30 AM–5:00 PM; Sunday 12:00 PM–4:00 PM

V, DEBIT

Robert and Karen Miller own this busy, cozy spot. It's the place for freshly house-roasted coffee, espresso or a latte. Everything is made in-house, from the

$$

Eco Café

10 Village Drive, Pigeon Lake   Tel: (780) 586-2627

Open Monday–Thursday 6:30 AM–8:00 PM

    Friday, Saturday 6:30 AM–9:00 PM

    Summer hours are longer.

V, MC, DEBIT

Next time you're driving Highway 2, contemplating the usual fast food choices for lunch, turn west at the Wetaskiwin turn off (Highway 13). In the Village at Pigeon Lake you'll find a crackerjack little restaurant called the Eco Café. At first glance this place looks like any other rural café, but there's something special happening here. Owner Tim Wood is living his dream: a restaurant serving local, seasonal product, expertly prepared, every day.

"The eggs are raised a few kilometers away. Sometimes we have to wait because the hens haven't laid yet." Now that's a fresh omelette. Tim and his wife, Deb, raise chickens, lamb and ducks. What they can't produce, they buy from local farmers, and they contract for elk, bison and beef to be raised to their specifications. A local grower supplies organic flour, stone-milled daily, that they make into breads, buns and pitas.

"My customers don't want pain au levain," says Tim. "They want a sandwich on fluffy homemade bread." Tim describes his menu as not haute, not gourmet, but simple and wholesome. The pizzas are Italian-style, thin crusts with a few tasty toppings: capicolla with roasted pepper spread, a drizzle of olive oil and fresh mushrooms. We love the grilled venison chop with a flavourful peppercorn reduction, crisp rosti potatoes and pan-roasted vegetables.

The menu changes twice a year reflecting what's in season. He insists on fresh, locally grown vegetables—Pic 'n' Pac out of Lacombe supplies peppers and tomatoes. "We can't get to the summer farmers' markets; we don't have time. We have no time for sleep in the summer! We have a lineup for 12 hours."

His vision of a primarily organic restaurant using local products has become a reality. "This is what I always thought restaurant food could be," he says. ✐

muffins (try the lemon blueberry) and carrot cake to the soups and the vegetarian chili. Want a real prairie specialty? It doesn't get any better than the rhubarb coffee cake. Fair Trade and regular coffee are available by the pound, whole bean or ground.

CAFÉS, BISTROS, DINERS AND NEIGHBOURHOOD JOINTS

$ **Hubie's 1955 Diner**
101–3722 57th Avenue   Tel: (403) 340-3795
Open Monday–Saturday 7:30 AM–4:00 PM; Sunday 9:00 AM–4:00 PM
CASH ONLY

Hubie's is a blast. It's a small, authentic '50s-style diner with jukeboxes in each booth and a soda fountain. This is homestyle cooking, with big, BIG breakfasts named after favourite Archie Comic characters. "Your fries are a patata until you order them," says the waitress in the authentic poodle skirt. Burgers are well garnished, and everybody loves the turkey dinner on Friday, with made-from-scratch gravy. This is a favourite coffee hangout for locals. A word of caution: smoky.

$$ **Las Palmeras**
3630 50th Avenue   Tel: (403) 346-8877 R
Open Monday–Thursday 11:30 AM–10:00 PM
        Friday, Saturday 11:30 AM–11:00 PM
        Sunday 12:00 PM–9:00 PM
V, MC, ENR, AE, DEBIT

Frank Lemus is from El Salvador, but he loves Mexican food, and that's what you'll get at his table. "My father is a great cook. He spent a lot of time in Mexico, and he developed most of these recipes himself" says Lemus, who has evidently followed in Dad's footsteps. There are the usual Tex Mex offerings—the giant tostada salad, the chicken fajitas—but look to the special dishes. The chicken al tequila is a favourite: chicken breast sautéed with peppers, mushrooms and house spices, flamed with a shot of tequila, and served with the traditional side of rice and beans. The marinated pork loin is charbroiled, and comes to the table still tender and full of its own natural juices.

For dessert, try this guilty pleasure: ice cream rolled in crushed cereal, deep-fried to a golden, crisp crust and served with chocolate sauce and whipped cream.

$$$ Manzzini's Pasta & Steak House

5018 45th Street   Tel: (403) 340–8806 R

Open Monday–Friday 11:00 AM–10:00 PM

Saturday 4:00 PM–10:00 PM

V, MC, ENR, DEBIT

Manzzini's ignores the whole north/south debate so often cited in the Italian kitchen, and goes both ways: red sauce, white sauce. You could pick a pasta or a meat dish and, with some discussion, customize it with the sauce of your choice. Or try the fettuccine alla gigi, the pasta bathed in a light, creamy tomato sauce with bacon, onions and mushrooms—it's outstanding. There are lots of steaks and ribs (either pork or beef) plus fish and seafood on this wide-ranging menu.

$$ Pho Thuy Duong Vietnamese Restaurant

Bay 4, 5108 52nd Street

Tel: (403) 343–2720

Open Monday–Saturday 11:00 AM–10:00 PM

V, MC, DEBIT

Pho means soup in Vietnamese, and at this small, family-owned spot it comes in vat-sized servings (even the small bowl is big). After stock and noodles, in goes the meat or fish. Add some thinly sliced onion and a handful of fresh bean sprouts to finish it, and you have a meal-in-a-bowl. Every item on the menu is numbered, which is handy for those of us who can't get our tongues around the names and would rather just sing out the numbers. Located in the heart of downtown Red Deer right behind Superstore, Pho Thuy Duong is perfect for lunch.

$$$ **Sakura Japanese Restaurant**

3731 50th Avenue   Tel: (403) 341-5502

Open Tuesday–Friday 11:30 AM–10:00 PM

   Saturday 4:00 PM–10:30 PM

   Sunday 12:00 PM–10:00 PM

V, MC, AE, DEBIT

Teppanyaki cooking is an evening's entertainment, and there's no denying the skill of a good teppan chef, his knife flashing, his vegetables flying, his jokes (Japanese snow, Japanese flying saucer) getting the requisite ripple of polite chuckles. There are various teppan choices—seafood, steak, chicken and vegetables. Both the quality of ingredients and the cooked-in-a-flash results are first-rate.

Sushi, sashimi, tempura and sukiyaki are also available, and the bento boxes are miniature works of edible art. For dessert, the green tea ice cream is subtly flavoured and refreshing.

$$$ **Shauney's**

4909 48th Street   Tel: (403) 342-2404

Open Monday–Friday 11:30 AM–10:00 PM

   Saturday 5:00 PM–11:00 PM

V, MC, ENR, AE, DEBIT

If you're looking for classic cuisine, Shauney's is the only game in town. When chef Dennis Albrecht and his business partner, Wendy Safron, took over this Red Deer landmark several years ago, they kept the traditional touches but updated the menu with contemporary versions of the classics. Albrecht loves to cook and insists on doing his own tableside specialties.

As well as the standard chicken-and-steak fare, he's happy to be cooking bison, ostrich, shark, swordfish or even alligator. For something a tad unusual, think of ostrich chateaubriand with a shallot and red wine sauce, or a rich-and-ritzy flambéed dessert.

〰 SPECIALTY GROCERY
ASIAN

Hong Kong Super Store

4815 48th Avenue

Tel: (403) 346-3131

Open Monday–Saturday 11:00 AM–6:00 PM

V, MC, DEBIT

The Wong family opened this Chinese specialty shop over a decade ago. It's a fine source for Asian produce like bok choy, suey choy, lo bok, lemongrass, ginger root, that sort of thing. They stock Asian groceries including coconut milk, the essential hot/sour/salty/sweet sauces for cooking (soy, bean, hoisin, oyster, chili) and lots of herbal and medicinal teas. It's a good place to buy rice and egg noodles and Asian candies.

Zen's Asian Foods

7–5108 52nd Street

Tel: (403) 343-1526

Open Monday–Saturday 10:00 AM–7:30 PM

Sunday 12:00 PM–5:00 PM

V, DEBIT

Zen's is the place for Filipino foodstuffs. Try the filled buns known as sio pau, with pork or chicken. Warmed for just a minute or so, they go down well with a cold beer. In the freezer case you'll find dim sum items and a small selection of seafood. They also carry sticky rice, pappadums, curry pastes, spices, sauces. It's a bit of pan-Asian exotica in the heartland.

EUROPEAN

Otherlands Imports
A3434 50th Avenue   Tel: (403) 341-6628
Open Monday–Friday 10:00 AM–5:30 PM; Saturday 10:00 AM–5:00 PM
V, DEBIT

> Frances Versluis's clientele of transplanted Dutch people must get just a little bit
> homesick when they step through the door. There are cookies and candies from
> Holland, Dutch salted liquorice, Honig soups. Here's your chance to pick up
> stroopies, the wafer sandwich cookies with brown sugar syrup between the lay-
> ers, beloved of all Dutch children. Heat them for just a minute, then eat them
> with ice cream. At Christmas, she brings in chocolate alphabet letters, foil-
> wrapped chocolate treats and marzipan. There are only two tables—a daily soup
> and sandwiches, your choice of deli meats on a kaiser. It's cozy.

MEATS AND FOWL

Baier's Sausage & Meats
6022 67A Street   Tel: (403) 346-1535
Open Monday–Wednesday, Saturday 9:00 AM–5:30 PM
    Thursday, Friday 9:00 AM–6:00 PM
V, MC, DEBIT

> Keith Baier is a traditional meat man who makes all his own sausage from scratch
> with no binders or fillers. He makes 35 varieties, including a tasty chorizo and a
> South African boar wurst. But that's not the only card in the Baier deck. He sells
> fish and chicken, plus top-quality Alberta pork and Alberta beef. Natural and cer-
> tified organic beef is available by special order, as is Alberta lamb.

Nossack Fine Meats
4951a 78th Street   Tel: (403) 346-5006
Open Monday–Friday 9:00 AM–5:00 PM
V, MC, DEBIT

> Nossack is a first-generation retail and wholesale meat processor with a fourth-
> generation sausage master at the helm. Karsten Nossack's family business spe-
> cializes in hams, pastramis and sausages. In the front, there's a deli counter plus
> soup and sandwich makings. The hot roast beef sandwich is the hearty, local
> favourite. Watch for their deli trailer at the Red Deer farmers' market on
> Saturdays, mid-May to mid-October.

THE DINOSAUR TRAIL

8

The early settlers who came upon the strange, contorted moonscape of south-central Alberta had seen nothing like it before. The earth looked gashed open—faults and folds, layers of shale, mudstone and sandstone, all visible. They called it the Badlands, and the eerie, wind-eroded shapes became known as Hoodoos. This was dinosaur country, and it is their historic presence that makes a visit to the Royal Tyrrel Museum and Dinosaur Provincial Park such a must for travellers.

But even dino-hunters have to eat. We begin in the pretty town of Drumheller.

◉ DINING OUT ON THE DINO TRAIL

$ **Bernie and the Boys**
305 4th Street W, Drumheller   Tel: (403) 823-3318
Open Tuesday–Sunday 11:00 AM–9:00 PM
V, MC, DEBIT

> Bernie Germain's non-smoking, family-style restaurant serves 60 flavours of milk-shakes, everything from chocolate to mango, and is home to the mammoth burger: 24 oz ground beef, 24 oz bread roll, fully loaded, weighing in at three pounds. If you can eat it in less than 14 minutes and 37 seconds (the current record), it's yours for free, and you might even get your picture in the paper. (No guarantee.) The people in this rose-coloured diner are deeply into fast food—fries, pizza, fish and chips, but on a Saturday night with the kids to feed, what more could you ask?

$$ **The Sizzling House**
160 Centre Street, Drumheller   Tel: (403) 823-8098
Open daily 11:00 AM–9:00 PM, summer hours are longer
V, MC, AE, DEBIT

> Three restaurants in Drumheller specialize in Chinese food, and each one has its fans, but the one we like best is The Sizzling House. Order the Manchurian beef

with honey and black bean, the steamed dumplings stuffed with minced barbecued pork, and the Mongol-style chicken. The sizzling shrimp, a true Szechuan dish, is wildly popular, especially with a Chinese beer. Thai curries are a good bet, green, red and yellow, with subtle underpinnings of flavour beneath the heat.

The Whistling Kettle
$$
Drumheller
109 Centre Street, across from the giant T-Rex   Tel: (403) 823-9997
Open Tuesday–Saturday after Labour Day; Monday–Saturday May 24–Labour Day
V, MC, DEBIT

> What was once a bungalow is now a tea house with a generous verandah running around two sides, very welcome on a summer afternoon when the heat settles over this valley. Good soups and sandwiches, terrific tea biscuits, and you'll love the quiche, but pies are owner Karen Lee Andrew's specialty, both savoury and sweet. Try the taco pie—salsa, ground beef and sour cream baked in a pie shell.
>
> On the sweet side, the sour cream rhubarb pie is so popular that regulars call ahead to reserve a slice. Also try the pumpkin pecan, the pineapple-laced French coconut, the fruit pies and the old-timey flapper pie.

The Last Chance Saloon   Tel: (403) 823-9189.
$$
Wayne
Open Monday–Saturday 12:00 PM–1:00 AM; Sunday 12:00 PM–7:00 PM
Closed Sundays October–April
V, MC, DEBIT

> Most of the 124 coal mines along the Dino Trail were depleted long ago, but the legacy of hard work and hospitality is very much alive. Nine bridges and 12 minutes southeast of Drumheller, make a hard right and pull up in front of the three-storey Rosedeer Hotel and Last Chance Saloon, owned by Fred and Alisia Dayman. It's been in the Dayman family for three generations, ever since Fred's great-uncle Alex bought the place in 1948.
>
> You order two beers. The bartender asks if you need glasses with the beer. You say yes. He plunks down a pair of sunglasses. Then he says "Whoops," and hands you one of the original gem jars Fred found in the basement one day. The noise level is high to extreme, the ambiance smoky/friendly. Somebody thumps tunefully on an old upright piano, somebody else strums a guitar. A guy in the corner raps out the beat with a pair of large bones. "Dino bones," says the red wine drinker beside you. "Pure T-Rex."
>
> This is a fun spot, and Alisia, Fred's wife, is a good cook. "When the weather cools down, I make all the soups and stews from scratch," she says. "We grill one

of the best steaks anywhere. It's all local beef, aged 21 days." A cook-it-yourself 12 oz. boneless sirloin, with beans, baked potato and garlic toast, done outside on the back patio, goes for $13. This is a fine place for a cold beer, a bison burger or a steak and a slab of Alisia's apple pie. She closes her kitchen around 8:00 PM, but the fast-food bar menu, mostly deep-fried, is still available. In the summer, Sunday is family day, and minors are allowed in the bar.

At sundown, step outside and watch the light change across the layered monochromes of this unearthly spot. You'll wish you could paint, because it's so strangely beautiful.

$$ Rosebud Country Inn

Main Street, Rosebud   Tel: (403) 677-2211 R
Open daily 8:00 AM–8:00 PM with seasonal closings
V, MC, AE, DEBIT

Sunlight streams into the small dining room with its oak furniture and mellow yellow walls. You can have a full buffet breakfast, lunch or dinner. Laurette Paris makes flavourful soups, and on weekends, main courses could be anything from barbecued chicken or steak to teriyaki salmon. Through the week there's a shorter menu offering casual dishes: baked spaghetti, chicken fajitas, chicken Caesar salad.

$$ The Rosebud Mercantile

Rosebud
Tel: (403) 677-2350
Dinner from 6:00 PM, before curtain time.
V, MC, DEBIT

Here's a tiny hamlet with a huge amount of talent, all concentrated in the Rosebud Theatre, a part of the Rosebud School of the Arts. Rosebud is all about dinner and the theatre, with a bountiful buffet in the old Mercantile. Seatings are staggered every 15 minutes, so the food is always hot and fresh and the lineups are short and friendly. It's a folksy ambiance with happy-faced students serving the food, singing at your table, and chatting up the customers.

Chef Patrick Murphy does his best to vary the menu as each show comes and goes. There's always seafood on the cold buffet, a huge roast at the carving station, and the

Big feast before little theatre takes place in the Rosebud Mercantile.

bus boys strongly endorse the teriyaki chicken when it's available. At Christmas try the farmhouse-style turkey dinner; Easter brings out the ham. About 220 people can be seated for the evening buffet, and everyone will be at the theatre by curtain time. NOTE: no alcoholic beverages are served.

That's Crafty! Tea Shop

$

www.thatscrafty.8m.com

Highway 9, 16 miles (26 km) west of Drumheller   Tel: (403) 677-2207

Open Monday to Saturday 10:00 AM–5:00 PM, March to December

V, MC, AE, DEBIT

An old dairy barn-turned-tea room makes a fine destination for a drive in the country, with tea served in delicate bone china. They offer a full menu—salads, soups, light fare—but don't miss the sweeter part of the repast: delicious cakes, cheesecakes, cinnamon buns, big fat muffins and the amazing chocolate fudge cake drizzled with warm caramel sauce.

The Doll Palace

$

400 Pioneer Trail, Hanna   Tel: (403) 854-2756

Open Wednesday–Sunday 9:00 AM–6:00 PM

V, MC

Just outside Hanna, Violetta Link operates her 50-seat café and amazing doll museum. Café tables are covered with flowered oilcloth, the lights are fluorescent, and in a back room are all 4,000 of her prized dolls. Most days around noon you'll find her sitting at a table near the pie case, wearing her spotless apron and watching her friends tuck into what they know will be good home cooking: cinnamon buns and tea biscuits in the morning, a roast at noon, and pie all the time.

"Our customers want their beef well-done, their chicken falling off the bone, and none of that spicy stuff," says Violetta. "No fried foods here. We all like a greasy hamburger once in awhile, but you'll have to go someplace else to get it."

JUDY SCHULTZ

She makes pies every day, usually 18 to 20, but she's made as many as 54—lemon meringue, saskatoon, apple. The regular lunch buffet is a bargain. For $7.95, you get a choice of salads including jellied, cole slaw, chunky vegetable, plus as much of the well-done roast beef and a second meat as you wish, with fluffy mashed potatoes, a vegetable and a river of gravy to pour over. Dessert is included if you want more jello. The famous pies cost extra and are worth it.

Food for Thought Deli

$

123 2nd Avenue W, Hanna   Tel: (403) 854-3850

Open Monday–Saturday 10:00 AM–5:00 PM

V, MC

> Victor and Beverley Fortinski and their daughter, Kari Duarte, a SAIT food serv-
> ice graduate, run this delightful spot. The shop has an impressive selection of cold
> meats, cheeses and freshly-baked bread. There are about six tables, and lunch
> always brings a special or two plus great homemade soup, a variety of salads, and
> desserts of the good-and-gooey genre. "On Fridays, we do Mom's corn and crab
> chowder. It's terrific," says Kari, who always saves a bowl for herself.

The Prairie Elevator Tea Room

$

Acadia Valley

May 24th to Thanksgiving, Lunch only   Tel: (403) 972-2028

CASH ONLY

> Somewhat off the Dino Trail, smack in the middle of the vast, rolling prairie sits
> the tiny village of Acadia Valley, where several years ago the local citizens wisely
> invested $1 to buy their Pool elevator. In saving the elevator, they got a museum

and a busy tea room.
"We're real pie people,"
says the friendly woman
named Pat, who man-
ages the food service.
"We have saskatoon pie
all summer, pumpkin
pie at Thanksgiving, and
our fruit kuchen is a
local specialty." The
community struggles a
bit to keep the elevator
up and running as a
museum, but they feel
it's worth the effort.
"We've managed for 11
years," says Pat. "There
aren't many elevators
left out here on the
prairie. Now we're a
destination!"

JUDY SCHULTZ

Tea Tyme and Porcelain Pleasures

4802 King Street, Coronation   Tel: (403) 578-2376

Open daily 10:00 AM–9:00 PM

CASH ONLY

It looks like a tea room and it sounds like a tea room, but it's also a lounge and a restaurant with a wide choice of main courses including soup, sandwiches, chili and lasagna. The tea aspect seems almost accidental, but it works, says Edna Redelback, who does it her own way. "No muffins, no cookies, no chocolate cake. We don't have a call for them here." Instead, she offers a delicious pumpkin cake, carrot cake, a light blueberry cheesecake and fruit tarts (apple, blueberry, peach.) One of the partners in this enterprise makes beautiful porcelain dolls for sale along with doll clothes and teddy bears.

Southern Alberta is a landscape out of a western movie, where wide open spaces are still home to antelope, and red-tailed hawks still wheel through the enormous blue sky. You can almost see the herds of buffalo that once roamed these plains. Today, irrigation defines the agricultural base. Some of Canada's sweetest corn is grown here, plus sugar beets and sunflowers, and it's home to a thriving bean industry. All of this near the place the ice age missed—the Cypress Hills.

MEDICINE HAT PANTRY
WHERE GOOD COOKS SHOP
SPECIALTY GROCERS

Nutter's #1
107–1601 Dunmore Road SE
Open Monday–Thursday, Saturday 9:00 AM–6:00 PM
     Friday 9:00 AM–9:00 PM; Sunday 12:00 PM–5:00 PM
V, MC, DEBIT

www.nutters.com
Tel: 1-800-665-5122

A home-grown company with headquarters in Medicine Hat, Nutter's is a reliable supplier of bulk products—nuts, dried fruit, grains, vitamin supplements and health foods. One of the secrets to the company's success has been its ability

to fit the local market, offering small delis in some outlets and extensive lines of specialty products in others. A family owned business started by Dr. Jim Cranston, it is now run by his nephew Donald Cranston and his daughter Lynn Cranston. Nutter's has 15 stores in Alberta and a total of 32 across the Western provinces. Check the web site for locations near you.

$ **Café Mundo**

105–579 3rd Street SE   Tel: (403) 528-2808

Open Monday–Saturday 8:00 AM–5:30 PM

V

> Denise Earl's coffee shop is a good place for cappuccino, latte, lunch or other casual indulgences. You'll find generously filled sandwiches, with ham and turkey being big favourites and their excellent cheddar cheese-dill muffin. They also make a dynamite turtle bar for any dedicated sweet tooth in the crowd.

RedCliff Bakery and Coffee Shop

$ 83rd Street SE, Redcliff   Tel: (403) 548-6050

Open Monday to Saturday

CASH ONLY

> It's a sociable place, full of temptations—Danish-style fruit pastries, cheese-and-egg pastries, delicious things to go with coffee. (No flavoured coffees here—what they pour is what you get.) When you leave, don't forget the bread. Several Medicine Hat restaurants buy their bread from this good old bakery.

BIG NIGHTS, SPLURGES AND CELEBRATIONS

Antique Country Dining Room

1 mile west of Redcliff, on Highway 1   Tel: (403) 548-2202

$$$ Open Tuesday–Thursday 4:30 PM–10:00 PM

Friday, Saturday 4:30 PM–11:00 PM

Sunday 4:30 PM–10:00 PM

V, MC, DEBIT

> Enid and Ivan Luk own and operate this 65-seat country dining room, with a patio in front, in a renovated bungalow on 53 acres of land. Ivan was one of SAIT's top grads in 1986, and he specializes in AAA Alberta beef. Prime rib is his signature dish, but you can have steak in almost any form, including with crab or lobster. If you're out for a drive in the country, it's an entertaining spot—Enid's goats and even a llama or two may amble by the large deck on a warm summer evening.

The Ribcage Grille

$$

505 2nd Avenue N, Vauxhall   Tel: (403) 654-2677

Open Tuesday–Sunday 1:00 AM–9:00 PM

V, MC, DEBIT

Leanne Meir, her father Dale Leeson and brother Brad Leeson own and operate this 55-seat family restaurant. It's a meat-and-potatoes spot, from the hamburger soup to the ribs, slow-roasted in their secret sauce, and finished on the grill. A half rack of six to eight pork side ribs is a good bet unless you're starving. "A full rack is more than most men can eat," says Leanne. "It's a foot and a half long."

The pulled pork sandwich comes on a kaiser (from Luigi's Bakery in Lethbridge), in a tangy-sweet barbecue sauce. They love their steaks: a huge (over 2 pounds) sirloin steak, T-bones, rib steaks, club steaks and a steak sandwich. "We're gaining a reputation for good food. We know it's fresh, we know where it comes from. My dad raises all our beef and pork," says Leanne.

The Vineyard on First

$$$

777–579 3rd Street SE

Tel: (403) 528-2666

Open Monday–Friday, lunch from 11:00 AM

 Dinner from 5:00 PM

V, MC, AE, DEBIT

Partners Raoul and Patricia Moran and Chef Andre Rainville, three people who really love food and wine, operate this elegant dining room. Raoul is a big fan of regional products, and his wine list includes a generous and well-chosen selection of VQAs from the Okanagan.

The menu emphasizes game. Try the elk chop with a savoury hunter sauce (wild and farmed mushrooms, red peppers, red onions, herbs), the buffalo rib-eye, ostrich with a triple berry sauce (blueberries, blackberries and raspberries) or even the ostrich burgers. Chef Rainville is from Falher, Alberta's honey capi-

Taber Cornfest

www.taber.ca

Tel: (403) 223-2265

On the last full weekend in August, somewhere between 10,000 and 12,000 people gather in Taber's Confederation Park for the annual Corn Festival. There'll be a midway, and tons of corn. In fact, says a regular, "Anything you can do with a cob of corn, we'll likely do it."

Corn-y events during the festival have included a corn eating contest with a three minute limit, a cornbread making contest, and a chili cookoff, because most people around Taber use corn in their chili. Then there's the corn stuffing contest: how many cobs can you stuff into a pair of coveralls while you're wearing them? The secret is to get a little person into big coveralls. The record is about 200 cobs. A number of growers dump huge loads of corn during the festival, and the attendees are invited to help themselves after the corn stuffing. ⊁

tal, so his honey-tarragon mustard sauce for the beef tenderloin is a touch of home. For dessert, we love the Spanish flan, an upbeat version of crème caramel with a red wine sauce. Yum.

⊘ THINGS TO DO BETWEEN MEALS

Cactus Clay

439 North Railway Street SE, Medicine Hat   Tel: (403) 580-5883

Open Monday–Sunday 10:00 AM–4:00 PM; seasonal closings

    January 10:00 AM–4:00 PM Saturday only

V, MC, DEBIT

Leslie Hirsch's pottery studio and shop is a mini-gallery, and we feel that every good cook should own at least one of her delightful oven-to-table pots, pitchers or casseroles. Eminently useful, her work is also beautiful to touch and to look at.

LETHBRIDGE

Lethbridge Pumpkin Festival   Tel: 1-800-661-1222

When the annual Lethbridge Pumpkin Festival is held in October, pumpkin lovers converge from all over the south. It's a charity event, sponsored by the Green Haven Garden Centre, and it includes a giant pumpkin auction. Seeds are given away in the spring, and plants are babied along all summer, until the week before Thanksgiving.

They sell pumpkin pie by the slice at the festival, but the giant pumpkins, the

ones that run to hundreds of pounds, are too fibrous to make good pies, and are grown strictly to astonish the crowd. "They're not really for eating. We have a live auction, and they'll be bought by local businesses. But we also sell a lot of Halloween-sized pumpkins, the ones you can carve or bake into a pie."

The 2002 local winner weighed in at 529 pounds. But then Kathy Peterson, from Vauxhall, came along with a 650 pound monster. "She got it on the truck with a forklift, and competed in Smoky Lake," says pumpkin fan Diana Greer. Funny thing about those giant pumpkins—sometimes they look a lot bigger than they are. "You never know what it's like on the inside," Diana says. "Not until you get it on the scale. It could be a lightweight."

◎ LETHBRIDGE PANTRY
WHERE GOOD COOKS SHOP
SPECIALTY GROCERS

The Alberta Meat Market
510 6th Avenue S   Tel: (403) 327-3492
Open Tuesday–Saturday 8:30 AM–5:00 PM
CASH ONLY

Ken Crighton's small meat shop is a fourth generation business started by his great-grandfather, George Crighton, way back in the 1920s. He's sad that the small local packer he once dealt with is now history, but he's still able to insist on good AA or AAA Alberta beef.

Simmons Hot Gourmet Products   www.firenbrimstone.com
22 Greenview Close   Tel: (403) 327-9087
Open Monday–Friday 9:00 AM–4:30 PM
V

Now, oh happy day, there's a hot sauce on the market that has layers of flavour—mustard, cucumber, mango—before it hits you with a scorching blast of scotch bonnet peppers backed up with other hot chilies. And it's made right here in Lethbridge. Basil's Fire & Brimestone Hot Gourmet Pepper Sauce is the invention of Basil Simmons, who knows a good hot sauce when he makes one.

The story began long ago and far away, with Simmons' grandmother Matilda, the woman who raised him back in Guyana. She was an expert in hot peppers. "She'd plant them, pick them, grind them, put them in the jar with the mangoes," says Simmons. "She made a wonderful sauce. We do it a little different now, we purée the mango, but the flavour is almost the same." This is the sauce that blasted Simmons into the international food spotlight, when he entered *Chile Pepper* magazine's Fiery Food Challenge in Fort Worth, Texas. Fire & Brimestone walked away with the Best International Hot Sauce award. The famous hot sauce is available in two strengths, colour coded—red for hot, green for mild—at IGA and Sunterra. ✒

"I try to age it for two full weeks, but people like that bright red colour," he says. "A lot of them won't buy it after it starts to darken, which is what happens when it puts on a little age." He specializes in custom-cut steaks and big juicy burger patties made without fillers.

Ken is known for dispensing cooking advice with his product. For the barbecue, he recommends pre-heating it well, then turning it down just as the steaks hit the grill. "But with a roast, a nice baron or a sirloin tip, low and slow is the way to go. When it's done, cover it and let it rest for about ten minutes so the juices get a chance to set. When you carve it, they won't all pour down on your toes. The juice stays in the meat, where you want it."

Bridge Berry Farms
RR 8-12-7

www.bridgeberries.com
Tel: (403) 327-9976

Open summer dawn to dusk, call for hours during the winter
V, MC, DEBIT

The farm grows organic black and red currants, chokecherries (native black cherry), saskatoons, and rhubarb, then processes the fruit into a superb line of jams, spreads, syrups, fruit leathers, pie fillings and juices. Former dairy farmer John Schussler has taken great care in the research and development of these great-tasting products. The fruit is the primary ingredient and there are no fillers, artificial flavours, nor preservatives. We find the syrups to be extremely useful in the kitchen. We love the saskatoon as a glaze for chicken and the black currant syrup is terrific as a pancake syrup or as the base for a game sauce. Look for them at most health food and specialty stores. The farm is a great spot to visit. In season, you can pick your own fruit and drive home with a big basket of luscious, juicy currants.

Sunnyrose Cheese Store
905 3rd Avenue S, Diamond City

Tel: (403) 328-2006

Open Monday–Saturday 9:00 AM–5:30 PM
V, MC, DEBIT

Sandra Vining manages this retail outlet for the cheese factory in the hamlet of Diamond City, about 10 minutes north of Lethbridge. Although you can buy imported cheeses here as well, Vining specializes in the locally made product, as well as jams, jellies, all kinds of condiments, and Zinter Brown's pepperpot jams.

Lethbridge has a large Dutch population, so the local Gouda in its many variations is a big favourite, but the factory also produces cheddar, marble and about a dozen flavours of Monterey jack.

COFFEE SHOPS AND TEA HOUSES

$

The Penny Coffee House

331 5th Street S   Tel: (403) 320-5282

Open Monday–Saturday 7:30 AM–10:01 PM (it's on the door)

    Sunday 9:01 AM–5:01 PM

V, MC, DEBIT

> Penny's is an outstanding coffee house. Order at the counter from the chalkboard menu—hearty soups, fresh, crispy salads and terrific sandwiches, all made with their homemade breads. The deli sandwiches, which are so packed with cold meats that they challenge the average jaw, are terrific, as are the all-veggie sandwiches. Lots of scrumptious cookies—peanut butter, chocolate chip, oatmeal and so forth. The cinnamon rolls are huge, the bottoms richly caramelized, almost candied. Don't leave without one.

CAFÉS, BISTROS, DINERS
AND NEIGHBOURHOOD JOINTS

$$

CoCo Pazzo

1264 3rd Avenue S   Tel: (403) 329-8979

Open Monday–Thursday 11:00 AM–11:00 PM

    Friday, Saturday 11:00 AM–12:00 AM; Sunday 5:00 PM–9:00 PM

V, MC, AE, DEBIT

> Chef Jarrod Gigliotti has been keeping Lethbridge pasta lovers happy for several years. Any of the veal dishes are a good bet. The Portofino is a felicitous marriage of sautéed veal with tiger prawns in sambuca-laced cream. Don't miss Trevi's Own Creation: pan-seared tenderloin with tiger prawns, capers and sliced mushrooms, in a lemony white wine sauce. If there's a secret to CoCo Pazzo's success, it's probably the tomato cream sauce known to devotees as the strascinati. This smooth blend of tomato, cream and Italian herbs is true comfort

food. Try it served with a plate of homemade gnocchi along with sautéed mushrooms and onions. CoCo Pazzo is owned by Tony Rose and the Suriano family, who also have a pasta factory (Let's Pasta) where the wonderful sauce is made in larger quantities and sold as a takeout item. People drive two hours from Calgary just to get their hands on the biggest possible container.

The Saigonese Restaurant

321 13th Street N
Tel: (403) 327-7225 R
Open Monday–Saturday 11:00 AM–10:00 PM
　　　　Sunday 12:00 PM–8:00 PM

$$ V, MC

The decor is minimal, but we don't care—the food's the thing. There are about 80 dishes on this menu, and nine of these are pho, traditional Vietnamese rice noodle soups in a delicate broth with beef, well-done or rare. You could begin with the rice rolls or crisp fried spring rolls, but for something different try the beef salad—thinly sliced beef laced with sweet, dark hoisin, served with iceberg lettuce, bean sprouts and cilantro. The bo saté (charbroiled marinated beef strips) is a spicy but not searingly hot dish, while the tom ga saté (grilled chicken breast and shrimp) has a milder, slightly sweet sauce. For a main course, spicy and mild are sensibly noted on the menu. The rice plates start with a rice base, then there's a choice of pork chops, curry chicken, shredded pork or crabmeat patty. Lots of variety. End with a satisfying glass of Vietnamese iced coffee.

Beantown, Alberta

Bow Island
Tel: (403) 545-6299

When you holiday in Greece, Spain, North Africa or South America, those authentic local bean dishes in quaint cafés could very well be made with Bow Island beans.

This southern Alberta community is a bean lover's paradise, with 55,000 acres of irrigated beans—small red, pinto, pink, great northern and black—and about 300 farmers involved in growing them. It's no wonder the big summer event is the Bow Island Bean Festival, and the town's mascot is a big fuzzy bean.

The beans go directly to Agricore United, Alberta Bean Division, and from there, about 98 per cent of them are exported around the world to 80-odd countries.

"We sell beans here in 10 k or 100 pound bags," says Wendy Keeler, in charge of bean cuisine for Agricore's plant. You can also buy dry beans at Grandma's Pantry in Taber, and local restaurants—Maggie's, Cucci's and Bow Gardens—all make good bean soup.

"You need time to cook with beans," Wendy says. "They're good for you, but they aren't fast food."

The Bean Festival is held in June, and a bean luncheon is served in conjunction with a rodeo. ⇐

Great Northern Roasted Garlic Bean Dip

    1 pound (500 g) dry great northerns, soaked and cooked
    1 cup (250 mL) dry white wine
    2 bulbs garlic, roasted and skinned
    2 bay leaves
    1 3-inch piece of lemon peel
    salt, pepper
    dash of Tabasco
    ½ cup mixed green herbs—cilantro, parsley, chives
    ½ cup (125 mL) extra virgin olive oil

Put drained beans in a pot with wine, roasted garlic, bay leaves, lemon peel, salt, pepper and Tabasco. Simmer for about 30 minutes. Remove bay leaves and lemon.

Cool beans in their liquid. Pour into a food processor and purée until smooth. Taste to correct the salt—it may need more. Stir in mixed herbs and olive oil. Serve on a rimmed plate, surrounded by pita bread and celery sticks for dipping. Serves 8 with pita bread.

BIG NIGHTS, SPLURGES & CELEBRATIONS

$$ **Hugo's**

314 8th Street S   Tel: (403) 320-0117 R

Open Monday–Wednesday 11:30 AM–12:00 AM

    Thursday–Saturday 11:00 AM–2:00 AM

    Sunday 4:00 PM–10:00 PM

V, MC, AE, DEBIT

Hugo's is one of those classic dining rooms that still prepares an excellent Caesar salad. Just the right amount of garlic and a subtle hit of anchovy, with crisp romaine and fresh tasting croutons. The excellent cedar planked salmon is finished with a rosemary-brown sugar glaze that brings out the natural sweetness of the fish. The grilled chicken breast with capicolla and provolone comes with penne. Or try the angel hair pasta with fresh vegetables in a lightly fragrant tomato sauce with herbal undertones. For dessert there's a selection of pies. NOTE: This is a no-minors restaurant, technically classified as a bar because smoking is allowed.

ALBERTA'S FOOD ARTISANS

Scattered across the agricultural landscape of mainstream farmers and ranchers are a number of small growers and producers who are choosing a different path. We've eaten their unique products in restaurants, or bought them in specialty grocery stores, possibly in bulk, or at farmers' markets. Their efforts in bringing to the table everything from wild turkey and Muscovy duck to heirloom tomatoes and lolla rossa lettuce enrich our entire food culture.

We've selected a few of these intrepid entrepreneurs to whet your appetite. You may have to search for their products, or even contact them directly, and it's worth the effort.

Barrhead Custom Meats

4708 62nd Avenue, Barrhead   Tel: (780) 674-3121

Open daily from 6:00 AM–5:00 PM

V, DEBIT

> Dennis and Bonnie Ranger have developed a clever market niche in providing smaller pork racks for restaurants sold under the brand name Novella Dolca. They make an elegant presentation as a single rack or with two racks in a crown roast, or they can be cut into magnificent chops. It truly is a different pork chop, as Dennis contracts with selected producers to raise their hogs outside in the fresh air and feed them a specific diet. The hogs are processed younger and smaller (about 100 pounds less than standard market weight for hogs) resulting in tender, flavourful meat that is then cut to each chef's specifications. Over 70 Alberta restaurants, including Teatro in Calgary and the Hardware Grill in Edmonton, serve this pork.

Bles Wold Dairy

                                     www.bles-wold.com

RR5, Lacombe   Tel: (403) 782-3322

Open Monday–Friday 9:00 AM–12:00 PM, 2:00 PM–6:00 PM

CASH ONLY

> One hour south of Edmonton on Highway 2, just past the Lacombe turnoff, is a small sign for Bles Wold Dairy. If you turn west immediately on to Range Road

27 and continue for 6 kilometres, you'll see an attractive blue clapboard farm-house on your left. You have arrived at the Bos-Eiler family farm, home to the 150 happy Holsteins that produce the milk for Bles Wold Dairy farm yogourt.

The farm is storybook-perfect with friendly dogs, a few curious goats and a barn full of contented cows. Wander over to the tasting room to sample the yogourts. If you're lucky, the Bos-Eiler's charming son Gerard will be available to take you on a brief tour of the operation.

Classic Smokers

www.classicsmokers.ca
5–3320 14th Avenue NE, Calgary   Tel: (403) 235-4531
Open Monday–Friday 8:00 AM–4:00 PM
CASH ONLY

Chris Gaudet runs a family business with his wife, his dad and his grandmother. Formerly a cook at La Chaumiere, where he handled the in-house smoking, Gaudet saw an opportunity for gourmet smoked fish in unique and surprising flavour combinations—tequila-lime, rosehip and lavender (developed for the Rimrock in Banff) and Thai chai, a heady blend of black tea, cardamom, cinnamon and ginger. His cold-smoked rainbow trout is available at The Cookbook Co Cooks and Boyd's Lobster Shop in Calgary.

Grainworks

www.grainworks.com
Vulcan   Tel: (403) 485-2808
Open daily 8:30 AM–5:00 PM
V

Dwayne and Doreen Smith are among the select group of Alberta producers who still farm the original homestead. They were certified organic back in 1986 and they grow a smorgasbord of grains: open-pollinated hard spring wheat, red spring wheat, soft white wheat, triticale, barley, flax, rye, oats, Durum wheat and Polish wheat. A true steward of the land, Dwayne uses crop rotation, under-seeding of clover, and permaculture, all to keep his soil healthy. He also plants shelter belts to conserve soil and encourage wildlife habitat.

The Smiths operate their own custom mill and seed cleaning plant to ensure consistent quality, and market their grains as flakes, flours and cereal mixes. Mighty Fine Flour, their house brand, retains both bran and germ. The Smiths also distribute organic beans, seeds, corn and basmati rice, and their products are generally available at Nutter's across the province, Save-on-Foods and The Big Fresh in Edmonton, and Community Natural Foods in Calgary.

"Farmers are told that in order to be successful, they must embrace new things," says Dwayne. "But we're looking backward, farming the way the first settlers did." And that's the way they like it. The Smiths are currently involved in a proposal to start field trials with heirloom grain varieties.

Hamilton's Barley and Flour
Olds

www.hamiltonsbarley.com
Tel: (403) 556-8493

CASH ONLY

Not to be confused with the chicken-producing Hamiltons, Alex and Donna Hamilton were a pair of city kids (he from Montreal, she from Calgary) who met while attending Olds Agricultural College. The rest, as they say, is history: They fell in love, married, and started farming. But why barley?

"This is barley country," says Donna. "Lots of rain and cool evenings because we're at a fairly high altitude, and barley has been a traditional crop here for years."

The Hamiltons are known for their soft-textured low-gluten barley flour, which is wonderful for muffins, cookies and fruit breads. It can be substituted for up to 25 per cent of the flour in traditional and whole-grain breads. The flour is available at Safeway and the Calgary Co-op stores.

Highwood Crossing Farm
Aldersyde
V

www.highwoodcrossing.com
Tel: (403) 652-1910

JULIE VAN ROSENDAAL

At Highwood, Tony and Penny Marshall produce and bottle cold-pressed organic canola oil and flaxseed oil. Their farm has been in the family for five generations, and Tony wryly observes that their operation might have been more at home in an earlier era. Their mission, to improve their land while producing healthful, chemical-free foods, has paid off. The cold-pressed canola oil is an intense golden-yellow, with an earthy aroma and a distinctive nutty flavour. Chefs use it as they do a top quality extra-virgin olive oil—for dipping bread or vegetables, for drizzling over soup, or in a flavourful salad dressing. Highwood's products are available in health food stores, high-end restaurants and specialty food markets throughout Alberta.

Highwood Crossing's Tony Marshall.

Pinzimonio, Alberta-Style

Here's a dish inspired by the Italian classic, pinzimonio, in which a top quality full-flavoured extra-virgin olive oil becomes a dip for vegetables, with nothing more added than a generous grinding of pepper and sea salt. We find that it translates beautifully with Highwood's distinctively flavoured canola oil. It's a great summer appetizer, especially after a trip to the farmers' market. Any young, fresh vegetable will work well.

Amounts as needed:
  sweet red and yellow bell peppers, sliced
  baby carrots, scrubbed, whole
  baby radishes, red and icicle
  asparagus tips, blanched
  baby cucumbers, scrubbed, quartered
  cherry tomatoes or quartered heirloom tomatoes, any variety

For each person, provide a small glass dish for the oil and a plate for the vegetables. Arrange vegetables in a basket for passing. Pour about 1/4 cup (50 mL) of Highwood Crossing oil into each dish. Season, and pass crusty bread. Delicious!

Hotchkiss Herbs and Produce
Calgary   Tel: (403) 236-8758
CASH ONLY

Here we have the entire salad bowl, certified organic. Consider: 33 varieties of heirloom tomatoes, among which are green, yellow, black, purple, striped and cherry. Hotchkiss, who you might call an artist in the garden, also grows seven colours of chard, a dozen varieties of lettuce, the standard beets plus golden and the delightful chioggia, as well as spinach and the widest variety of herbs we've seen. A big part of his business has become custom growing for quality-conscious chefs. Home orders are available at (403) 371-7230.

Hoven Farms
Eckville   www.hovenfarms.com
V, MC   Tel: 1-800-311-2333

Laurie and Tim Hoven farm with Tim's parents, Cecil and Carole, on land home-steaded in 1908. Today their beef is organic, raised on grass and dry aged for superior flavour and texture. From November until mid-April, the Hovens get together with two other farm families, the vegetable-growing Lunds and the chicken-producing Hamiltons. Twice a month, they set up a market at the

Blackfoot Inn in Calgary. In case you miss ordering, don't worry; Laurie says they always bring a little extra.

Jerry Kitt's First Nature Farms

Goodfare

CASH ONLY

www.firstnaturefarms.ab.ca

Tel: (780) 356-2239

Jerry Kitt is a bit of a pioneer. He believes in the merits of contented livestock, and is most noted for his wild turkeys, which won a gold medal for Team Canada in the world culinary olympics.

At home, his birds, both chickens and turkeys, live in big, moveable outdoor pens. When fresh pasture is needed, he simply moves pen and birds together, quietly and with little disturbance to the birds. "Once they arrive on their new pasture, with a fresh banquet of weeds, grasses, flowers and bugs, they get so happy they make a little noise, like a chuckle," says Jerry. "I call it a cluckle."

He records the contented cluckling so he can play it back to them on the way to market. "It's music to a turkeys ears," he says. Look for his domestic turkeys and chickens at Excel Foods, Planet Organic and Sunterra Lendrum in Edmonton, and they're usually at the Old Strathcona Farmers Market the first Saturday of the month. Community Natural Food and Horizon Meats carry them in Calgary. These birds have intense flavour, shrink very little during roasting, and the leftover carcass makes the world's best turkey soup. The Kitt family won the Alberta SPCA Farmer of the Year Award in 1996. They continue to farm in the Peace Country, and have added beef, bison and eggs to their roster.

Lauriston Highland Farm

Calmar

CASH ONLY

www.lauristonfarm.com

Tel: (780) 985-3863

Victor and Lesley Jackson raise the unique Highland cattle breed on their ranch southwest of Edmonton. Do check out the informative web site explaining their philosophy of raising cattle, information on the breed and buying the beef. This is the only retail source that we are aware of for this high-quality beef—dry-aged, lean, with a high moisture content. It can occasionally be found on the menu at Bricco in Calmar.

Lund's Organic Farm

RR 3, Site 18, Box 7, Innisfail

CASH ONLY

www.lundsorganic.com

Tel: (403) 227-2693

Gert and Betty Lund emigrated to Canada from Denmark in 1981, looking for a different way of life. Although they began as dairy farmers, they became one of Alberta's first certified organic vegetable farmers in 1988. "We grow cold-weather crops," says Gert. "No corn, no cucumbers, no tomatoes. But we do grow fantastic carrots!"

In addition to those delicious carrots, Gert is proud of their short-season tender lettuces, and the wide variety of potatoes, ranging from standard yellows and reds to the more exotic blues and fingerlings. The Lund's vegetables are available at the Sunnyside Market, Amaranth Whole Foods and Community Natural Foods in Calgary year-round, and at the Red Deer and Calgary Blackfoot farmers' markets in the summer. The Lund family participates in the winter market at the Blackfoot Inn along with the Hovens and the Hamiltons. There are plans to be available at more grocery stores across the province and to contract their vegetables to restaurants. But up until now, as Gert says, "There has been more market than crop."

MO-NA Food Enterprises

www.monafood.ca
9320 60th Avenue, Edmonton
Tel: (780) 435-4370
CASH ONLY

MO-NA Food Enterprises began as a happy accident, when Rita and Otto Holzbauer, recent immigrants from Europe, went for a walk in the woods. It was May of 1980, and to their delight and surprise, they discovered many of the same wild mushrooms they'd known and loved back home. They began picking, and timing their harvest with a stopwatch. It was so abundant that they decided to go into business drying and selling the mushrooms. But Agriculture Canada, fearing

Dave Jensen, Taber Corn

In corn season, Dave Jensen works at night. Later, when you and I are sitting down to lunch, he'll think about going to bed. After 18 hours in a cornfield, he could use a little sleep.

Jensen is a Taber corn grower, one of several who at the end of the season spend their nights in a field so their daily quota of cobs can be harvested before sunrise, while it's still cool. "That's what makes the difference here," says Jensen, who's been growing corn for nearly 30 years. "Long hot days, cool nights and lots of water. If it wasn't for irrigation, we wouldn't harvest a single ear of corn."

By the time the reefer is loaded there'll be 650 mesh sacks on board, 5 dozen cobs to a sack, destined for roadside stands all over Alberta. And there'll be no shortage of buyers—the entire province waits for Taber corn. The season usually lasts about six weeks, depending on the first hard frost.

Most of the varieties grown around Taber are of the peaches and cream persuasion, a bi-coloured sugar-enchanced corn bred for extra sweetness. "We're after good tip fill, small kernels, lots of rows. We want it early and sweet, with good flavour and a fresh taste that lasts." He suggests the ultimate test of a cob of corn is to nibble a few kernels raw. " If you like it raw, you'll like it cooked." ✎

mass poisonings from deadly toadstools, was prudently slow, finally giving them the green light three days before Christmas of 1980. They've never looked back.

They have a booth at the Edmonton City and Millwoods farmers' markets and the Sherwood Park market. Today, the Holzbauers ship approximately two dozen varieties of dried wild mushrooms to most of Europe, many parts of Asia and around the province. They keep threatening to retire, but so far it's just an ugly rumour.

Robins Organic Farm
Barrhead

www.organicscanada.com
Tel: (780) 674-5812

CASH ONLY

Scott Robins grows organic green fillet beans (long French beans with superb flavour), broccoli, carrots, Rote Esterling and Yukon Gold potatoes, and red and yellow peppers. His lettuces—arugula, lolla rossa, green leaf, and good peppery mustard greens—are delicious for adding extra flavour to a summer salad.

Most of the seed Robins uses is from last year's crop, proven to grow well on his land and in this challenging climate. Other seed is sourced from certified organic farms and seed houses across North America. Several good restaurants use Robins' produce and he has been custom growing for Ross Munro at the Westin among others. These stellar vegetables can be found at the Big Fresh, Sunterra and from the Good Earth Produce Company in Edmonton.

Sunworks Farm
Armena

sunworks@telusplanet.net
Tel: (780) 672-9799

V, MC, DEBIT

The Hamilton family sells its certified organic pasture-raised meats at farmers' markets in and around Edmonton and Calgary and at the farm gate, as well as supplying chefs in the province. Along with chicken, turkey and the unusual tree-roosting Muscovy duck, they produce eggs, pork and beef. Try the excellent mildly-spiced turkey breakfast sausage. Pasture-raised chicken is lean and flavourful. As the birds are not water-processed, the birds look smaller in the grocery case. Don't be put off, they are meaty and, due to the leanness of the meat, cook very quickly.

Wagyu Canada Quality Marbled Beef
3501 57th Street, Camrose

www.wagyucanada.com
Tel: (780) 672-2990

Patrick and Kimberley McCarthy produce a deliberately marbled beef, a cross-breed from Japanese Wagyu sires and mostly Angus cross females. They call it Kobe-style, after a Japanese beef breed known for its succulence, flavour, exceptional tenderness and (yes) high intra-muscular fat. In Japan, a small serving of this luxury meat in a restaurant costs hundreds of dollars. In Alberta, it's available at the Westin Pradera, the Japanese Village, Eastbound Café and at retail at A Cut Above Deli in Edmonton, at The Belvedere in Calgary and at the Banffshire Club and Eden (Rimrock Hotel) in Banff.

◉ ALBERTA RANCHERS
GENTLE ON THE LAND

Bearded Ladies Buffalo Company www.beardedladiesbuffalo.com
Foremost Tel: (403)867-2094

Way down near Foremost, in the extreme south of the province, Diane and Norm MacKenzie raise bison on 8,000 acres of rare short-grass prairie. This timeless landscape was homestead-ed in 1904 by Norm's grandfather, Murdo MacKenzie.

Every morning before the birds start to sing, the MacKenzies wake to the soft grunts of bison moth-ers with their babies at heel, ambling past the bed-room window. No wonder Diane loves the prairie. The sights and sounds around her have scarcely changed in a century. The bison are once again in harmony with the landscape and the other creatures that have always lived there: coyotes, deer, antelope. Bison use the prairie gently, grazing native grasses in coulees with poetic names like Chin and Etzikom.

> ### Bison Steak on a Kaiser
>
> 1 kaiser roll, split
> 6 oz bison steak (sirloin)
> 1 thinly sliced onion
> handful yellow and red pepper strips
> handful mushrooms, sliced
> 1 tsp (5 mL) butter
> 1 tsp (5 mL) mayonnaise
> 1 small jalapeno, diced
> grated Cheddar or Monterey Jack cheese
>
> Grill steak to medium rare (approximately 3 min-utes per side). Allow to rest 5 minutes for juices to set. Slice thinly, diagonally across the grain. Sauté onion, pepper and mushrooms in butter. Mix may-onnaise with jalapeno and spread on roll. Fill roll with sliced meat, top with sautéed vegetables and sprinkle with cheese. Serves 1.

For Diane, the best part of the day comes later, when they can finally sit down to dinner. "The crickets sing, we watch the sunset, and I think about how lucky we are to live here."

Cooking Bison

Bison is the west's original red meat. The cuts look like beef, but are leaner and need to be handled differently. Familiar names are used: chuck, rib, loin, tenderloin, sirloin, top and bottom round. Cook the cuts from the rib, loin, sirloin and tenderloin with dry heat, and braise or stew hip and chuck cuts. These cuts are eminently suited to marinating.

Because bison has less fat than other red meats, it will cook about one-third faster. It also has 30 per cent less water than beef, so it's important not to overcook it. For more information on bison check out the association web site: www.albertabuffalo.com.

Roasting Bison Meat

For rib, sirloin and tenderloin roasts: season to taste. Place on a rack in a roasting pan without a lid. Cook at a lower temperature (325 F, 160 C) for about 30 minutes per kilogram for medium-rare. Remove from oven when instant-read meat thermometer in centre of roast reaches 140 C; it will continue to cook to another 10 degrees while the juices set. Cook steaks and roasts to rare or medium-rare. For sirloin tip and hip cuts: place roast in preheated 325 F oven (160 C) for 30 minutes uncovered. Add about a cup of water or stock to the pan and reduce heat to 300 F (140 C). Cover and cook for about 30 minutes per kilo. Remove from oven at 300 F (140 C)—it will continue to cook.

Bearded Ladies is primarily a breeding stock company. However, some stock does go to market. Their beef jerky is available at Head-Smashed-In Buffalo Jump and at local grocery stores. Diane is also developing a line of additive-free sausage made by Old Country Sausage in Raymond, south of Lethbridge.

TK Ranch Natural Meats
Coronation
Tel: (403) 857-2404 / 1-888-857-2624

TK Ranch was started in 1956 by Thomas Koehler Biggs, who traded a New York lifestyle for the backcountry of east-central Alberta. Today, TK Ranch guards some of the last virgin fescue in the province. In places you can still see the faint outline of tipi circles.

Other than 700 acres of hay, these grasslands have never seen a plough and, if Dylan and Colleen Biggs have anything to say about it, they never will. They know intensive agriculture doesn't work on fragile prairie. It was tried by the pioneers. Then came the 30s, and the wind. It dried up the exposed soil and blew it away, carrying the hopes and dreams of many families with it.

"The ability of this land to support future generations depends completely on our willingness to sustain it now," says Colleen. That means treating the land gently. "The soil surface must be covered, and the native northern fescue is perfect for that," says Dylan. "We're careful not to overgraze, which would leave bare spots."

The Biggs family philosophy of treading lightly on this land is reflected in what they produce on it: naturally raised beef that has never seen a growth hormone, an antibiotic or a feedlot. "We finish our cattle on the range in the summer instead of sending it to a feed lot. In the winter the animals get lots of hay and a grain supplement," Colleen says.

Humane treatment of animals is also part of their philosophy. Dylan teaches his low-stress handling techniques to cattlemen across North America. "You don't have to yell, you don't have to use stock prods or whips," says Dylan. "These animals aren't pets, but you can read them, and you can get them to go where you want."

TK Ranch Natural Meats products are available at selected Safeway stores in Calgary and Edmonton in the natural foods section, Community Natural Foods in Calgary and Planet Organic Market in both Edmonton and Calgary. All the beef is dry aged a minimum of 21 days.

If It Ain't Alberta, It Ain't Beef

To Albertans, beef is more than a great barbecue item. It's part of our history. It has become a cultural icon, involving cowboys around the campfire, roundups at branding time, the bawling of a calf separated from its mama. It speaks of hard work and heartbreak, cattle drives and stampedes, foothills and parkland, and (if someone has a guitar) ghost riders in the sky.

The beef industry in Alberta may be part legend, but it also represents the biggest chunk of our agriculture industry, which is second only to petroleum. Today, Alberta beef is the benchmark against which other beef is judged. While 17 per cent of what we produce is consumed right here in the province, 24 per cent is sold to Quebec, the United States takes 28 per cent, and 29 per cent goes to the rest of Canada. Two per cent is shipped overseas.

For many restaurants, beef is the signature dish. Such a place is Tom Goodchild's Moose Factory and his Sawmill group of restaurants in Edmonton, where they serve 110 tonnes of prime cuts in a year. Small wonder that Goodchild and his crew recently received the Alberta Cattle Commission Restaurant of the Year award.

"We sell about 40,000 steaks a month at four restaurants in Edmonton," says Len McCullough, director of operations. "New York, sirloin, filet mignon, prime rib. And it's all Alberta AAA grain-fed beef, aged 28 days."

For beef lovers in Alberta, it doesn't get any better than that. ✑

Beef Tenderloin with Toasted Spice Rub and Garlic Chutney Sauce

This deliciously simple tenderloin comes from Carol Corneau, sous chef at Gourmet Goodies Catering in Edmonton. The recipe is used with permission from the Alberta Cattle Commission.

2 lbs (1 kg) prepared beef tenderloin
¼ cup (50 mL) fennel seeds
¼ cup (50 mL) whole cumin seeds
2 cinnamon sticks
¼ cup (50mL) black peppercorns, coarsely crushed
2 tbsps (30mL) granulated garlic (see note)
canola oil

Crush fennel, cumin and cinnamon into fine pieces, but do not powder. In a heavy pan over medium heat, toast spices until aromatic and slightly coloured (2–5 minutes). Remove from heat and add crushed peppercorns and granulated garlic. Cool, then pound slightly in mortar. Spread onto cookie sheet. Coat tenderloin in oil and roll in spice rub to completely coat. Cover and refrigerate overnight. Barbecue over medium heat until desired doneness, about 10 minutes for each inch of thickness for medium rare. Let rest approximately 10 minutes before carving. To serve, slice across the grain. Serve with garlic chutney sauce and grilled leeks.

NOTE: Use granulated garlic as opposed to fresh garlic, as fresh garlic has a tendency to burn easily on the barbecue. Granulated garlic can be found in the bulk section of Save-On-Foods.

GARLIC CHUTNEY SAUCE

¼ cup (50mL) mango chutney (we used Major Grey)
juice of 1 lemon and 1 lime
¼ cup (50mL) water
¼ cup (50mL) white wine
4 cloves garlic, crushed
1 tbsp (15 mL) fresh cilantro, chopped
1 small jalapeno, chopped
½ cup (125mL) canola oil

In food processor, mix all ingredients except oil. Slowly drizzle in oil to thicken sauce. Serves 6.

Canadians are fond of complaining about the state of our cheese. Now that we've processed it, coloured it, sliced, diced, liquified and extruded it, all in the name of convenience, there's something missing. The taste, we mutter. Where's the taste?

Fortunately, there are still some cheesemakers who care deeply about the taste of a handmade, patiently aged cheese. Even better, some of them are in central Alberta, where artisan cheese makers are returning to those traditional methods and reaping the rewards: gold medals and happy customers.

Leoni-Grana www.leonigrana.com
Round Hill Tel: (780) 672-1698
4304 52nd Street, Camrose

Emanuela Leoni's cheese is about 30 per cent milk, 70 per cent hard work. Her cheese is an artisan recipe, used in Italy for seven centuries. It takes a whole day to make 8 wheels, with 250 litres of milk in each 15-kilogram cheese.

Taste a big pale wheel and it will remind you of young Italian granas, nutty, with a mild flavour that holds the promise of greater intensity as it ages. The similarity is no accident. Leoni came to Canada from the dairy-rich Po Valley in Italy, home of the famous Parmigiano-Reggiano cheese.

"I wasn't sure Alberta milk or Alberta air were right for grana," Leoni says. So she embarked on a formidable project, making trial cheeses with 15 different farms and sampling them after one, two and three years. Near Round Hill, she found the ideal dairy farm with a large herd of pampered Holsteins.

"In the late spring when the grass is new and freshly green, I make my cheese. I use fresh morning and evening milk. The cows are right here, which eliminates transporting and pumping. This means no foaming. And that's a good thing, because foaming stresses the milk. Also, we de-cream to 1.8 per cent, using gravity, not centrifuge."

In her spotless white boots and crisp lab coat, she's all science. But, like fellow cheese maker Virginia Saputo of Natricia, she combines science with art and passion. Cheesemaking is a fussy business, subject to the whims of nature, and each step takes concentration. Most of the time you'll hear Leoni's favourite country and western music playing in the dairy, but not during the making of the cheese. "Everybody has to focus, every minute. Things can go wrong. I can't allow distractions."

In the aging room, each cheese is dated and stamped with the name Leoni-Grana and (she's proud of this) a maple leaf.

Grana is extremely low in lactose, found in the whey, 98 per cent of which is drained off. Thus, lactose-intolerant people can often eat Leoni's cheese with no ill effects. It's also 33 per cent protein and only 28 per cent fat, which makes it leaner than most cheese.

Natricia Dairy   www.natricia.com

5710–49th Street, Ponoka   Tel: (403) 783-8945

Open Monday–Friday 9:00 AM–5:00 PM

Saturday 10:00 AM–2:00 PM

Like Emanuela Leoni, Virginia Saputo knows that cheesemaking is part science (witness the high-tech factory and adjoining lab), part art.

Virginia is passionate about the quality of her cheeses: the ash-rolled Pyramide, the St. Maure, the surface-ripened Cabecou, the petit Crottin de Chavignol, the fresh chèvre. They ship most of their production to eager clients in New York, Montreal, Toronto and Los Angeles.

Goat cheese is traditionally sold by age, growing more expensive, flavourful and aromatic as time passes. Although it takes a connoisseur to appreciate the whiff and tang of an aging goat cheese (joyfully referred to by cheese lovers as smelly), it only grows more delectable as the outside crust begins to show some age and the inside turns runny and golden, with a liquid layer around the buttery centre.

"I babysit my cheese," says Saputo. She worries that some people fear goat cheese because they think it has a strong, goaty flavour. "If you can taste goat, it's poor-quality milk," she stresses. "You won't taste goat in any of our cheeses."

Goat milk is about 4 per cent butterfat, skimmed to 2 per cent for cheese. It's high in vitamins A and C, calcium and iron, lower in cholesterol than many cheeses and easily digested.

Sylvan Star Gouda   sylvanstar@telusplanet.net

RR 1, Red Deer   Tel: (403) 340-1560

Take Sylvan Lake turnoff west from Highway 2

Open Monday–Saturday 11:00 AM–6:00 PM

John and Janny Schalkwyk are champion cheesemakers. Their 18-month-old gouda won the top prize, a gold medal in the prestigious Grand Prix of Cheese, sponsored by Dairy Farmers of Canada.

They make cheese every second day, year-round, starting at 4:00 AM.

They've always done it this way; it's a family craft, a traditional method learned in the Netherlands. "I can feel when the cheese is ready and it's time to go into the moulds," John says.

If you've ever wondered why cheese costs what it does, the following look at the cheesemaking procedure should help explain. To begin, 12 litres of milk go into every kilogram of cheese. Each wheel of cheese must be brined, pressed, brushed and turned frequently during the ripening. Then John hand-coats it with five layers of food-grade wax to protect it from moulds and dirt. Finally it goes to the aging room, John's cathedral of cheese, where row upon row of golden wheels are stacked ceiling-high. After that it takes six months of aging for a mild cheese, 18 months for his prize-winning gouda.

John's aging room is humidity controlled because Alberta's climate can dry the cheese too fast. (As a cheese ages, it loses weight. In one year, a cheese will shrink 20 per cent.) And what about that gold medal? "I know I make good cheese, but it's better when the competition says so."

Good cooks need good tools, and these dedicated food lovers have chosen to turn their talents to pots and pans.

Where do you look for a krumkakker? Where to find six different potato peelers under one roof? Or the newest high-tech pan from space-age materials?

Every big name in cookware is available at these stores. As well, Italian, French and Spanish ceramics, English china, plus art-quality pottery and glassware by local artisans. It's a feast. Check out these stores—our favourites—while you're on the trail.

ALONG THE COWBOY TRAIL

Pots 'n' Peppers
212 1st Street W, Cochrane   Tel: (403) 932-1175
Open Monday–Saturday 10:00 AM–6:00 PM
      Sunday 11:00 AM–5:00 PM
V, MC, DEBIT

Pots 'n' Peppers is reason enough to go to Cochrane. This store has fun with the cowboy theme, befitting Cochrane's image as a bastion of the old West. Need a

cowboy dishtowel? This is the place. But this is no tacky souvenir shop. Its western theme is carried through the hand-thrown pottery by Brushworks, made by two Calgary sisters. Lots of heavy equipment for serious cooks— all lines of All Clad cookware, Kitchen Aid mixers in a rainbow of colours. Cookbooks, condiments and teas round out the selection.

The Compleat Cook

Bankers Hall   Tel: (403) 264-0449

Open Monday–Wednesday 10:00 AM–6:00 PM

    Thursday, Friday 10:00–8:00 PM; Saturday 10:00 AM–5:30 PM

V, MC, AE, DEBIT

Diane Ferguson and Linda Hayes say their long-time staff are the soul of their business. "We call ourselves the old girls. Customers like dealing with people they know, and we do know our stuff," says Diane. "We're all serious cooks."

The Compleat Cook is far more than a gadget store, and it has real depth in every category. Who else would carry six different potato peelers? We found the full line of Portmeirion and the Spring line of aluminium cookware from Switzerland, along with an extensive linen selection. The stores (additional locations in Dalhousie Station and Willow Park as well) are gorgeous.

The Cookbook Co Cooks

                                      www.cookbookcooks.com

732 11th Avenue SW   Tel: (403) 265-6066

Open Monday–Friday 10:00 AM–8:00 PM

    Saturday 10:00 AM–5:30 PM; Sunday 12:00 PM–5:00 PM

V, MC, ENR, AE, DEBIT

People come from across the province to take classes with the Cookbook Co's intriguing mix of celebrity chefs. We're talking big names: Donna Hay, Jeffrey Alford, Caprial Spence. The format is a demo followed by a convivial dinner. Other classes feature accomplished local culinary celebrities such as personal chef Karen Miller, Italian cuisine aficionado Alsan Shewchuk and 'cue devotee Kathy Richardier. You can learn to make Brazilian tapas, stuff a sausage, or grill in a southwestern style, all in the downstairs kitchen.

Evening and specialty classes are available, along with the ongoing specialty dinners. They have an excellent newsletter—ask to be put on the list.

The Happy Cooker

Strathcona Square   Tel: (403) 242-6788

Open Monday–Wednesday, Saturday 10:00–6:00 PM

    Thursday, Friday 10:00 AM–8:00 PM

    Sunday 12:00 PM–5:00 PM

V, MC, AE, DEBIT

Other locations in Glenmore Landing and Market Mall. These are technical kitchen stores—no dishes, no tabletop items like placemats and napkin rings but

Gail Norton
The Cookbook Co Cooks

Calgary is home to one of the most unusual cookbook stores. It's also a catering company, a cooking school, a source of specialty ingredients and a destination for chefs from across

North America. Gail Norton's Cookbook Co has become a heady mix of retail and food events.

Gail and her mother Jean opened a cookbook store on the second floor of an old house on 17th Avenue in 1984. Five years later, they grew into a slightly larger space in Mount Royal village, an upscale shopping centre. Needing more room to cater, to teach and to have a special place for cookbook authors to come and cook, they moved again in 1996.

That's when the fun began. While they were at it, why not sell a little cheese and some exotic, hard-to-find ingredients? Maybe someone could sell wine in the back. And they'd need a little bread. The result was the Building Bloc, where they now share space with Metrovino and Brûlée Patisserie—an inspired mix.

The cookbook selection is still the best in town, from local interest food books to professional tomes and best-sellers. Downstairs is a large professional kitchen that holds 24 for classes and 42 for the frequent specialty dinners, cooked by star chefs and cookbook authors. ✍

lots of serious equipment. Of note is the state-of-the-art Scan Pan 2001, tough non-stick pans made in Denmark. Made of pressure-cast aluminum with a titanium ceramic coating, they are extremely durable. Maguerite McVicar offers cooking classes at the Glenmore Landing store to introduce customers to new flavours and new equipment. A typical lineup might include Thai and Mexican cooking fondues and hors d'oeuvres.

Italian Centre

824 1st Avenue NE
Tel: (403) 263-5535
Open Monday–Saturday 9:00 AM –6:00 PM
V, MC, AE, DEBIT

> A good place for authentic Italian kitchen essentials—pasta machines, espresso makers, gorgeous hand-painted platters, bowls and jugs.

Kilian

www.kilian.ca
1110 Kensington Road NW
Tel: (403) 270-8800
Open Monday–Wednesday 10:00 AM–6:00 PM
    Thursday 10:00 AM–8:30 PM
    Friday 10:00 AM–6:00 PM
    Saturday 10:00 AM–5:30 PM
A, MC, AE, DEBIT

> Brothers Frank and Gunnar Kilian believe in the basic principle of good design: form follows function. Their big, beautiful store is an homage to modern design, where you'll find the latest in espresso machines by Frances Ford, the super-trendy Dualit toaster, everything by Alessi and the Danish masters of design, including Danesco kitchen products. They love Silga cookware from Italy—excellent value. Look for the professional mandolines from France, and Global knives.

Scuola di Cucina

809 1st Avenue NE (Above Italian Gourmet Foods)   www.merlogourmet.com   Tel: (403) 263-6996
Open September–November, January–June sessions

> Peter Beluschi teaches classic Italian cooking techniques to groups no larger than 16. His classes are fun and very popular—he has a following. Don't delay in booking, these highly entertaining classes are well-priced and fill quickly.

Southern Alberta Institute of Technology (SAIT)

1301 16th Avenue NW   Tel: (403) 284-8615
V, MC, DEBIT

> The professional course is an accelerated 12-month program. Students then go on to an apprenticeship, followed by the red seal diploma exam, after which they can call themselves chefs. Part of the training involves working in SAIT's

Highwood Dining Room. SAIT also offers courses for non-professional enthusiasts to bone up on everything from sushi to artisan breads. Call for information and the most recent calendar.

ON THE ROCKY MOUNTAIN HERITAGE TRAIL

Colorful Cook

721 8th Street (Shaman Lane), Canmore　　　　　　　Tel: (403) 678-3922
Open Monday–Thursday, Saturday 10:00 AM–6:00 PM
　　Friday 10:00–9:00 PM; Sunday 11:00 AM–5:00 PM
V, MC, AE, DEBIT

"Kitchenware is a lot like fashion. There are classics, and there are fads, and we carry both," says Julia Phillips, owner of this delightful store tucked just off Canmore's main street. The store has quality in every price range. Highlights include cooking accessories that we think are mountain necessities: Swissmar raclette pans and cast iron fondue pots by Frontignac that weigh a ton and cook beautifully. There's a large and varied selection of glassware.

Jasper Rock and Jade

620A Connaught Drive, Jasper　　　　　　　Tel: (780) 852-3631
Open summer daily 10:00 AM–9:00 PM
Open winter daily 10:00 AM–6:00 PM
V, MC, AE, DEBIT

Honey pots, casseroles, teapots from local potter Louise Maguire—this is beautiful giftware of a culinary nature. The store sells Danesco fondue pots, Good Grips gadgets and the well-made Zyliss kitchen tools. It's a handy place to know about when the can opener doesn't make it into the camping gear.

EDMONTON

Bosch Kitchen Centre　　　　　　　www.bosch-kitchen.com

9766 51st Avenue　　　　　　　Tel: (780) 437-3134
Open Monday–Wednesday, Friday 9:00 AM–5:00 PM
　　Thursday 9:00 AM–8:00 PM; Saturday 10:00 AM–5:00 PM
V, MC, AE, DEBIT

This is serious European cookware. Bosch professional-quality kitchen equipment includes the fabulous Kitchen Centre with its multiple options and attachments, plus mixers, grain mills, American Harvest dehydrators, pressure cookers, Henckels knives and useful gadgets. Bosch also has bakeware from Wilton in every size and shape under the sun as well as the raw materials—grains and chocolate supplies.

Demonstration cooking classes are free if you're buying equipment; $10 per class for non-buyers.

Call the Kettle Black

www.kettle.ab.ca
12523 102nd Avenue
Tel: (780) 448-2861
Open Monday–Wednesday, Friday,
    Saturday 10:00 AM–5:30 PM
    Thursday 10:00 AM–8:00 PM
    Sunday 12:00 PM–4:00 PM
V, MC, DEBIT

Darcy Kaser's shop focuses on high-end, semi professional cookware, including the trendy new Emeril line from All Clad. He's fond of small appliances and has a big selection of everything from toasters and juicers to state-of-the-art food processors, plus a lot of practical bakeware. Kaser also carries the colourful Emile Henri line and other gorgeous things for tablescapes: glassware, handsome platters and bar accessories.

G Dennis & Co

10746 82nd (Whyte) Avenue
Tel: (780) 438-4117
Open Monday–Wednesday, Friday
    Saturday 10:00 AM–5:30 PM
    Thursday 10:00 AM–8:00 PM
    Sunday 12:00 PM–5:00 PM
V, MC, AE, DEBIT

The shop hums with activity. In the demon-

Gail Hall
Caterer Par Excellence

When there's a big party in the offing in Edmonton, Gail Hall's name is certain to come up. Her award-winning catering company, Gourmet Goodies, started small, when Hall left a career in social services to do what she really loved: cook and entertain congenial people.

These days she has no time to cook, and little time to entertain. The company has grown by leaps and bounds. "The most important thing I've learned in this business is to focus on what the customer wants," she says. "That's why we grew as a company, so we could meet customer expectations. Not just food, but the total picture."

Hall actively supports the culinary scene in Edmonton and is quick to offer apprenticeship and employment opportunities to cooking school grads. She's the past chair of Cuisine Canada, a national organization of food professionals dedicated to recognizing and promoting Canadian food.

One of Hall's new directions is an annual culinary tour to a food destination. She's done Santa Fe, New York and Italy. And now there is a chic little takeout store, Gourmet Goodies To Go, in the same building, offering everything for tonight's dinner, oven-ready specials that change daily, plus baked goods, chocolates, condiments, frozen stocks, and sauces. Good place to compose a wonderful gift basket. ✍

stration kitchen, 12 people can enjoy a convivial session with local chefs, learning the secrets of Cajun cooking, artisan bread, Thai food, hors d'oeuvres and so forth. Ask to be put on the mailing list. Schedules change quarterly and classes fill up fast.

In the retail area, you'll find open-stock Bopla dishes from Switzerland, Global knives and every size of whisk imaginable. The Henckels man holds occasional knife-sharpening clinics, and on most Saturdays from 12:00 PM to 3:00 PM there are cooking demonstrations.

Gourmet Goodies

10665 109th Street

Open Monday–Saturday 8:30 AM–5:00 PM

V, MC, AE

www.gourmetgoodies.ab.ca

Tel: (780) 438-1234

Gail Hall's big catering kitchen makes an ideal spot for hands-on cooking classes, which she has offered since 1988. Classes range from culinary fundamentals to preparing a four-course Provençal dinner. Or get a group of friends together and book a private class.

Le Gnome

1814 West Edmonton Mall

Open Monday–Friday 10:00 AM–9:00 PM; Saturday 10:00 AM–6:00 PM

    Sunday 12:00 PM–6:00 PM

V, MC, AE, DEBIT

Tel: (780) 444-1137

A one-stop shop for kitchen equipment enthusiasts. The baking section alone could be a single store. Staff knowledge is encyclopedic when it comes to cooking and cooks' tools, everything from a small-dollar gadget to the highest-end professional cookware. Le Gnome has one of the best selections in all of Canada. Owner Pnina Staav stocks special items for each season: cookie presses and seed grinders at Christmas, gravy separators at Thanksgiving. Tableware lines include Denby and Portmeirion, all in open stock. The store stocks the complete line of Rosle from Switzerland and Emile Henri from France, as well as Good Grips gadgets, Henckels cast iron cookware, Cuisinart cookware and All Clad.

Northern Alberta Institute of Technology (NAIT)

www.nait.ab.ca/culinary/dining/index.htm

11762 106th Street   Tel: (780) 471-7655

NAIT offers a two-year professional culinary arts program. Following the completion of the required apprenticeship, fledgling chefs are eligible to write the red seal exam. Working in NAIT's full-service dining room is part of the program.

Under the outstanding mentorship of people like the late John Butler, Canadian culinary team alumni Nigel Webber and Vinod Varshney, who now heads the program, this school offers some of the best professional training in Canada, and produces outstanding graduates.

There are 40-odd non-credit classes offered to the general public, in topics as diverse as cake decorating, bartending and meat cutting.

Zenari's

10180 101st Street (Manulife Place)

Tel: (780) 423-5409

Open Monday–Wednesday 7:00 AM–6:30 PM
　　　Thursday and Friday 7:00 AM–9:30 PM
　　　Saturday 9:00 AM–5:30 PM

V, MC, AE, ENR

Most people come here for the early morning lattes and deli lunches, but Adriano Zenari also carries beautiful up-market Italian ceramics—platters, pitchers, tureens, art-quality espresso pots—and hand-blown containers for balsamic vinegars. There is a small selection of very good cookware and lots of quality gadgets. At the other side of the deli you'll find a veritable pantry of gourmet items including sauces, oils, balsamic vinegars and luxury condiments.

Prairie Pedlar

5018 39th Street, Lloydminster   Tel: (780) 875-0370
Open Monday–Friday 9:00 AM–6:00 PM
    Saturday 10:00 AM–5:30 PM
V, MC, DEBIT

> Although not strictly a cookware shop, owner Janice Lorenz chooses her stock
> with a lot of care. She always offers a strong line of Danesco among the custom
> draperies and decorative accessories. Henckels products are well represented.

◉ PEACE COUNTRY

Kettles and Company

603 Prairie Plaza, Grande Prairie   Tel: (780) 532-4049
Open Monday–Wednesday, Saturday 9:30 AM–6:00 PM
    Thursday, Friday 9:30 AM–9:00 PM
    Sunday 12:00 PM–5:00 PM
V, MC, DEBIT

> Henckels cast iron, Emile Henri cast and enamel cookware from France, and
> Cuisinart cookware from France. Look around, and you'll find odd treasures like
> poppyseed grinders and krumkakker irons.

◉ CENTRAL ALBERTA

Culinary and Gift Shoppe

5017 50th Avenue (Main Street), Lacombe   Tel: (403) 782-1682
Open Monday–Saturday 9:30 AM–5:30 PM
V, MC, DEBIT

> Here's a moderately sized kitchen store that packs in a full line of almost every-
> thing an enthusiastic cook could want: Cole and Mason pepper grinders, beauti-
> ful Emile Henri, the Danesco line and Tramontina knives.
>
> They also handle our favourite hot sauce, Basil's Fire and Brimestone from
> Lethbridge. Store owners Blaine and Helen Lee used this sauce to make their
> super-hot chili, which won first prize at a recent Lacombe Days chili cook-off.

Rosewood

103A–4900 Molly Banister Drive   Tel: (403) 346-5919
Bower Place Shopping Centre, Red Deer
Open Monday–Friday 9:30 AM–9:00 PM; Saturday 9:30 AM–6:00 PM
      Sunday 11:00 AM–5:00 PM
V, MC, DEBIT

> Darlene Friesen's mid-sized store carries many
> gadgets—garlic presses, potato peelers, pickle
> forks, you name it—along with a big selection
> of beautiful dishes from Fitz and Floyd and
> Portmeirion. She also stocks Henckels and All
> Clad cookware, and a fun, casual line of linens.

ON THE DINO TRAIL

Jungling Works

299 1st Street W, Drumheller
Tel: (403) 823-2208
Open Monday–Saturday 10:00 AM–5:00 PM
      Sunday 12:00 PM–4:00 PM
V, MC, DEBIT

> Talk about atmosphere. Jungling Works occu-
> pies the main floor of the original Drumheller
> Bakery, and some things haven't changed since
> the building went up in 1920. Selection ranges
> from gourmet oils and vinegar to Kootenay

Forge fireplace tools and the essential wiener cooker. Proprietors Debra Jungling
and David Carter live above the store with the winsome shop dog, Cuddles.

THE CONDIMENT QUEENS

Remember Grandma's green tomato relish? Sweet, spicy and toothsome, it was her way of using up the last of a bumper crop when the weather closed in early.

Today, few of us have the time or skill to recreate Grandma's favourite chili sauce, but we'd still love to eat it with our eggs. Those wonderful condiments that appeared on so many tables and at so many farm fairs have changed over the years, evolving from catsup to chutney, to salsas and hot sauce.

In Alberta, creative cooks have turned treasured family recipes into cottage industries. Their products are often available for a short time, in limited quantities, at farmers' markets, on specialty shelves or directly from the producer. They're worth the search. The Leduc Food Processing Development Centre, brainchild of Alberta Agriculture, has been crucial to the success of many condiment makers, including Palette Fine Foods and Zinter Brown, among others.

MacFarlane's Farm Fresh Preserves, Lyalta   macfarlanejam@yahoo.ca
Several years ago, Sharon MacFarlane started making preserves—syrups, mustards, pickles, jams and jellies—to sell at the local farmers' market. Every Saturday, she sold out.

Her dilled beans had just the right amount of dill and crunch. The horseradish jelly, her unique recipe, had texture and not too much heat. The horseradish jelly came out of experiments to find a replacement for jalapeno jelly. "Everybody was making that. The horseradish jelly isn't easy," she says. "The fumes bring tears to your eyes."

Meanwhile, Sharon continues to fill 20,000 jars every year: dilled baby corn, bartender's onions, dilled sugar peas, dilled okra, Grandma's chili sauce and several dozen other jams, jellies and mustards. They're available at the Millarville farmers' market, specialty food stores and craft shows across the province, and at the Treasure Barrel in Edmonton, as well as by mail order.

Zinter Brown Taste Treats, Edmonton   www.zinterbrown.ab.ca
Joanne Zinter has always loved making condiments. Her business started with a couple

of favourite home recipes for antipasto and jalapeno jelly. After that came orange brandied cranberries. She began selling her wares at farmers' markets, but didn't stop there. Many new flavours and fusions were on the burner: peachy mango chutney, her award-winning roasted garlic and onion jam, the roasted garlic pepper pot, the raspberry pepper pot.

In order to make large amounts that could be bottled and sold at retail, Joanne tested the recipes in her own kitchen, working up to a commercial batch of 1,200 small jars, with the help of the Food Processing Development Centre in Leduc. Today she makes 15 different products, filling 60,000 jars a year, and is distributed throughout North America. Available at Zenari's in Edmonton and the Cookbook Co Cooks in Calgary.

Sultana Ali, Edmonton   masala@telusplanet.net

In 1996, Fijian-born Naazima Ali teamed up with husband Tim Marsh to develop a commercial version of her mom's favourite masala, an aromatic spice mixture traditionally used in East Asian and Indian cooking.

Building on the belief that families no longer have time to search out the best-quality ingredients, roast and grind their own spices and put them together, Sultana Ali does it for them.

The product, marketed as Homemade Magic Curry Powder, is redolent of bay leaves, curry leaves, fennel and turmeric. She also has a splendid apple chutney called the Awesome Apple Chutney, available in mild and hot.

All the labels include the intriguing phrase "remind my belly of old New Delhi." Sultana Ali products are available at The Cookbook Co in Calgary and at G Dennis & Co in Edmonton, among others.

Palette Fine Foods, Calgary   www.palettefinefoods.com

Calgarian Marnie Fudge has deep roots in food. She founded the specialty produce business, the Basil Ranch, several years ago, then moved on to create Palette Fine Foods, which debuted in 2001 with a line of eight rubs, jams, jellies and honeys.

Alberta honey is cleverly paired with star anise (amazing on duck), lavender or chili in three excellent combinations. The purple basil jelly makes cream cheese taste like a party and it's even better with Natricia Dairy's ash-ripened St. Maure goat cheese. The golden raspberry jam has the distinct yin/yang sweetness/tanginess of the berry picked at its peak ripeness.

The Palette products are available at Caban stores across the country, Sunterra in both Edmonton and Calgary, Urban Fare in Edmonton and Cornucopia market, Cookbook Co, Wrayton's and Janice Beaton Fine Cheese in Calgary.

WINE AND BEER

PRIVATIZATION
ALBERTA'S LIQUOR STORES
GO MAINSTREAM

Buying beer and wine in Alberta used to be so simple. Just trot on down to the vendor's, pay with cash and bring it on home in a plain brown bag.

In the mid-'80s, a limited form of privatization was legislated, bringing into being 13 private stores across the province, able to source wines directly from producers as opposed to having to use an agent. By 1991, the number of stores had grown to 30. They had a narrow mandate: wine only, no restaurant sales and no selling below the government markup. However, store owners did have freedom within their licenses to source new wines previously unknown to Albertans.

Most of these early licensees took the opportunity to become authorities on wine in their own communities. They began offering courses, tastings and wine-purchase plans. In the mid-'90s, the government brought in a flat tax on wines and spirits, sold off their own stores and leased out the massive St. Albert warehouse. The government got out of the physical distribution of wine, but still controls it through regulations concerning importation, sales and licensing. A few of those original wine stores (now known as the G6) were able to maintain their relationships with producers and buy in small quantities without using an agent/distributor.

Today we can say the program has been a success, certainly for the Alberta taxpayer. Tax revenues from wines and spirits have kept pace with consumption, and the government is out of the costly business of stocking and retailing alcoholic products. Alberta is now considered to be one of the most open markets in the world and producers flock to it. There are now over 700 stores in the province. They range from local mini-mart style stores—tiny in size, with limited selection and no product knowledge—to major stores that take the business and the romance of wine very seriously indeed.

We think the following are worthy of a visit.

Eau Claire Wine Market

Open Monday–Friday 10:00 AM–9:00 PM   Tel: (403) 262-9463

     Saturday 10:00 AM–6:30 PM; Sunday 10:00 AM–5:30 PM

V, MC, AE, DEBIT

Chock full of well-chosen wines! There's a strong emphasis on value and a good, solid selection of everyday wines, though collectors will certainly find enough to interest them. The selection of Canadian VQA includes several wines from Burrowing Owl, Quail's Gate, Cedarcreek, Sumac Ridge and Tinhorn Creek, stellar BC producers. Check out the Spanish selections ranging from under $10 to vintage Gran Riservas.

J Webb Wine Merchant   www.jwebb.net

C157–1600 90th Avenue SW (Glenmore Landing)   Tel: (403) 253-9463

Open Monday–Friday 10:00 AM–9:00 PM

     Saturday 10:00 AM–6:00 PM; Sunday 11:00 AM–5:00 PM

V, MC, DEBIT

This is a well-established wine shop with a strong French, Italian and US selection. Check out the intriguing stock of wines from Argentina, Portugal and Spain, such as the producers Ochoa and Guelbenzo in the Navarra region. There is a quarterly newsletter and an extensive web site. The store carries spirits, beer, ports and sherries as well.

Kensington Wine Market

www.kensingtonwinemarket.com

1257 Kensington Road NW

Tel: (403) 283 8000

Open Monday–Wednesday, Saturday 10:00 AM–8:00 PM

     Thursday, Friday 10:00 AM–9:00 PM

     Sunday 12:00 PM–6:00 PM

V, MC, AE, DEBIT

Owners Nancy Carten and Richard Lindseth carry an eclectic selection in all price ranges. The store has a strong focus on wine education, with classes offered throughout the year. They also teach wine classes for the Calgary Board of Education. Kensington's strengths are in Bordeaux, New World wines and what the wine trade calls cult wines from

JULIE VAN ROSENDAAL

the United States. These very expensive small production wines can have the wine lovers affectionately known as wine geeks frothing at the mouth. Pay them no mind, they're just exercising their palates.

Scotch lovers can choose from over 100 single malt scotches. This extensive selection earned Kensington Wine Market a listing in the *Malt Advocate* as having one of the best single malt selections in the world.

Merlo Vinoteca

813 1st Avenue NE

Open Tuesday–Friday 10:00 AM–6:00 PM
    Saturday 10:00 AM–5:30 PM

V, MC, AE, ENR, DEBIT

www.merlogourmet.com
Tel: (403) 269-1338

Franca and Peter Beluschi source rare and wonderful Italian wine. Have a serious look at Chiantis including bottlings from Fontodi, and Enzo Baglietti, a Barolo producer who makes single-vineyard, modern-style, fruit-forward Dolcettos and Barbarescos. Excellent selection of grappa.

MetroVino

722 11th Avenue SW

Open Monday–Friday 10:00 AM–8:00 PM
    Saturday 10:00 AM–5:30 PM
    Sunday 12:00 PM–5:00 PM

V, MC, AE, DEBIT

www.metrovino.com
Tel: (403) 205-3356

This is a happy place for intrepid lovers of food and wine. It's a well-designed shop in the back of The Cookbook Co. (You can also reach it off the alley to the north of the building.) The atmosphere is relaxed and the passion for wine is evident in the selections. Of note: French, especially from the south and other lesser-known regions. American choices are strong in zinfandel, sangiovese and syrah. The proximity of MetroVino to the Cookbook Co leads to some interesting cross promotion of the which-wine-with-which-cheese sort.

The store reflects its idiosyncratic owner, Richard Harvey, often seen in a beret betraying his status as a dyed-in-the-wool Francophile. Richard teaches the international sommelier guild courses in both Edmonton and Calgary. At the end of

Miles of wine at MetroVino.

term we imagine him bussing newly minted sommeliers on both downy cheeks, adjusting their crisp new berets to a jaunty angle while exhorting: "Go forth and taste! Remember, rosé is not just white zinfandel!"

Willow Park Wines & Spirits

www.winealberta.com

10801 Bonaventure Drive SE

Tel: (403) 296-1640

Open Monday, Tuesday 10:00 AM–11:00 PM

 Wednesday, Thursday 10:00 AM–12:00 AM

 Friday, Saturday 10:00 AM–1:00 AM

 Sundays and holidays 10:00 AM–9:00 PM

V, MC, AE, DEBIT

The largest store in the province has a phenomenal selection. What it lacks in atmosphere it certainly makes up for in quantity and a staff well versed in their wines. Do visit the cellar in the basement; you'll find lots of treats there. The store offers a wine-in-barrel program, crate of the month, tastings, classes and the spectacular charity auction held in the fall to benefit the Alberta Children's Hospital.

The Wine Cellar at Vineyard South

www.thewinecellar.ca

600–9737 Macleod Trail South

Tel: (403) 640-1111

Open Monday–Friday 10:00 AM–9:30 PM

 Saturday 10:00 AM–8:00 PM

 Sunday 11:00 PM–6:00 PM

V, MC, AE, DEBIT

The heavy hitters of US wine can be found in this tasteful shop: Pahlmeyer, Raymond, Rochioli. It's one of the few sources in the province for Domaine Romanee Conti and there are wonderful Italian selections reflecting the passion of the former owner Joseph D'Angelus. The shop is now operated by Frank Kennedy and we expect more of the same good things.

The Wine Shop

www.wineshopcal.com

815A 17th Avenue SW

Tel: (403) 229-9463

Open Monday–Friday 10:00 AM–8:00 PM

 Saturday 10:00 AM–6:00 PM; Sunday 12:00 PM–5:00 PM

V, MC, AE, DEBIT

One of the original 13 stores licensed in 1986, The Wine Shop continues to offer its customers excellent quality Spanish, Aussie and lesser-known French wines in its wide-ranging inventory. Better-known name producers such as Drouhin and Robert Mondavi round out the selections. Genial, low-key staff make it easy to try something new.

Banff Wine Store

302 Caribou Street, Lower Level, Banff
Tel: (403) 762-3465
Open daily 10:00 AM–11:00 PM
V, MC, AE, DEBIT

Owner Mark Saumer carries several VQA wines from both BC and Ontario, including an eclectic selection of ice wines. He's strong in French and Australian wines and many selections are exclusive to this store. (Saumer belongs to the G6, a buying consortium set up by some independent-minded merchants to help them source hard-to-get wines; thus the exclusive selections.) Tastings, special wine events and wine classes are offered. Staff members are well versed in their subject and hold definite opinions on wine and its place in the world.

Liquor World

Tel: (403) 762-2518

202 Wolf Street, Banff
Open daily 10:00 AM–11:00 PM
V MC DEBIT

Genial manager Larry Moskal is a well-known fixture on the Banff wine scene, whose tenure dates back to ALCB days. This large, brightly lit store carries the general selection of spirits, beers and wines that you would expect from a good quality chain, but truly shines in its stock of lesser known wines from Chile, Italy and Spain. The VQA selection, especially from British Columbia, is especially broad. If you can't find what you're looking for ask Larry or one of his cheerful staff; they'll search it out.

Jasper Liquor Store and Wine Cellar

606 Patricia Street, Jasper

Open summer daily 10:00 AM–10:00 PM

Open winter daily 10:00 AM–8:00 PM

V, MC, AE, DEBIT

jasperwine@incentre.net

Tel: (780) 852-5682

> The main floor looks like any standard liquor store. In the basement, however, someone with a wide-ranging palate has had fun stocking the shelves. There's real depth here. Lots of cigar-chomping reds from the United States and Australia, obscure yet tasty French bottlings, Canadian VQA in spades and a smattering of Try Me! wines from Spain, Chile and Argentina.

❧ EDMONTON

123 Street Liquor Store

10505 123rd Street

Open Sunday–Thursday 10:00 AM–10:00 PM

Friday, Saturday 10:00 AM–11:00 PM

V, MC, DEBIT

Tel: (780) 420-1650

> If it's sold in Alberta, you'll find it here. The selection of wines and spirits is truly extensive: deep verticals (successive vintages of one particular wine) of prestige bottlings and horizontals (different wine or producer, same vintage).
>
> There's a great selection of higher-end Californian, Italian and French and Aussie reds.

Crestwood Fine Wine

www.crestwoodwines.com

9658 142nd Street

Tel: (780) 488-7800

Open Monday–Saturday 10:00 AM–8:00 PM

Sunday 12:00 PM–6:00 PM

V, MC, DEBIT

> This cozy shop, conveniently located next to Urban Fare, has a little bit of everything. We can always find a bottle to have with dinner. The frequent tastings are relaxed and convivial— it's a wine-snob free zone.

Cozy, convenient shopping at Crestwood Wines.

Cristall's Wine Market

5854 111th Street   Tel: (780) 455-8888
Open Monday–Wednesday 10:00 AM–8:00 PM
      Thursday–Saturday 10:00 AM–10:00 PM
      Sunday 12:00 PM–6:00 PM
V, MC, AE, DEBIT

Strengths at Cristall's are in Australian and Californian wines, especially Zinfandels. They have a hefty selection from Spain. As well, they carry Canadian VQA from Tinhorn Creek, Cedar Creek, and offerings from Burrowing Owl. With its low key "guy" atmosphere—lots of wine crates and flats of beer sitting around—Cristall's is a completely unintimidating place to learn, talk about and purchase wine. They offer informal tastings, case discounts and an email newsletter.

Grapes and Grains

                                                    www.grapes-n-grains.com
9500 170th Street   Tel: (780) 444-2121
Open Monday–Saturday 10:00 AM–10:00 PM
      Sunday 12:00 PM–6:00 PM
V, MC, AE, DEBIT

This west end store carries over 1,500 wines including ports, classed growth Bordeaux, wines from the Alsace and the Rhone and the heavy hitters of the US and Australian wine world such as Penfold's, Hardy's, Stags Leap, St. Francis and Far Niente. Weekly educational tastings are supplemented by a wine room that is available for private tastings.

Liquor Depot

                                                    www.liquordepot.com
208–6655 178th Street (Callingwood Shopping Centre)   Tel: (780) 483-4600
Open daily 10:00 AM–12:00 AM
V, MC, DEBIT

Once a garden variety liquor store chain, a complete revamp of the wine program has changed the selection considerably. Callingwood is the flagship store but you'll find a large selection at the Riverbend, Whyte Avenue and Jasper Avenue wine markets as well.

Under the direction of Grant Smith and certified sommelier Robynn Gustafson, there are intelligent choices at every turn, not just in the big name highly-rated wines but in the under $20 everyday category. You'll find good buys here. And lots of them—they say it's the largest selection in Alberta. Watch this outfit for more good moves.

Liquor Select

www.liquorselect.com
8924 149th Street
Tel: (780) 481-6868
Open Monday–Thursday 10:00 AM–10:00 PM
    Friday, Saturday 10:00 AM–11:00 PM
    Sunday, 12:00 PM–8:00 PM
V, MC, AE, DEBIT

    This compact (filled to the rafters) store
    was chosen retailer of the year in 2002
    by its peers, the Alberta Liquor Store
Association. Great staff, loads of customer services, excellent selection were the
reasons. We like the choices of sake and Japanese plum wine, lesser-known and
well-priced Italians, lots of VQA, and depth in French, especially Bordeaux.

Vinomania Manulife Place

10180 101st Street   Tel: (780) 428-VINO
Open Monday–Wednesday 10:00 AM–5:30 PM; Thursday 10:00 AM 8:00 PM
    Friday 10:00 PM–6:30 PM; Saturday 10:00 AM–5:30 PM

Wines and Spirits Warehouse Cost Plus

11452 Jasper Avenue   Tel: (780) 488-7973
Open Monday, Tuesday 10:00 AM-7:00 PM
    Wednesday 10:00 AM–9:00 PM; Thursday, Friday 10:00 PM–10.00 PM
    Saturday 10:00 AM–9:00 PM; Sunday 12:00 PM–5:00 PM
V, MC, AE, DEBIT

    Both of these Edmonton stores are owned by Gurvinder Bhatia, a lawyer who left
his practice to follow the siren call of the grape. His strengths are in vintage port
and Australian, Italian (including grappa) and California wines. The Vinomania
store in Manulife has an added plus. It's home to VinoAerobics, amusing evenings
designed for people to meet, eat and sample. They're part singles night, part wine
education; call it what you like, some fine bottlings get opened and tasted.

The Wine Cellar

     www.thewinecellar.ab.ca
12421 102nd Avenue   Tel: (780) 488-9463
Open Monday–Friday 10:30 AM–6:00 PM; Saturday 10:00 AM–5:30 PM
V, MC, DEBIT

    The Wine Cellar was the first private wine store in Alberta. Founder Hank
Gillespie had forged his own path through the maze of deregulation and privati-

zation. Strengths are in California (Pahlmeyer, Rochioli) and French bottlings, especially Bordeaux and Burgundy. At first glance the selection appears to be largely high-end, but wine-savvy staff will help you shop in your price range. High-quality classes and a newsletter are available to those who are serious about learning more. Note: The Wine Cellar is an all-wine store.

❧ PEACE COUNTRY

The Grapevine
9506 100th Street, Grande Prairie   Tel: (780) 538-3555
Open Monday–Thursday 10:00 AM–10:00 PM
    Friday, Saturday 10:00 AM–10:30 PM; Sunday 11:00 AM–7:00 PM
V, MC, AE, DEBIT

    The owner, Terry Dola, was, with her husband, one of the original 1986 licensees. The Grapevine is still very much a specialty store, carrying over 3,000 wines plus nearly 100 different scotches, one of the largest selections of Scotch whisky in the province. They also have an extensive stock of imported beer.

❧ ON THE DINO TRAIL

Andrew Hilton Wines & Spirits
212 3rd Avenue S, Lethbridge   Tel: (403) 320-9464
Open Monday–Saturday 10:00 AM–9:00 PM; Sunday 12:00 PM–5:00 PM
V, MC, DEBIT

    Max Baines opened his store in 1986. Customer service and an impressive selection of thousands of wines from every wine-making country make this store a favourite in the community, particularly with restaurant buyers. Best selection is in Canadian VQA and rare Australian and French bottlings, especially Bordeaux and Champagne.

Alley Kat Brewing

www.alleykatbeer.com

9929 60th Avenue, Edmonton

Tel: (780) 436–8922

Open Monday–Friday 9:00 AM–5:00 PM

V, DEBIT

Owner Neil Herbst is a busy guy. He makes the beer, conducts the tours and holds the tastings. His brewery is in a nondescript industrial park on Edmonton's south side, but he makes some interesting beers.

Try his Olde Deuteronomy barley wine (the secret ingredient in many a good cook's braised beef) and Aprikat, an apricot-flavoured beer. Alley Kat is on tap around town and is available by the six pack. All of the beers are unpasteurized, so they have a shorter shelf life than factory beer. They must be kept refrigerated, and should be quaffed as soon as possible. Watch for their seasonally available beers such as Ein Prosit for Octoberfest.

Big Rock Brewery

www.bigrockbeer.com

5555 76th Avenue SE, Calgary

Tel: (403) 720-3239

Open for tours Monday–Wednesday 1:30 PM

Big Rock Brewery, named after a local geological oddity (a big rock), was founded in 1985 by Calgary entrepreneur Ed McNally.

"In the early days people thought I was an idiot to start a brewery," says McNally. Beer drinkers are happy that he persevered. Today Big Rock is an Alberta success story, a public company listed on the Nasdaq and the TSE. Big Rock beers are sold throughout North America and are still developed by the original brewmaster, Bernd Peiper. The distinctive labels are by Calgary artist Dirk van Wyk.

The beers are unpasteurized, follow the Bavarian quality standard (using only water, hops, malt and yeast) and are individually batch-brewed and micro-filtered through an advanced sterile filtering system that gives the beer a longer shelf life—up to six months. The lineup includes several top-fermented ales: Traditional Ale, Grasshopper Wheat, McNally's Extra and Warthog.

Brewsters Brewing Company
www.brewstersbrewingco.com

CALGARY
Eau Claire, 101 Barclay Parade
Tel: (403) 233-2739
Open Monday–Thursday 11:00 AM–1:00 AM
    Friday, Saturday 11:00 AM–2:00 AM
    Sunday 11:00 AM–10:00 PM
V, MC, DC, AE, DEBIT
    Other Calgary locations: 834 11th Avenue
    SW, 265-2739; 176–755 Lake Bonavista
    Drive SE, 225-2739; 25 Crowfoot Terrace
    NW, 208-2739

EDMONTON
Meadowlark Shopping Centre
15820 87th Avenue
Tel: (780) 421-4677 (HOPS)
Open Monday–Thursday 11:00 AM–1:00 AM
    Friday, Saturday 11:00 AM–2:00 AM
    Sunday 11:00 AM–12:00 AM
V, MC, DC, AE, DEBIT
    Other Edmonton locations: 11620 104th
    Avenue, 482-4677 (HOPS)

LETHBRIDGE
1814 Mayor McGrath Drive
Tel: (403) 328-9000
Open Monday–Thursday 11:00 AM–1:00 AM
    Friday, Saturday 11:00 AM–2:00 AM
    Sunday 11:00 AM–12:00 AM
V, MC, DC, AE, DEBIT

Brewsters Brewing Company

The Brewsters Brewing Company has grown from one location in Regina (opened in 1989) to 10 locations in Alberta and Saskatchewan.

"Our restaurants don't pretend to serve haute cuisine, but the food is well prepared, consistent and has authentic flavours, just like our beers," says general manager Don McDonald. Menus are standardized throughout the group with some regional twists in each city. "Our chefs use the beers as an ingredient in their pantry. They cook mussels in it, create soups and stews with it, and dip halibut in a lager batter for fish and chips."

Asian and East Indian influences reflect the traditional home cooking of some of the chefs, who make dishes like Kashmir butter chicken and Asian ginger chicken. The burgers are top-notch. Try the Bow Valley buffalo burger with Brewsters own beer-laced BBQ sauce and Swiss cheese. ⬳

Grizzly Paw Brewing Company
622 Main Street, Canmore
Open daily 11:00 AM–12:00 AM
V, MC, AE, DEBIT

www.thegrizzlypaw.com
Tel: (403) 678-9983

    The Grizzly Paw Brewing Company was opened in 1996 by two transplanted
Edmontonians, Niall Fraser and Alex Burnett. The two are self-taught, having

begun as intense full-mash home brewers. They've gone from 50 litre home-brewed batches to 1000 litre batches of seven ales, one lager and a variety of seasonal beers. Eight beers are on tap at any given time. In two rustic rooms and on their heated patio, they serve good pub grub with their beer. We like the sun-dried tomato pâté, a potato and leek soup made lively with a splash of Grumpy Bear Honey wheat. Or hold out for the double-trouble pizza made with Italian and Mundare sausage, aged mozzarella, jack and cheddar cheeses with fresh mushrooms and roasted red peppers.

$$ **Wildwood Grill & Brewing Company**

www.creativeri.com

2417 4th Street SW, Calgary   Tel: (403) 228-0100

Open Sunday–Thursday 11:30 AM–3:00 PM, 5:00 PM–10:00 PM

Friday, Saturday 11:30 AM–3:00 PM, 5:00 PM–11:00 PM

V, MC, AE, DEBIT

Brewmaster Jim Anderson apprenticed in Germany, and has a degree in bio-chemistry. His beers are handcrafted liquid art, never pasteurized or cold-fil-tered. Look for the Elusive Trout Stout, made in the Irish tradition, with under-tones of coffee and chocolate. Then there's the Bugaboo Bitter, an aromatic English-style bitter, quite hoppy on the palate.

Wildwood has a ski lodge ambiance with an extensive casual menu down-stairs in the brew pub. Amazing sandwiches: barbecue sauce-glazed shaved pork loin with caramelized onions and aged white cheddar, grilled flat bread with arti-chokes, spinach, Alberta feta and mozzarella cheese. Or have the excellent bangers and mash with garlic-mashed Yukon gold potatoes with grainy mustard and fried onions. The key to this inventive menu is executive chef Josef Wiewer, who holds forth upstairs in the dining room. (See also page 55.)

THE WAY WE COOK

Alberta has always had wonderful cooks, and it's fair to say that the great majority of them have always been women.

In the good old days, women didn't cook professionally, and they were modest about their culinary skills. Beyond a recipe or two in the local church cookbook for Linda's sweet pickles or Grandma Kowalchuk's cabbage rolls, fame didn't visit their kitchens.

Still, decades of Sunday roasts and flaky piecrusts taught each succeeding generation that nobody cooked like Mom.

In the mid-'70s, Alberta saw a minor culinary revolution that spread throughout Canada, when Mom came out of the kitchen and into the publishing world with the self-published, coil-back cookbook. Determined women, good cooks to be sure, were literally putting their money where their mouths had always been. Sometimes the books followed a theme: muffins, squares, casseroles. Most were collections of the familiar dishes we all loved, from Caesar salad to Nanaimo bars. If there was a certain sameness about these books, there was also a spirit of generosity and hospitality that has always marked Western people.

The Best of Bridge Publishing, Calgary

Way back in 1975, *The Best of Bridge* hit the market and became an instant bestseller. It was a fat coil-back cookbook with a glossy red cover, written by a group of women who had been friends and bridge partners for several years.

Since then, the women of the bridge group have parlayed their original collection of favourite recipes into six more volumes in the format stuffed with recipes for dishes people love to eat, sprinkled with goofy jokes and one-liners. Their recipes, made with familiar ingredients, were designed to feed family and friends. The joyfully fattening desserts and do-ahead casseroles in the early books evolved into more healthful fare in later volumes. Eventually they landed their own television show. With the sixth volume, *The Best of The Best and More*, book sales topped 2.5 million.

The Best of Bridge has had many imitators, but nobody did it as well as those savvy women who continue to refer to themselves as "the girls." The last word goes to them. "To answer the questions we're always asked: yes, we're still good friends; no, we're not all divorced; yes, we've made money (where has it gone?); and no, we don't play bridge anymore." Their latest book, *A Year of the Best*, is a collaboration with Calgary chef Vincent Parkinson.

The Atco Gas Blue Flame Kitchen

There's been a Blue Flame Kitchen in Alberta for over 70 years. With offices in Edmonton and Calgary, its original mandate was to educate consumers in the use of natural gas appliances. But it quickly morphed into a source of information and recipes for home cooks all over the province. For many years, staff taught cooking classes around the province, and their barbecue courses were wildly popular.

Now, Barbara Barnes and her team of eight home economists test recipes for their Christmas cookbook, and for their semi-annual barbecue cookbook. They also answer consumer queries on everything from home canning to party food. "We get about 55,000 calls a year," says Barnes. "Last year 6,400 of them were in August—the height of canning season."

The Atco Gas Blue Flame Kitchen is as close as your phone: (780) 420-1010 in Edmonton; 1-877-420-9090 toll free; (306) 825-5010 in Lloydminster; 1-800-840-3393 (call Monday to Friday from 10:00 AM 4:00 PM) to order cookbooks.

Jean Paré, Company's Coming, Edmonton

From modest beginnings as a caterer in her hometown of Vermilion, Jean Paré is the undisputed queen of the cookbook publishing industry. Her phenomenal success is the envy of the North American publishing world.

Jean's mission was simple: good home cooking with easily available ingredients. Starting in 1981 with her first book, *Company's Coming: 150 Delicious Squares*, she has produced 50 titles (and counting) on every imaginable aspect of home cooking. Having sold more than 16 million books, including translations in French and Spanish, Company's Coming routinely ships books to India, Australia and many other countries.

Working closely with son Grant Lovig, granddaughter Amanda Jean, and other family members, she now has a professional test kitchen, The Recipe Factory, and a television series.

Julie Van Rosendaal: One Smart Cookie

When you win the Stampede Chili Cookoff at 12 years of age, odds are pretty good that you should be a cook. So it's no surprise that Julie Van Rosendaal ended up in a singular part of the food world—as a cookie expert.

Her entrepreneurial spirit started to surface when she developed a low-fat cookie to satisfy her dad's sweet tooth and help keep his cholesterol in check. Inspired by the success of The Best of Bridge, Julie wrote *One Smart Cookie* which was self-published in the fall of 2000, with over 200 recipes for cookies, squares, brownies and biscotti, all reduced in fat. During this time, while baking and eating cookies every day, Julie lost half her body weight in two years. Newly svelte, she's planning projects, which include securing a contract to supply frozen dough to supermarkets, and the next volume in a series of low-fat cookbooks.

Butter Tart Squares One Smart Cookie

¼ cup (50 mL) butter, softened
⅓ cup (75 mL) packed brown sugar
1 cup (250 mL) flour
pinch salt

1 large egg
2 large egg whites
1 ½ cups (375 mL) brown sugar
1 tbsp (15 mL) flour
¼ tsp (1 mL) baking powder
pinch salt
1 tsp (5 mL) vanilla
1 cup (250 mL) raisins
⅓ cup (65 mL) chopped pecans

Preheat oven to 375 F (180 C). In medium bowl, beat butter, and brown sugar until creamy. Add flour and salt and stir until well combined and crumbly. Press into an 8" x 8" pan sprayed with non-stick coating. Bake 10–15 minutes, until golden brown around the edges. Using same bowl, combine egg, whites, brown sugar, flour, baking powder, salt and vanilla and stir until smooth. Stir in raisins and pecans. Pour over base and return to oven for 25 to 30 minutes, until golden and bubbly around the edges. The topping will puff up as it bakes and then settle. Cool completely in pan on wire rack. Makes 16 squares with 4.8 g of fat, 21% of calories from fat.

FARMERS' MARKETS AND U-PICKS

FARMERS' MARKETS

There's a lesson to be learned from the little pig who went to market: get up early and be there when it opens, or the best potatoes will be on their way out the door just as you're going in. You know the pig we're talking about. The ambitious one, with two lazy brothers and a good recipe for wolf soup. Probably he was a sociable type, as most pigs are. Market enthusiast that he was, he went to visit as much as to shop.

Each market develops its own flavour, and dedicated shoppers tend to adopt one market and call it theirs. Here are three we've adopted for ourselves.

Millarville Market

On a golden fall day, the Millarville Market is breathtaking. Everything about Millarville's outdoor/indoor market reflects its fortunate location—where prairie meets mountain, from the hearty rancher's breakfast that has become a tradition or the beloved and portable bacon-on-a-bun, to the pickups overflowing with local vegetables, preserves, flowers and baking.

Millarville's exceptional artistic community makes high-quality crafts available for sale, which account for about half the market. The Christmas market, held on a November weekend, is the time to buy unique gifts, a gorgeous wreath or some freshly roasted chestnuts from a local boy scout.

Saturday morning at Millarville.

JULIE VAN ROSENDAAL

St. Albert Market

St. Albert's sprawling Saturday market feels like a European street market—a throwback to the days when city people bought all their food directly from the farmers who grew it. There's a sidewalk café near the fountain, gaily coloured tarps snapping in the breeze, strolling musicians and the smell of fresh coffee. It's a great spot for a Saturday outing and the place to buy flats of local strawberries for jams, the Hutterite saskatoon pies, pyrohys from Two Babas and a Stove. Feast your eyes on luscious tomatoes, peppers and eggplants of every size and colour including the hard-to-find white eggplant. People walking back to their cars are toting massive armloads of fresh flowers and a bag of potatoes. We love it all.

Busy summer Saturday at St. Albert's Market.

The Old Strathcona Market

We adopted the Old Strathcona Farmers Market in Edmonton while watching it struggle to stay alive, and then fight to maintain its identity as a true farmers' market. Here, the faces, food and crafts are pure prairie.

Milling about this former Edmonton Transit bus barn, we find out whose lettuce got rained out, whose strawberries are ready for jam, who will have saskatoons next week. These vendors aren't playing at farming. They're serious gamblers, whose wins and losses turn on the whim of the weather. While the town sleeps, they're out in the field, weeding, picking, packing the truck, filling thermoses so they can work straight through, coffee cup in one hand, bunch of carrots in the other. It's a thriving Saturday village, quite at home in the midst of the larger village, also called Old Strathcona.

Many Alberta towns hold regular market days throughout the summer months, and there's usually a sign posted near the highway. Travellers with a spare half hour will always find a welcome, plus a cup of coffee and home baking, in these friendly spots. Pack up the kids and go. You'll be glad you did. Note that this is a listing of accredited markets only. Times, dates and even locations are subject to change, so we've included phone numbers.

CALGARY

Bearspaw Lions
0.6 miles (1 km) west of city limits along Highway 1A   Tel: (403) 239-0201
Open June–October Sunday 11:00 AM–3:00 PM
> Special Christmas markets in November

Calgary Blackfoot
5600 11th Street SE   Tel: (403) 243-0065
Open end of May–October 31, Friday, Saturday 8:00 AM–5:00 PM
> Sunday 10:00 AM–4:00 PM
> This is one of the oldest and most authentic markets in Alberta, a must-go-to for market lovers. Features "Calgary's Favourite Pie Contest."

Calgary Hillhurst/Sunnyside
1320 5th Avenue NW   Tel: (403) 283 0554
(Hillhurst–Sunnyside Community Centre)
Open June–October 3, Wednesday 3:30 PM–8:00 PM
> Special Thanksgiving market

Grassroots Northland
Northland Village Mall parking lot   Tel: (403) 239-8231; (403) 239-1023
Open second Tuesday in June–September 30 4:00 PM–8:00 PM

EDMONTON

Edmonton Beverly Towne
3945 118th Avenue   Tel: (780) 477-6333
Open May–September, Tuesday 4:00 PM–8:00 PM
> Special Christmas market

Edmonton Callingwood

6655 178th Street (the Marketplace at Callingwood)
Tel: (780) 487-8649
Open May–October 31 Sunday, Wednesday

Choosing bedding plants at the Old Strathcona Farmers Market.

Edmonton Capilano

5004 98th Avenue
(Capilano Shopping Centre)
Tel: (780) 459-6082
Open year-round, Saturday 9:30 AM–5:00 PM

Edmonton City

10165 97th Street
Tel: (780) 424-9001
Open year-round Tuesday–Friday 10:00 AM–5:00 PM
        Saturday 7:00 AM–2:00 PM
        Special markets during bedding plant season

Edmonton Millwoods

7207 28th Avenue
(Parking lot, Millwoods Recreation Centre)
Tel: (780) 476-9445
Open June–September Thursday 5:00 PM–8:00 PM
        Special markets throughout the year

Edmonton Old Strathcona

103rd Street and 83rd Avenue (Old Bus Barn)
Tel: (780) 439-1844
Open year-round Saturday 8:00 AM–3:00 PM
        Special markets throughout the year

Edmonton Westmount

Westmount Shopping Centre
Tel: (780) 459-6082
Open year-round Thursday 10:00 AM–5:00 PM

OTHERS AROUND ALBERTA

Camrose
4702 50th Avenue (Elks Hall), Camrose   Tel: (780) 672-8930
Open year-round Saturday 8:00 AM–12:00 PM
    Special Christmas markets in December

Devon
Community Centre on Haven Avenue   Tel: (780) 987 4016
Open June–October, Thursday 2:00 PM–6:00 PM
    Special Christmas market in November

Lethbridge Exhibition
3401 Parkside Drive South (Whoop-up Pavilion)   Tel: (403) 328-4491
Open June–October 31 Saturday 8:00 AM–12:30 PM
    Special market during Fair Week (July) in Pioneer Park

Millarville Fairground
      Tel: (403) 931 2404
Open June 16–October 6, Saturday 8:30 AM–12:00 PM

Red Deer
43rd Street and 48th Avenue   Tel: (403) 346-6443
Open mid-May–early October Saturday 8:00 AM–12:30 PM

St. Albert
Grandin Park Plaza (spring and fall location)   Tel: (780) 458-2833
St. Anne's and St. Thomas (downtown location for summer)
Open April 1–June 24, Saturday 10:00 AM–3:00 PM
    Moves to downtown July 1; moves back to Plaza from October to mid-December

Sherwood Park
Festival Way Parking Lot   Tel: (780) 464-3354
Open May–September 30 Wednesday 5:00 PM–8:30 PM
    Special market on Canada Day (July 1)

Vegreville
5002–55th Avenue (Elks Hall)   Tel: (780) 632 7482
Open March–December 31, Friday 7:30 AM–12:00 PM
    Special markets for Father's Day, Thanksgiving, Christmas

Vermillion

5018–49th Avenue (Elks Hall)   Tel: (780) 853-4669
Open February–December, Tuesday 10:00 AM–1:00 PM
    Special Christmas markets through December

Wetaskiwin

Wetaskiwin Mall   Tel: (780) 352-3157
Open January 5–June 28, Wednesday 11:00 AM–4:00 PM

Drill Hall   Tel: (780) 352-3157
Open July 5–December 20, Wednesday 6:00 PM–8:00 PM

◉ U-PICK GARDENS

U-pick gardens are flourishing in Alberta. Fifteen years ago, there were three U-pick growers in the greater Edmonton area. Now there are thirty, plus dozens of others throughout the province.

    U-picks welcome pick-it-yourselfers to their garden patches from early morning, daily during the season. Many also offer custom-picking. If you call ahead, they'll have your order picked and ready for you to take home.

    For a complete listing of every U-pick in the province, call the toll-free number, 1-800-661-2642. Ask for the latest edition of the *Come to Our Farms* brochure, with maps, complete listings and phone numbers.

The Alberta Market Gardeners' Association offers these tips to improve your visit to a U-pick:

- Wear loose, comfortable clothing.
- Bring a picnic cooler to keep berries and vegetables at optimum temperature until you get home.
- Remember those UV rays: bring a sun hat and sunscreen. Also take along some mosquito repellent.
- Call ahead to be sure the farm is open and has a good supply of what you want that day. ✒

IN AND AROUND CALGARY

Premium Organic Farm

Highway 22X east to 88 Street, 1 mile (1.6 km) north   Tel: (403) 203-1095
on 88 Street, 1.7 miles (2.8 km) east,
0.75 miles (1.2 km) north on west side of road
    Available: Mixed vegetables, all organic

The Saskatoon Farm

19 km south of Calgary on Highway 2,   Tel: (403) 938-6245
3 km east on 338th Avenue at train display (near Okotoks)
    Available: saskatoons and bedding plants

IN AND AROUND EDMONTON

Park Berry Fields, Sherwood Park

2.5 km east of Highway 21 on   Tel: (780) 922-6973
Township Road 530 (Baseline Road)
    Available: Strawberries, saskatoons, raspberries

Peas on Earth

At 50th Street and 160th Avenue in northeast   Tel: (780) 478-1075
Edmonton, across from Little Mountain Cemetery
    Available: Peas, potatoes, strawberries and other small fruit, organic produce

Prairie Gardens and Greenhouses

1 km past Bon Accord on Highway 28 (97th Street),   Tel: (780) 921-2272
2 km left on Lily Lake Road
    Available: Strawberries, pumpkins, potatoes

The Strawberry Farm, Spruce Grove

4.6 km south of Zender Ford in   Tel: (780) 963-3841
Spruce Grove on Golden Spike Road
    Available: strawberries and organic produce.

Zaychuk Berry, Vegetable Farms & Greenhouses

1.6 km south of Highway 37 on 34th Street   Tel: (780) 472-2600
or 1 block west of Manning Freeway on 167th Avenue,
8 km north on Zaychuk Road.
    Available: Greenhouse tomatoes

OTHERS AROUND ALBERTA

Baker Creek Berry Company, High River

7 km west of High River on 12th Avenue   Tel: (403) 652-4381
    Available: Saskatoons, strawberries (June bearing and day neutral), raspberries
    and other small fruits

Berry Acres, Lethbridge

6.2 km east of Lethbridge on Jail Road off 43 Street   Tel: (403) 320-8501
    Available: Raspberries, saskatoons and black currants

Dunvegan Gardens, Fairview

25 km south of Fairview on Highway 2,   Tel: (780) 835-4459
east of Dunvegan Provincial Park
    Available: Several types of vegetables, corn festival on Labour Day

The Garden of Eat'n, Grande Prairie

4.8 km east, 1.6 km south of Sexmith   Tel: (780) 568-4505
(follow Morningview Park Golf Course signs)
    Available: Strawberries, raspberries and other fruit

Linda's Market Gardens, Smoky Lake

On Highway 28 at west entrance to Smoky Lake   Tel: (780) 656-2401
    Available: A wide variety of vegetables and strawberries; pumpkin days

Mr. V's Field and Forest

                                                        www.mrvs.net
5 miles (8 km) west of Boyle on Highway 63, at junction   Tel: (780) 689-2944
with Secondary Highway 663, Athabasca
Open May–September Monday–Saturday 10:00 AM–6:00 PM
    Sunday 12:00 PM–5:00 PM
    Available: strawberries, saskatoons, raspberries, vegetables, herbs, fresh and
    dried flowers, bedding plants, ranch beef, pork and lamb

Pearson's Berry Farms, Bowden

17.5 miles (28 km) West of Bowden on Highway 587   Tel: (403) 224-3011
Open daily 9:00 AM–9:00 PM
    As well as growing and processing prairie berries, the Pearsons now serve brunch
    on Sunday, by reservation only. Their adjacent gift store carries pies (filled with
    berries, naturally!) spreads, jellies, pioneer marmalades, and Joyce Pearson's own
    tomato-onion relish. Weather permitting, saskatoons, chokecherries and high
    bush cranberries may be available. Call ahead.

Poplar Bluff Farm

8 miles (13 km) south of Strathmore on Secondary   Tel: (403) 934-5400
Highway 817, 1.2 miles (2 km) west on north side, Strathmore
    Available: Asparagus, potatoes and organic produce

Suncrest Colony, Coronation

East of Castor on Highway 12 to Highway 36, Tel: (403) 882-2476
15 km south to Suncrest Road sign, 5.5 km east to the colony gate
> Available: June-bearing strawberries, peas, cucumbers

Tam Andersen
Prairie Gardens and Greenhouses

"U-pick is not a plant-it-and-they-will-come business, especially not out here where we are," says Tam Andersen, AKA "That Strawberry Woman." She's easy to spot, wandering about the yard in her strawberry-print blouse and strawberry earrings, often with a baby in her arms.

"Marketing is everything," says Andersen. And she does it so well. Her Prairie Gardens and Greenhouses near Bon Accord, with picnic area and playground plus 12 acres of strawberries, has become a favourite destination among u-pick fans. Andersen watches 200 to 300 pails of berries leave her farm daily, twice that many on a weekend.

Although she also grows peas, spuds and pumpkins, strawberries are her true passion. She can tell you anything you'd need to know about them—whether they're June-bearing or one of the day-neutral varieties, how to pick, store and cook with them.

The annual July strawberry festival and the October pumpkin festival have become must-do events for many people. For a recent berry fest, more than 1,500 hungry people showed up to eat strawberry shortcake. ✐

TASTEMAKERS

Alberta's emerging culinary community wasn't found under a cabbage. It exists and thrives because of the people you're about to meet in this chapter.

Their vision, good taste, passion and hard work have changed the way we eat.

GRASSROOTS GOES UPTOWN
THE PRICE FAMILY OF ACME

"When you have a big family like ours, you spend a lot of time working things out around the kitchen table." So says Flo Price, matriarch of one of Alberta's most forward-thinking farm families.

Stan and Flo Price raised seven kids on their farm near Acme. Today, five are actively involved in their fully integrated farm-to-table food operations. The Prices employ hundreds of people in every aspect of the food business, producing, processing and retailing their pork and beef to their own exacting specifications.

Dave Price runs the pork production, with 8,000 breeding sows. Doug looks after their beef—40,000 head in three feedlots. Ray is in charge of the pork processing plants, and looks after the financial end of the business. Glen is president of the retail outlets known as Sunterra Market. Art is the chairman of the board. The other two Price offspring, Al and Joyce, aren't directly involved in the company, "but they're always here when we need them," says Flo.

It's one thing for a farm family to raise and process meat. It's another to suddenly jump into the cutthroat world of upscale retail groceries, and Flo has a theory about such leaps of faith: "In this country, if you want to do something badly enough, you have no excuse not to try."

Thus was born the first Sunterra Market, with the Price's own products available fresh or cooked for takeout.

"Our family enterprise succeeds because we all have a strong work ethic. Stan was involved with the Pork Board, he was away a lot, so our kids have been doing a man's work on the farm since they were 10 years old."

The other thing they all have is passion. If that means working an 18-hour day, so be it. "When we hire new chefs, they come out to the farm and I give them a tour, so they know we are still farmers. Our kids all love the land, and they value it," says Flo, emphatically. In 2002, Stan Price was inducted into the Alberta Agriculture Hall of Fame.

A CHEF WITH WINNING WAYS
SIMON SMOTKOWICZ

In 1975, when Simon Smotkowicz was a newly minted chef, he left his home in Toulouse, France, and came to Canada.

He's the executive chef of Edmonton's Shaw Conference Centre, but Smotkowicz is better known around the international food world as the past-manager of Culinary Team Canada. Through that team he played a big role in putting Alberta products, and Alberta chefs, on the culinary map.

After many years and many triumphant trips to Europe and Asia to cook for Canada, chef Smotkowicz and his team could fill a small museum with their medals and honours. In that capacity, he has had a tremendous influence on young chefs coming up in the culinary world. "If you stay in your own little corner, you

JANICE MCGREGOR

stagnate," he says. "Our student teams are so important. They're the new kids on the block, and they're excited about the possibilities. About the future."

He remembers when it wasn't that way. "My father didn't want me to be a chef, just a domestic. In those days, a chef's job was not respected. Today, chefs are stars," he says. "Our profession is attracting better people with a passion for the job.

"We have such excellent ingredients here now. So many small producers who are dedicated to their craft," says Smotkowitz. "I'd like to think that chefs have had something to do with that."

ALBERTA'S IRON CHEF
MICHAEL NOBLE

Michael Noble, chef and part-owner of Calgary's Catch, believes in thinking outside the proverbial box. "I've done a lot of that. With the Bocuse D'Or, and especially the Iron Chef," he says. "These were life-changing experiences."

A man who despises routine, Noble is in love with the restaurant business. "I reach

for perfection every day. I learn something new every day. You achieve perfection by building culture—the food culture of a city. I want people to be excited about what oysters are coming in next week."

Noble stresses regional ingredients, and is making some happy local discoveries, like Central Alberta's vibrant cheese community and its passionate producers. "I didn't expect this. Sylvan Star gouda is incredible."

He wishes the growing season was longer here, and he sees Alberta's food industry as still emerging. "We've featured farmed tilapia on the menu, from somewhere southeast of Calgary. We tried Manitoba pickerel, but it's a hard sell. I guess Prairie fish isn't sexy. They want shark, or swordfish, or red bandit from the Queen Charlottes." Michael Noble is following his heart. "I was born in Alberta," he says. "Thirty years later, it feels good to be back."

FOOD AND WINE IMPRESARIO
PETER BLATTMANN

Peter Blattmann has been in the business of giving people what they want for a long time. Starting in his parents' winery at age six, Blattmann has developed a career that has taken him from Germany, Switzerland and England to France, Morocco and now Canada. He started the International wine and food series at the Banff Springs Hotel in 1991. "I came back to the Banff Springs in 1989 and immediately challenged everyone to create one of the premier wine and food events in North America," says Blattmann. "They thought I was out of my mind!"

The International wine and food series started with six California producers in 1991. Blattmann orchestrated these celebrations annually, attracting food and wine lovers from all over the world. The events always sell out.

Like any good impresario, Blattmann knows when to close one show and bring on the next. "The Spanish event in 2000 was the last of the individual country themes. I'm taking the event upscale, something very fine, very exclusive.

The third act of Blattmann's career is a bold move. He's taking his show on the road. While continuing to produce wine and food events for the Banff Springs, Blattmann is busy designing and leading personal gourmet tours to Europe and beyond.

GOOD FOOD, GOOD WINE, GOOD FRIENDS
WOMEN WHO DISH

In Calgary, they're known as The Women Who Dish. There are nine of them now, each one involved in some aspect of the food industry, and they've recently published their second cookbook, *Double Dishing: The Dishing Women Entertain.*

Meet the crew: Pam Fortier of Decadent Desserts; caterer Karen Miller; restaurateurs Rhonda Siebens and Judy Wood; wine lover Janet Webb; Gail Norton, whose wonderful store has nurtured the Calgary food community with its cooking school, specialty foods, catering, and *City Palate* magazine; talented food writers Cinda Chavich and Dee Hobsbawn-Smith; and food stylist-chef Shelley Robinson.

Two books later they're a tight-knit little group. "We get together. We cook for each other. We socialize," Gail Norton explains. "We have nine competent, articulate, creative women involved, and it's always a good time. The biggest controversy we've ever had was whether to have nametags, and which dresses to wear for the picture."

They're an entertaining bunch, but they dismiss the insanity that sometimes surrounds food events. Janet Webb sums up their philosophy: "Get a bottle of wine and some good bread and cheese, and just sit around," she says. "That's fun."

ROCKY MOUNTAIN RESTAURANTEURS
GEORGE AND ANDRÉ SCHWARZ

"When my brother and I first came here, moose walked down Banff Avenue. Nobody was out after 8:00 PM. In November, you wouldn't have seen even one parked car."

So says George Schwarz, co-owner with brother Andre of Giorgio's in Banff and the Post Hotel in Lake Louise.

The Schwarz brothers' career started here in 1974, with a restaurant called Felices on Wolf Street. It became Ticino and the brothers sold it five years later. Then came Giorgio's, a consistently popular Italian eatery on Banff Avenue. "We always had good food and good service, even then," says George of the early years.

In 1978 Sir Norman Watson, the owner of a run-down lodge on the Pipestone River near Lake Louise, was looking for somebody to carry through his dream of a chic small hotel, patterned after the Post Hotels in Switzerland. In 1986 the brothers

Schwarz, in partnership with Husky Oil, rebuilt the Post into the elegant hostelry that it is today. Now the Post is a member of the prestigious Relais and Chateaux, a European-based organization of privately owned country hotels of particular character, always with an outstanding restaurant. (See also pages 65, 77.)

George Schwartz

Another project, Storm Mountain Lodge, remains dear to Schwarz's heart. For five years the brothers have been working with Parks Canada on plans to develop an intimate 47-room inn on the original site. They remain confident that the project will go ahead. "We must be patient in the parks. It's important, and the decisions made affect everyone," says George, always the diplomat.

He has scaled back a little, taking a day off occasionally, and he no longer works 15-hour days. He remains as straightforward as ever about his business. "We're just two ski instructors who ended up in the restaurant business."

SWEET MAN IN CALGARY
BERNARD CALLEBAUT

It's been 20 years of Alberta winters, and many tonnes of chocolate have crossed the counter, but he still loves his work. Two decades after he opened his first Alberta shop, Bernard Callebaut, chocolate maker, has lost none of his Belgian charm.

"We'll use about 660,000 pounds of chocolate this year," he says happily. It's a production day, and all day long he's been up to his ears in his favourite commodity. Brief pause, then a snippet of science: "Did you know that cocoa butter is good for your arteries?"

If he sounds like he has chocolate in his veins, it's probably because he was born in a house across from his family's chocolate factory back in Belgium. "At six, I could jump from my bedroom window to the factory. Chocolate is in all my memories. All my history." But make no mistake, Callebaut is an Alberta company. "I wanted to leave Belgium, get some space. Wanted to be near the mountains," he says. "This province had a good business attitude."

The secret of making great chocolate? Start with the know-how. "After the knowledge, you need a good apprenticeship. Mine was with a small, artisinal chocolate maker. His influence is still with me."

And through it all, you need creativity. "If you're quality-oriented, you'll just keep getting better. You cannot stand still," he says. "I'm still learning."

Although he professes to love all chocolate equally, Callebaut is especially crazy about certain combinations. "We had rose champagne with chocolate at our wedding. It was very romantic."

"Then there's the best one of all: chocolate with coffee. They grow together, so they go together. They have similar properties. They're both dark and delicious . . . It's the natural combination."

(And yes, he does use Tide to keep those uniforms snowy-white.)

TRIBUTE TO AN ORIGINAL
JEAN HOARE

Jean Hoare was an Alberta original. She was a generous, intelligent, hospitable woman who became a legend in her own time. Better than that, she was a darned fine cook.

For 20 years, this silver-haired dynamo ran a restaurant. At first it was at Driftwillow Ranch, where she served country-style food in her own home at the tail-end of a narrow dirt road. "Turn west where the Pulteney elevators used to be," she'd say. "Go four miles on the gravel, cross a Texas gate, through the coulee and come on up the hill."

When her restaurant outgrew the house, she moved to an old NATO supply depot near Claresholm. It became known as the Flying N, and guests—some famous, a few infamous and a lot of ordinary folk she called friends—arrived by plane, car and horseback to eat Jean's trade-mark western cuisine. She fed everybody from Bing Crosby to Pierre Berton.

Wonderful things came out of her kitchen: flapjacks with wild rosehip syrup, deer in beer, spit-roasted buffalo and the best T bone steaks in the country.

In *The Best Little Cookbook in the West*, Calgary author Nancy Millar quoted Jean in a modest moment. "The restaurant had only two things going for it: My appalling ignorance of the basics of normal restaurant operations, and the curiosity of people who couldn't resist checking out this crazy lady who lived in the middle of nowhere and had the audacity to serve six-course meals that took three hours to eat."

Jean set the highest standards in food and hospitality—standards that would hold up well today. Although she closed her restaurant for the last time on New Year's Eve, 1981, Jean went on to write several cookbooks, travel the world and enjoy life to the last drop. She died in the year 2000 while sitting at her kitchen table, having coffee with a friend, and eating a cookie. She was 85 years old.

LISTINGS BY CATEGORY

ALPHABETICAL LISTING